NOTABLE
WOMEN AUTHORS
OF THE DAY. By
HELEN C. BLACK

WITH PORTRAITS

Essay Index Reprint Series

BOOKS FOR LIBRARIES PRESS
FREEPORT, NEW YORK

First Published 1893
Reprinted 1972

Library of Congress Cataloging in Publication Data

Black, Helen C
   Notable women authors of the day.

   (Essay index reprint series)
   "First published 1893."
   1.   Authors, Women--Biography. 2.   Authors,
English--Biography. I.   Title.
PR115.B6   1972   820.9'008 ⌐B˥   74-38758
ISBN 0-8369-2637-4

PRINTED IN THE UNITED STATES OF AMERICA
BY
NEW WORLD BOOK MANUFACTURING CO., INC.
HALLANDALE, FLORIDA 33009

CONTENTS.

NOTABLE WOMEN AUTHORS OF THE DAY.

MRS LYNN LINTON

NOTABLE WOMEN AUTHORS.

MRS. LYNN LINTON.

A BLUE sky and a bright sun belie the typical foggy month of November, and while entering the elevator which glides rapidly and smoothly to the eighth floor of the gigantic pile of buildings once cynically termed "Hankey's Folly"—now Queen Anne's Mansions—you feel justified in anticipating a glorious view over the great city. You step out into a corridor where are arranged a stand of grenades with a couple of hydrants, backed by printed directions for their use, and are shown into the library of the distinguished author; but ere there is time to look around, the door opens, and Mrs. Lynn Linton enters.

Her personality may be described thus : tall, upright, and stately in appearance, the keen, but kindly bright blue eyes smiling through the gold-rimmed glasses which she always wears. She is clad in a suitable black dress, trimmed with jet, a white lace cap partially covers the thick grey hair, which escapes in a tiny natural curl or two on each side of the smooth, in-

▲

tellectual forehead. The eyebrows—far apart—are straight and level, but shaded off so delicately that they impart a look of benignity and softness to the aristocratic nose, while the curves of the well-cut lips indicate straightforwardness, sincerity of disposition, and power. Can it be possible that you had felt a momentary trepidation before meeting the gifted woman for whose genius you have ever entertained the greatest reverence? But Mrs. Lynn Linton will have none of it! Her kind and friendly greeting puts you at once at ease. She says that she has an hour or two to spare, that her work is well on, and that there is no immediate fear of her being disturbed by an emissary from the printers, so you settle down to have a good talk, and to learn from your hostess some particulars of her early life, and her subsequent eventful career.

Mrs. Lynn Linton was born at Keswick; her father being the vicar of Crosthwaite, Cumberland. When only five months old, her mother (a daughter of Dr. Goodenough, Bishop of Carlisle) died, leaving a family of twelve children. She was brought up plainly and frugally, with no particular advantages of education; nevertheless, at an early age she developed a strong taste for reading and a thirst for knowledge. Casting aside her childish story books, she dived into such ancient literature and chronicles as she found on her father's book-shelves, and at the age of eleven determined to train herself to be a writer. About this time she became keenly interested in Polish affairs, in which her favourite brother took an active part. In those days there were not the same facilities for pro-

curing books as in later years, but the young child-
student managed to overcome all obstacles, and educated herself, mastering French, German, and Italian.
The one aim and end to which her ambition was
directed buoyed her up through early years of what
were somewhat rough times to the shy, nervous,
short-sighted girl, who always seemed in everyone's way.

To this repression and self-training may be attri-
buted the independence of thought, the thoroughness,
the originality of idea, as well as the deep sympathy
with young and struggling authors which are Mrs.
Lynn Linton's prevailing characteristics. One of her
earliest recollections is of the poet Southey, and that to
this day she can recall to mind his peculiar face, his
dark eyes, full of fire, his eagle nose, and thin figure.
She wrote her first novel, " Azeth, the Egyptian," when
she came to London, at the age of twenty-three, and
from that day to this has supported herself entirely by
her pen ; but she says that this "first book" gave her a
whole year's hard work to write, and she thinks it is
now probably " unreadable." For her second, " Amy-
mone," she will ever have the tenderest memories, and
the blue eyes kindle when she remarks that it was the
means of bringing her into contact with Walter Savage
Landor, and securing for her his lasting sympathy and
friendship. She says he was her literary father, her
guide, philosopher, and friend, and that one of her
dearest treasures is a large packet of letters from the
poet, beginning " My dear daughter," and signed
"Father" only, or " Your affectionate father," as
well as those verses which he addressed to her,

ending with the line, "Pure heart, and lofty soul, Eliza Lynn."

Between the production of "Realities: a Tale," in 1851, and "Witch Stories," there was a gap of ten years, which the young writer devoted principally to journalism. She was, indeed, the first of women journalists. She contributed to several of the daily papers and magazines. Presently a series of pungent and clever essays began in the *Saturday Review*, which increased its fame, and took the world by storm. "The Girl of the Period," "The Shrieking Sisterhood," "Paying One's Shot," "Mature Sirens," have now passed into proverbs. They made a famous topic of conversation at dinner-tables, and proved a decided hit. For many years a certain lady of rank had the credit of the series, until at last, after many futile efforts, Mrs. Lynn Linton was allowed to collect her own papers and publish them under her own name.

"I never mind how much I slash," says Mrs. Lynn Linton, "because I always feel I am not slashing at a personality, but at a type. Thackeray never drew Becky Sharp from one individual; we all know a Becky Sharp."

In 1858 the young writer married Mr. Linton, the well-known wood engraver, and in 1861 began again the interrupted series of fifteen novels, amongst which were "Under which Lord?" "Patricia Kemball," "The True Story of Joshua Davidson," "Lizzie Lorton of Greyrigg," "Sowing the Wind," "The Atonement of Leam Dundas," "The World Well Lost," "The Rebel of the Family," "My Love," "Paston Carew, Miser and Millionaire," "Jane Stewart," "Through the Long

Night," and "Christopher Kirkland." This last is deeply interesting, as a history of the author herself, her theories, philosophy, and religious opinions.

The writing table in the cosy library—or as Mrs. Lynn Linton often calls it, "the workroom"—is placed slantways to catch the best light, and commands a beautiful view from the windows, full south over the Surrey hills.

The cut-glass inkstand has been in constant use for over fifty years. Papers, reviews, and books of reference are tidily heaped up; the table is full, but in perfect order; commenting on this to your hostess, she says it is "part of her nature, she could ·find anything in the dark." She is altogether a believer in method, regularity, and punctuality, which last quality gained for her from Charles Dickens the remark that she was "good for anything, and thoroughly reliable."

Opening a well-worn "Dictionary of Greek and Roman Antiquities" lying on a side-table close at hand, Mrs. Lynn Linton remarks it was bought with nearly her first earnings, and that she has by degrees purchased nearly all the books, which seem to occupy every available recess. The two deep cases opposite are filled with treasures of literature, and the tall revolving bookstand contains chiefly her collection of favourite poets—Landor, Arnold, Swinburne.

A Persian carpet of subdued tints covers the floor; on a large round table, over which hangs a lamp of graceful design, is heaped, with extreme precision, a mass of journals, magazines, and periodicals; not a paper is awry. The great accumulation of literature has indeed necessitated the fitting up of two tall, narrow recesses at the other end of the room, each neatly hidden by a long tapestry curtain. A tender light comes into Mrs. Lynn Linton's face as she points out three photographs hanging on the wall. The first is of her beloved brother, " without fear or favour," who died of a broken heart after the death of an adored wife; the second is of her " father " Landor; and the third is of Mr. Linton—" brother, father, husband," she says, with infinite tenderness for the memory of all three.

Asking if you may be allowed to see the famous view from the drawing-room, which you had heard " looks over St. James's Park and Carlton Terrace, and embraces the whole of the park from Buckingham Palace to the Horse Guards," " *Did* embrace it," amends Mrs. Linton, mournfully, " but come and see." She takes you to the opposite side of the flat, into a rather long drawing-room, the windows of which look due south over the uninterrupted view one might reasonably have expected to see. Alas! a tall and ugly erection of bricks and mortar has sprung up to the left, obscuring a portion of the prospect. " They have given me only a vista," says Mrs. Lynn Linton, " where I once had a view." What is left, however, is very fine, and from the great height above ground the people look like pigmies dotted about. Queen Caroline once talked of shutting up this lovely park, and converting it into a noble garden far the palace. She consulted Walpole as to the probable cost; the witty minister replied, " Only three crowns, your Majesty," and the idea was abandoned.

There is a peculiarly long, narrow frame hanging
on the opposite side of the wall, and as Mrs. Lynn
Linton permits an inspection of everything, you
examine it carefully, while she explains the subject.
It is nearly four yards long, and represents the Par-
thenon frieze—the Panathenaic procession—and the
fight of the Amazons and Athenians, reduced and
restored by John Herring. As the slate matrix was
broken, it is now extremely valuable. It is in plaster
of Paris, mounted on red, and is the property of Mr.
Linton, who has bequeathed it to the National Gallery
in America. The small statuette of "Margaret,"
modelled by Geefs, is another and very rare gem.
Mrs. Lynn Linton is also the possessor of a quaint grey
vase, a relic of the Great Exhibition of 1851. On one
little table, covered with an Oriental cloth, crowded
with favourite photographs, the portrait of a graceful,
pretty girl occupies a prominent place. "That is my
Beatrice, my Bee, my dear adopted daughter," she says,
"dear as if she were my own; and these," pointing to
two large framed pictures, "are both likenesses of my
friend Mr. Fuller, a nephew of Sir Arthur Helps.
We first became friends through correspondence. He
sent me his book, 'Culmshire Folk.' His wife invited
me to Ireland last year, and the result was my first
and last political work about that country."

You ask Mrs. Lynn Linton to tell you about some
of the celebrated people whom she has met. After
musing awhile, she mentions Captain Maconochie (the
convicts' friend), Sir Charles Babbage, Kinglake, Miss
Jane Porter, Mrs. Milner Gibson—"she was my social
godmother; but these all belonged to a past generation.

In later years I was more or less on intimate terms
with Harrison Ainsworth, George Eliot, Sir Henry
Layard, Sir Henry Rawlinson, Tom Taylor, Thackeray,
Dickens, Yates, Wilkie Collins, Swinburne, Sir Roderick
Murchison, Rider Haggard, Dr. Elliotson, and William
Spottiswoode, late President of the Royal Society. *He*
was a prince among men, and I loved and reverenced
his noble character."

Unlike many literary women, Mrs. Lynn Linton is a
great adept with her needle. The beautiful silk em-
broideries—of which she is very proud—cushions,
chair seats, and the handsome fire-screen are all the
work of her skilful fingers, and made from her own
designs. The big green frog and the swallows hanging
on the left are a present from Mr. Oswald Crawfurd,
the famous consul at Oporto. The Tunis plates and
various photographs indicate that your hostess has
made sundry journeys abroad, and travelled in many
foreign lands where she has picked up a few picturesque "bits" as mementos of the places which she
visited; but she says her most cherished possession
is the gold cinquecento basket standing yonder, the
gift of Walter Savage Landor.

Yet more books! Each recess in the opposite
wall is well filled, also the low dwarf bookcase
under the large mirror, and another under the
Herring "slate."

You are curious to know if Mrs. Lynn Linton reads
and is influenced by criticisms on her works? She
says she has never striven for popularity, and has
boldly put forth her opinions, without caring for the
consequences. She was once called "selfish." *Selfish!*

Have you not known, and been told by a score of young authors, that they owe their success and a deep debt of gratitude to her! In despair, one after another has taken to her an article, a story, a three-volume novel, a play; what not? With patience she would pore over a crabbed manuscript, word by word, suggesting, correcting, improving, advising. She has a large number of young friends, who confide all their troubles, hopes, and wishes to her, with the certainty of absolute sympathy and wise counsel. Far from being stern or severe as some of her books might lead one to think, she is bubbling over with the milk of human kindness, and her chief desire is to be of use or help to some one. The tender, motherly manner casts its spell over you too, and you find yourself presently pouring out confidences as if she were an old acquaintance.

Mrs. Lynn Linton generally enjoys the best of health. She keeps early hours, works in the morning, takes plenty of exercise, and " plain living " keeps the *mens sana in corpore sano* for " high thinking." Although in her sixth decade, she possesses a splendid physique, of which she is pardonably proud. She says she finds residing in her exalted flat far preferable to a house. There she is out of the reach of burglars and beggars ; she lives at less expense, combined with incomparably more comfort; whilst the servants of the gigantic establishment all respect her, and " Ellen," who has been there for eleven years, she calls her " child," and looks upon her as a personal friend.

But the clock strikes. You have been unconscionable. The time has sped so rapidly that the promised hour

has doubled itself.   You say good-bye, and as Mrs.
Lynn Linton kindly asks you to come again on her
"Saturdays, to one or to all," you look down on the
small white hand which holds yours, and notice the
long slender fingers.   The memory of its hearty clasp
remains on your mind as you are conveyed down the
eight stories of Queen Anne's Mansions, and so, into
the street, where you become one of the aforenamed
"pigmies."

MRS RIDDELL

MRS. RIDDELL.

THE sleepy little village of Upper Halliford, Middlesex, has one peculiar charm. Though within ten
minutes' walk of Walton Bridge, it lies quite off the
main line of traffic, and is consequently free from the
visits of Cockney tourists, affording in this, as in
many other respects, a striking contrast to Lower
Halliford, which, situated on a lovely reach of the
Thames, welcomes annually thousands of visitors.

There the inevitable steam-launch cuts its swift
way through the water; there boating-men, clad in
all the colours of the rainbow, are to be met with,
on or after Good Friday, when the "season" begins;
there persistent fishermen, seated in punts warily
moored, angle day after day, and all day long, for
the bream, roach, and gudgeon, to be found in such
abundance; there furnished houses let at high rents;
willows dip their branches in the river, and from
thence the trees of Oatlands show well on the
upland on the opposite sides of the glistening Thames.

It was between Lower Halliford and Walton
Bridge—half of which is in Surrey and half in
Middlesex—that, at a point called the Coway Stakes,

Julius Cæsar is believed to have crossed the river. The name " Coway Stakes " originated in the fact that there Cassivelaunus fortified the banks, and filled the river with sharp-pointed stakes to prevent the enemy from crossing the stream, but notwithstanding these precautions the Roman leader and his legions accomplished their purpose, and, a little way above where the Ship Hotel (so well known to boating-men), now stands, a terrible battle was fought in the year 54 B.C. between the Britons and Romans.   Several relics have been dug up about this part of the Thames, also a number of the stakes taken from the bed of the river, black with age, but still sound.

Any one who cares to walk on to Walton should make a point of visiting the old Church of St. Mary—an edifice of great antiquity—in order to see a curious relic, dated 1632, a scold's bit, or bridle, bearing the following inscription :—

> " Chester to Walton sends a bridle
> To curb women's tongues that talk too idle."

Upper Halliford, unlike Lower Halliford, or Walton, has nothing to show in the way of beauty or relic. It boasts no history, it has no legend, or old church, or historic mansion.   It is only a quaint little hamlet, which might be a hundred miles from the bustle and roar of London ; there, however, the famous author of " George Geith of Fen Court " has for the last seven years made her home, where she lives in absolute seclusion.

Her little cottage stands slightly back from the

high road. It is built flush with the ground, and covered with trellis-work, which in summer time is concealed by clustering white roses and clematis. The porch is in the centre, and the rooms on each side have broad bay windows. There is a large field in front, and so many evergreens about the cottage, that, when snow comes, the place looks like a winter "transformation scene."

A great, old-fashioned garden stretches far out at the back, and it was chiefly the tranquillity and privacy of this delightful garden, with its grand old hedge of holly, now bright with red berries, which attracted Mrs. Riddell, and decided her to settle down, away from the world, after long and fierce buffeting with the stormy seas of sorrow, disappointment, losses, and bereavement, of which she has had so large a share.

The gentle, quiet face tells its tale of early struggles, heavy burdens, severe trials; yet time has not laid its ruthless hand over-harshly on the author. Not a silver hair is visible on the soft, brown hair, which is simply rolled into a neat coil, high on the back of her head, and fastened by a large tortoise-shell comb. The deep grey eyes are undimmed, and wear a look of peace and resignation, nobly won; while "ever and anon of griefs subdued, there comes a token" which recalls the past. But Mrs. Riddell can smile sweetly, and when she smiles, two—yes two—absolutely girlish dimples light up the expressive countenance. She is tall, has a good carriage, and is dressed in black; she has worn no colours for over ten years.

The little room is very simply but prettily fur-

nished. It is lighted by one bay window reaching to
the ground in front, and a glass door at the side. Soft,
white rugs lie here and there on the dark red carpet,
and an old-fashioned bookcase contains the works of
her favourite authors. There are no particular curiosities or decorations to be seen, save one valuable bit
of old Dresden china, two or three plates of ancient
Crown Derby, together with a couple of quaint
Delhi-work salvers, and a few pictures hanging on
the walls. Of these last, two are particularly attractive. One is the Head of a Christ crowned
with thorns, beautifully painted on copper; the
other, over the fire place, represents the Castle of
Carrigfergus, which, though built nearly a thousand
years ago, is still strong enough to hold a troop of
soldiers.

Mrs. Riddell was born in Ireland, at The Barn,
Carrigfergus. She was the youngest daughter of Mr.
James Cowan, who held the post of High Sheriff for
the county of that town.

"Yes, I am from the north—the black north," says
your hostess in a low, soft voice. "My grandfather
was in the navy, and my great-grandfather fought at
Culloden, so I may fairly claim to be English, Scotch,
and Irish. My mother, Ellen Kilshaw, was a beautiful, graceful, and accomplished English woman. On
most subjects people have two opinions, but I never
heard a second opinion about my mother. Even
amongst those who only knew her in later life, when
stricken with disease, and changed by long years of
sorrow, she stands out a distinct personality, as one
of those possessed of the manners, appearance, and

ideas, that we associate with the highest bred women of the past!"

"And she was good as she was beautiful. I wish you could hear how rich and poor who knew her in the old time at The Barn still speak of her. As for me, while I speak, the grief of her death seems sharp and present as on that sixteenth of December when she left me."

Last autumn, after a lapse of twenty-five years, Mrs. Riddell revisited her native place. "Such of our old friends as were left," she says, "I found as kind as ever."

It must have been sad, yet sweet, for the author to recall the old reminiscences of her girlish home as she saw once more the pretty bungalow-like house, with its gardens, hot-houses, and vineries, and to visit again the spot where, at the age of fifteen, she remembers writing her first story.

"It was on a bright moonlight night," she says—"I can see it now flooding the gardens—that I began it, and I wrote week after week, never ceasing until it was finished. Need I add it was never published?"

She goes on eloquently to tell you of yet further recollections of the old house, the memory of her father's lingering illness, and the low, sweet tones of her mother's voice as she read aloud to him for hours together. "From my father," says Mrs. Riddell, "I think I got the few brains I possess. Undoubtedly he was a very clever man, but *I* never knew him at his best, for as far as my memory goes back he was always more or less a sufferer, blessed with the most tender and devoted wife man ever had."

On her father's death the property passed into other hands, and with but a small jointure the broken-hearted widow and her daughter left their old home. They lived afterwards, for a while, in the charming village of Dundonald in the County Down, where the young author subsequently laid the scene of her novel, "Berna Boyle," and then, after a good deal of meditation, they decided to come to London. In later years she wrote three other Irish stories, "The Earl's Promise," "The Nun's Curse," and "Maxwell Drewitt," which last contains an exciting account of an election at Connemara.

"I have often wished," says Mrs. Riddell, "we never had so decided, yet in that case, I do not think I ever should have achieved the smallest success, and even before we left, with bitter tears, a place where we had the kindest friends, and knew much happiness, my mother's death was—though neither of us then knew the fact—a certainty. The illness of which she died had then taken hold of her. She had always a great horror of pain mental and physical; she was keenly sensitive, and mercifully before the agonising period of her complaint arrived, the nerves of sensation were paralysed; first or last she never lost a night's sleep the whole of the ten weeks, during which I fought with death for her, and—was beaten.

Mrs. Riddell's first impressions of London are well worth recording. Coming as strangers to a strange land, throughout the length and breadth of the great metropolis, she says, "We did not know a single creature! During the first fortnight, indeed, I really thought I should break my heart. I had never taken

kindly to new places, and, remembering the sweet
hamlet and the loving friends left behind, London
seemed to me horrible ! I could not eat ; I could
not sleep ; I could only walk over the ' stony-hearted
streets ' and offer my manuscripts to publisher after
publisher, who unanimously declined them." The
desolation of her spirit can be more easily imagined
than described. Conceive the situation of the young
girl, burning to earn a living by her pen, knowing
that it was within her to do so, yet unacquainted with
a single literary or other person ; friendless, unknown,
with an invalid mother, and terribly insufficient means!
And when, at last, she sold a story, called " Moors
and Fens," that beloved mother had passed away ;
and your eyes moisten as the daughter mentions the
touching and filial use to which her first twenty
pounds were applied.

But Mrs. Riddell has something pleasant to say
for those who declined her MSS., and it must be
related in her own words : " Looking back I *must*
say, as a rule, they were all very kind to me. I
was too ignorant and heartsore to understand how
gracious they were to my simplicity, even more than
to my youth. Yet I shall never forget how charming
Mr. George Bentley's manner seemed the first day I
saw him. His father—the kindest, most impulsive,
most sympathetic of men—was alive then, and for
many a year afterwards ; but it so happened that Mr.
George Bentley was the partner whom I saw, and,"
she adds smiling, and naïvely, " though he, like everyone else, refused my work, still I left his office not
unhappy, but thinking much more about how courteous

B

and nice he was than of how entirely the wrong person in the wrong place I seemed to be. Ere long,
with some publishers I became quite on friendly
terms, and I have now known three generations of
the Bentleys."

After a short silence Mrs. Riddell resumes the subject, saying, " I must name also Mr. Charles Skeet,
of King William Street, who was good enough to
keep my mother supplied with books. Long as it is
since he retired from business, our friendship remained
unbroken until his death. He was most kind to me
always. He published ' The Rich Husband,' ' Too
Much Alone,' ' The World and the Church,' and ' Alaric
Spencer.' "

" I could always, when the day was frightfully cold
—and *what* a winter that was when I first came
to London—turn into Mr. Newby's snug and warm
office in Welbeck Street, and have a talk with him
and his ' woman of business.' I am glad to mention
her name—Miss Springett. She was a lady, always
kind, nice, and capable ; she remained with him till
her death, I believe. Everyone was good to me in
those days ; but, indeed, I have received, all my
life through, an enormous amount of kindness, and
have not a word to say against a world which has
treated me far better than I deserved."

A year after the death of her mother the young
author married. Mr. Riddell belonged to an old
Staffordshire family, a branch of the Scotch Riddells,
of long descent and gentle blood. "Courageous and
hopeful, gifted with indomitable energy," says his
widow, "endowed with marvellous persistence and

perseverance; modestly conscious of talents which ought to have made their mark, he, when a mere lad, began his long quest after fortune, one single favour from whom he was never destined to receive."

Gifted with much inventive genius, Mr. Riddell was also possessed of considerable general knowledge, and was deeply versed in literature, medicine, science, and mathematics. To him his wife turned for all the information she needed in her novels; the chemistry in "Too Much Alone," the engineering in "City and Suburb." He supplied all the business details in "George Geith," and "The Race for Wealth"; while in "Mortomley's Estate" Mrs. Riddell says she has "but told the simple story of what, when in ill-health and broken in spirit, he had to encounter before ruin, total and complete, overtook him." Too early in youth overweighted with a heavy burden, under which a strong man might have found it hard to stagger, she declares that, "in spite of harassing trouble and continuous misfortune, their twenty-three years of married life were happy as few lives are, simply by reason of his sweet, patient temper, and his child-like faith." Suddenly and unexpectedly, the end came, and the crowning sorrow of a much-tried life was laid upon the devoted wife when death claimed her gifted husband. Over that grief a veil must be drawn. Suffice it to say that it is a sorrow which will ever be keen in her remembrance "Until the day break and the shadows flee away."

"I never remember the time," Mrs. Riddell says, "when I did not compose. Before I was old enough to hold a pen I used to get my mother to write down

my childish ideas, and a friend remarked to me quite
lately that she distinctly remembers my being discouraged in the habit, as it was feared I might be led
into telling untruths. In my very early days I read
everything I could lay hands on, the Koran included,
when about eight years old. I thought it most
interesting."

Mrs. Riddell describes the way in which the situations and characters of her books are often suggested.
She observes everything almost unconsciously; but if
asked, directly after, her impressions, she could scarcely
describe them. Later on, perhaps, when between the
border-land of sleep and waking, scenes, words, people
whom she has noticed seem to be photographed on the
brain; sentences form themselves, and in the morning
she is able to reproduce them at length.

The intimate knowledge of the city possessed by
this novelist is the result of personal experience.
Whilst on her once fruitless expeditions to publishers
she learnt every short cut, every alley and lane by
heart. Little as she relished these excursions at the
time, they laid the foundation for many a scene afterwards so faithfully depicted in " George Geith," " City
and Suburb" (in which most of the poetry was quoted
from the works of her young sister-in-law, a genius
who died at the age of nineteen), " Daisies and Butter-
cups," "The Struggle for Fame," " Mitre Court," " My
First Love, and My Last Love," " The Earl's Promise,"
and also that entrancing book, " The Senior Partner,"
in which the old Scotch merchant, M'Cullagh, " plain
auld Rab," worthy but saving old gentleman, is a
distinct creation. "In all the old city churches and

graveyards, such, indeed, as are left," Mrs. Riddell says, sorrowfully, "you could take no better guide than myself; but, alas! many of the old landmarks are now pulled down to make room for the ever increasing business of the great metropolis."

"Austin Friars" described her first home after her marriage, when, without much practical knowledge of business, she was greatly impressed by the lives of business men. This old house is now a thing of the past, and the Cannon Street railway runs over the place where it once stood.

The author's latest work—a story of seaside life, and her twenty-ninth novel—is called "Grays Point," and will be brought out in three volumes in the coming year. She lately was invited to write an article for *The Lady of the House*, a new journal which appeared in Dublin last year, and this is the first time that she has ever written a line for an Irish paper. Of her own books, Mrs. Riddell says that she prefers "The Mystery in Palace Gardens" and "Too Much Alone." The latter she considers made her name, though the first edition was only a short one, and but four copies were sent out for review. "A Mad Tour, or A Journey Undertaken in an Insane Moment through Central Europe on Foot," in one volume, is a recent work, and describes accurately her own experiences in company with a young friend. It gives a bright and amusing account of their misadventures.

Mrs. Riddell's latest published novel in three volumes, "The Head of the Firm," fully bears out the high literary reputation of the author of "George

Geith." Carefully and conscientiously worked out, each character is drawn with an unerring hand, and sustains its interest to the final page, whilst here and there are not wanting those touches of humour which have always distinguished her works.

After a snug luncheon in the comfortable dining-room, in which, by the way, unexpected little steps and deep cupboards seem to be built promiscuously—as, indeed, they are throughout the cottage—your hostess takes you round the garden, which is well worth seeing, mid-winter though it be. She points out the great height of the holly hedge, and laments that she has been obliged to have twelve feet cut off the top. Notwithstanding, it is still twenty feet high. The japonica is the admiration of passers-by in the early spring, being then covered with a mass of scarlet flowers. The apricot tree is sadly in want of root pruning, but, as she says, " I cannot persuade the old gardener to do it, and as I am never equal to arguing, I let him take his own way." There is an extra-ordinary plant which you have never seen before; its flowers are green, and Mrs. Riddell says that she never saw one like it except in her old home. The huge weeping ash, although now bereft of leaves, is a great feature, and the high box borders divide large squares of ground, wherein good old bushes of lavender, rue and lad's love grow profusely.

Your hostess points out the adjoining cottage, the home of her old gardener, aged eighty, and remarks that another old man who preceded him begged from a neighbour enough elm to make him a coffin. It was given to him, and the hitherto unnecessary article made. He kept the gruesome object for some time, but finding it took up too much room in his small abode, he altered it into a cupboard.

A turn round the last walk leads to the poultry-yard, which is a great delight to Mrs. Riddell. She has several fine breeds of fowls and geese, amongst which last are two handsome but noisy specimens from Japan. One little peculiarity of interest must be noticed. The wall which supports the granary steps is pierced by two holes for dog kennels, an arrangement of great antiquity.

Mrs. Riddell loves walking. The church she attends lies rather more than two miles away towards Laleham, which place Arnold left with so much regret, and where Matthew Arnold is buried. She speaks of Littleton in the neighbourhood as being the village she described in "For Dick's Sake," and says, laughing, "It has stood still for over two hundred years. There is no resident rector or squire, or doctor, or lawyer, or publican, or farrier, but it is a sweetly peaceful spot, and the woods in primrose time are a sight to behold, whilst at Sunbury," she adds, "to show you how little change may take place, in one hundred years there have been only two vicars, and one of them is alive now!"

But it is getting dark, and tea is ordered as a preparation for your cold journey; whilst sipping it, she says that as you are so much interested in her own early "struggle for fame," she will mention one more anecdote à propos of Mr. Newby, as it is amusing, and she relates it thus: "In those early days he—Mr. Newby—was good enough to take a book of mine. Of course he only knew

me by my maiden name, because after my mother's
death Welbeck Street lay quite out of my way,
and I fear I ungratefully forgot the cheerful fire,
and the talks about authors, which were once so
pleasant.

" For this reason he knew nothing of my doings.
The years came and the years went, till after the
crash came in our affairs ; when I was looking about
me for every five-pound note I could get, I bethought
me of this and another old book, which I can never
sufficiently regret republishing.   Well, I found I
could sell both of them, and forthwith repaired, after
all that time, to Mr. Newby's, where nothing looked
much changed, and no one seemed much older,
except myself, who had lived many lives in the
interval.

" Of course both Mr. Newby and Miss Springett
had a vague memory of me, when I reminded the
former that he had published ' Zuriel's Grandchild.'
What I wanted was a copy of the book.   He feared
he had not one, but promised to ascertain.   I can see
them both now in that warm, comfortable back room,
into which, as a girl, I had often gone shivering.

" He took a seat on one side of a large table, she on
the other.   I sat facing Mr. Newby—a most anxious
woman, yet amused.

" ' Have you,' he said delicately, ' gone on at all
with literature ? '

" ' Oh, yes,' I answered.

" ' Have you—published anything ? ' with great
caution, so as not to hurt my feelings.

" ' Several books,' I replied.

" ' Indeed ! ! !' *amazed.* ' Might I ask the names ? ' —tentatively.

" ' Well, amongst others, " George Geith." '

" A dead silence ensued, during which I had the comfort of feeling that they both felt sure I was saying what was not true. I sat quite quiet, and so did they. If I had not been so burdened with care I must have laughed out loud. As it happened, I comported myself, as I have often done since, in many difficult and humorous positions, with decent gravity, and then this came from Mr. Newby, the while the ribbons on Miss Springett's cap were tremulous :

" ' *If*—you *really* wrote " George Geith," *then* indeed you have achieved a success !' "

And so you part ; with loving tender sympathy. Though the morn of this distinguished woman's life has been so clouded, the noon so stormy, the noble, self-reliant spirit has battled through it bravely and patiently, and you leave her with the inwardly-breathed prayer that " at evening time there shall come light ! "

MRS. L. B. WALFORD.

A THICK fog obscures the whole of London. You grope your way through Liverpool Street station with considerable risk, now colliding with a truck full of luggage, anon canoning against an angry passenger. Not a yard can be seen in advance, more by good luck than good guiding the right train is somehow found, and, half an hour later, it is delightful to find the enemy is left behind, and that there is once more cheerful daylight. The sun at first looks like a sullen ball of fire, but presently, shaking off, as it were, the heavy clouds, he begins to shine out brightly, as, after a drive of something under a mile from the station, the carriage turns into the old-fashioned lodge gates of wrought iron on the left. A long road between two low wire fencings, running nearly straight through the park, which is dotted about with clumps of trees and spinneys, suddenly rounds into a wide space in front ot the house, and breaks off into one of those quaint old rights-of-way which are so common in this part of Essex.

Cranbrooke Hall is a substantial red-brick, many-windowed building, dating nearly two centuries back,

MRS L. B. WALFORD

but it has been greatly added to and improved during recent years. The lofty, spacious entrance-hall, laid down with parquet, branches out into five reception rooms, opening one into another, all facing south, and overlooking some seven-hundred-and-fifty feet of lawn, bordered by a lake formed of clear, running water, the overflow of a spring which is a hundred-and-fifty feet deep, and has never yet been known to run dry. This is, in its turn, bounded by a shrubbery, which leads round to one of the principal features of the Cranbrooke Gardens, the "Lovers' Walk," an ivy colonnade, carpeted with thick, soft moss.

Passing through the ante-room, a door opens on the left, and the picture which presents itself to the eye is a thoroughly domestic one. A huge fire, heaped with acacia logs, blazes brightly in the low deep grate, flanked with brass dogs; tall standard lamps shed a soft light over a merry family group; a silver urn stands on the cosy five o'clock tea table, where a young, fair girl presides. A few guests are present, and two younger daughters of the house are flitting in and out with plates of Scotch scones, cakes, and muffins. The three nursery little ones have come down to say good-night; the youngest, a fair-haired, blue-eyed little maiden of four years, is nestling on her mother's lap. Rising from amidst them, Mrs. Walford comes forward to welcome you. She wears a pretty steel-blue tea-gown, richly embroidered in silks by her own hand; for your hostess loves needlework, and looks on it as a great resource for a weary brain. She has a

clear, fair complexion, dark brown hair, and laughing
grey-blue eyes; and the bright, sunny smile, which
in childhood gained for her the pet name of "the
laughing girl," lights up her expressive countenance,
and just reveals two rows of white, even teeth. She
gives you the impression of being a thoroughly
happy, contented, and sweet-tempered woman, and
her subsequent conversation assures you that your
judgment has been correct.

Mrs. Walford is of Scottish birth. Her father
was the second son of Sir James Colquhoun, the
tenth Baronet of Luss, to whom Burke wrote on
one occasion that he was "*the* Baronet of Scotland,
just as Sir William Watkin Wynn was *the* Baronet
of Wales." For seven hundred years the Colquhouns
of Luss have held the same lands, and, unlike those
of many other ancient families, they are still in
as flourishing, or, rather, more flourishing condition, than they have ever been. The Sir James
Colquhoun who—with four of his keepers and a
ghillie boy—was drowned in Loch Lomond, nearly
seventeen years ago, was a widower with an only son,
the present baronet. Mrs. Walford's mother was
the daughter of Mr. Fuller-Maitland of Stanstead,
Essex.

Whilst the other visitors are leaving, the opportunity arises of examining the room more minutely.
The polished oak floor is covered here and there
with Persian carpets; near the door is a lovely
Dutch marqueterie bureau, a husband's gift to a
busy wife, and at which most of her well-known
novels were written. Mrs. Walford says they "fur-

nished their home as a jackdaw does his nest, stick
by stick. From many an old farm-house and wayside
inn they collected piece after piece, handsome old
oak cabinets, chests and chairs, scarcely a single
article having passed through the dealers' hands,"
indeed, you shrewdly suspect that the large carved
settle whereon you are seated has been part of some
despoiled church or sacred edifice.

On a table yonder stands a miniature set of china
under glass, "Jane Eyre's own doll's tea service,"
by which Mrs. Walford sets great store, as she
became possessed of it when visiting the house
of Charlotte Brontë. The dainty, antique spinning-wheel known as "Lady Helen's wheel" (it
belonged to an ancient dame of the Colquhoun
family) is so old that the woodwork has begun
to crumble away; but a more modern specimen
opposite, covered with a cloud of flax, is often
used by your hostess's own nimble fingers. The
relic she treasures above all, however, is a
gold "mazer," inherited by Mr. Walford through
a long line of ancestors. This is a real curiosity, there being but few of these "mazers"
now left in England. The little "silver table"
holds many a prized bit of old Highland silver,
including one which was picked up on the field of
Bannockburn. Big bowls of Oriental china are filled
with *pot-pourri*, which gives out a delicious fragrance.
This, Mrs. Walford adds to afresh every year from
an old recipe. Her children laughingly declare that
"whenever they go out to gather flowers for the
tables, mother, with a pair of scissors in hand, has

snipped off all the finest roses and quietly slipped them into her pocket."

Mrs. Walford has inherited her literary tastes. Her father's well-known book, "The Moor and the Loch," now in its eighth edition, and full of spirited engravings, is considered as a classic amongst sportsmen; and who has not read and laughed over, in by-gone days, "Holiday House," and other delightful stories, by her grand-aunt, Catherine Sinclair, daughter of Sir John Sinclair of Ulbster, himself one of the most distinguished men of his day? In spite of Catherine Sinclair and her sister being authors (the latter was known as the "good" Lady Colquhoun, and the writer of many religious books for the Scottish poor), so little was literary reputation then thought of by some members of the family that, when Sir Walter Scott appeared at Rossdhu to take notes for "Rob Roy," he was shown round *by the butler*, and never forgave the affront. In consequence he never mentioned the Colquhouns in that great romance or in the "Lady of the Lake."

Speaking of Rossdhu, you tell your hostess that you have been taken over those ancestral halls and round the great picture galleries, and had noticed with much surprise that there was no portrait of her to be seen. This omission may however some day be repaired.

Mrs. Walford remarks that it was not until after her marriage that she took seriously to novel writing. Whilst yet in her teens she was wont to steal out into the shrubbery with paper and pencil and write short stories, one of which was called "Macgregor, our Chieftain," but as she burnt these early effusions as fast as they were written, nothing remains of Macgregor's adventures. In 1872 delicacy of health prevented her pursuing the active out-of-door life which she had always enjoyed; so, as the necessity arose for finding vent for her energy, the young author spent a long period of bodily rest in mental activity, its first fruits being " Mr. Smith: A part of his Life." This character was drawn from life; even the name was the same, and he was found dead as described in the book. She sent the MS. anonymously to Mr. John Blackwood, the late distinguished editor of *Blackwood*, who—much struck with its promise—at once accepted and published it.

Brought up from her childhood in the stately homes of her own people, now in Scotland, now in England, and reared in the atmosphere of healthy country life, Mrs. Walford has been enabled to write with the frankness and accuracy which make her books so thoroughly characteristic and enjoyable.

A propos of " Mr. Smith," an amusing anecdote is told. The Queen had had the story read to her twice, and, being much interested in it, expressed a wish to see the author. She was presented on her marriage by the Duchess of Roxburghe, who on the occasion happened to take the place of the Mistress of the Robes, absent from indisposition. It is said that as the young novelist made her curtsey before the Royal presence, the Duchess softly breathed into Her Majesty's ear the words, "Mr. Smith."

A series of short stories soon followed this first success and appeared in *Blackwood*, beginning with

"Nan, a Summer Scene," and under this name they
have since been collected and published in one volume.
" Pauline " next ran through the same magazine as a
serial ; " Cousins " was written in 1879 ; " Troublesome
Daughters" followed in the ensuing year.   " The
Baby's Grandmother," which is perhaps the most
popular of all, was written in 1885.   Then came " A
Stiff-necked Generation," " A Mere Child," " A Sage
of Sixteen," " The Havoc of a Smile," " The Mischief
of Monica." The latter book is more on the lines
of " Mr. Smith" than any of Mrs. Walford's recent
works of fiction, and proved a great success in
Longman's Magazine.   Then came " A Pinch of
Experience," and later on, she wrote a series of
Biographical studies on "Famous Authoresses of
Bygone Days," for *Far and Near*, an American
Magazine.   This is coming out as a Christmas gift or
prize book.   A little volume of Christmas Tales illustrated by T. Pym (Mrs. Levett) is shortly to appear, and
will be called " For Grown-up Children," being stories
about children *for* grown-up people.   Besides this,
she is a constant contributor to the *St. James's
Gazette.*   She also writes a weekly letter for the
American *Critic* on literary subjects ; one called an
" Epidemic of Smartness" made a special sensation ;
and she has, in addition, stories in two Christmas
numbers, *The Queen* and *Atalanta.*

One great aim of this author has ever been to make
herself thoroughly acquainted with all the details of
her subject.   So particular is she to ensure absolute
accuracy, that every item of military life is submitted to one or other of her soldier brothers (two of

these were respectively in the 4th Dragoon Guards
and the 42nd Black Watch), and every detail of
sport to her father; indeed, so well up was she in
the latter, that a reviewer of "Mr. Smith"—when
the sex of the author was yet unknown—caustically
observed, that the writer was "more up in wood-
cock shooting than in religion!" the young author
not having yet learnt to verify a quotation, even
from Holy Writ.

An ardent lover of the old Scottish kirk, Mrs.
Walford says that she "would go any distance to hear
a good, long sermon from some of its divines." She
is an indefatigable walker, and has traversed on foot
twenty-three miles, from Arrochar to Inveraray—
"from milestone to milestone" she is careful to add,
knowing what Scotch and Welsh miles are supposed
to be. She is extremely fond of poetry, and has a
good collection of her chief favourites, whilst she
keeps habitually on her own table copies of Tennyson,
Jean Ingelow, and Coventry Patmore's work.

In earlier days your hostess gave much of her
time to water-colour drawing, but her children have
claimed for the decoration of their schoolroom all
her pictures, the majority of which, they proudly
remark, were "exhibited and hung on the line in
the R.A. of Edinburgh." Mrs. Walford is just saying that she was married at St. John's, Edinburgh,
when the door opens and in comes the bridegroom on
that occasion. He is a native of another part of
Essex, in which county his forefathers have held
lands for several centuries, his grandfather having
been High Sheriff in the famous "Waterloo year."

He is a magistrate for the part in which he now lives,
and, amidst the claims of a busy life, he finds time
to sit on the bench perhaps oftener than do many of
his less occupied colleagues. Looking at the noble,
genial face, you secretly wonder if he can ever
find it in his heart to pass severe sentences on
offenders. He is extremely popular, has made a distinct mark for himself in his own circle, and it is his
wife's pride to recognise that he will never be known
as "Mrs. Walford's husband."

An hour later you are taken into the dining-room,
through the ante-room, in the latter, a table near
the great bay windows is filled with all the newest
books and magazines ; these are regularly changed
and brought up to date by Mrs. Walford, and are a
constant source of attraction to visitors. On your
left at dinner sits your host's elder son, " Desborough,"
a fine manly young fellow, just of age ; he is full of
intelligence, and possesses great powers of observation. He is delightfully entertaining throughout
the meal, and asking him about the pictures, which
literally cover the walls, he explains that they are
a complete collection of Boydell's fine old Shake-
spearian engravings, and, he adds modestly, these, and
all the many etchings and pictures in the house,
were framed by his father.

It is quite apparent in this happy home that there
is perfect love and sympathy between the parents
and the children. The children are as proud of
their good, distinguished-looking father as they are
of their pretty, gifted mother ; the elder ones are
keenly interested in her books, and look out eagerly

for the new copies, each confiscating one for his or
her own room. Mr. and Mrs. Walford have ever been
in touch with each individual member of their family.
The children have never been put aside for her work,
and they are constantly with their mother. They
have all inherited her talent for drawing, and many
of them bid fair to be no mean proficients in the art.

On the following morning your hostess announces
that she has "given herself a holiday" and she
proposes to take you out for a turn. The season is
late and, though within but a very few weeks of
Christmas, the sun is shining brightly over the grounds
and the air is pleasantly warm. What was once
said of a famous lawn at Oxford may well be applied
to Cranbrooke Hall. A stranger inquired of a solemn
old gardener what was done to keep it so fine and
smooth? "Well, sir," was the reply, with the utmost
gravity and good faith, "first we sows the seed, and
then we rolls it and we mows it for three hundred
years." Skating will soon be largely indulged in on
the glittering lake, and many merry moonlight parties
are looked forward to during the coming severe
weather, which is predicted by the great holly trees
covered with red berries. After a stroll round the
pleasant demesne, and a peep into the vineries, in
which is the old black Hamburg vine, sister of the
famous one at Hampton Court, you return through
the billiard-room into the Camellia house, which, a
little later on will be a mass of bloom, sometimes as
many as two thousand being in flower at a time, in
every variety of colour.

The billiard table is decorated at the sides with

groups of hand-painted flowers, exquisitely designed, and the cues are arranged in a round oak niche, which you feel sure once contained the image of a saint in some old cathedral. Just above the seat backs, and extending all round the room, is a perfect picture gallery of friends' photographs, placed closely side by side, and above these there is a wealth of engravings and etchings which would take days to examine.

Mrs. Walford has had three old-fashioned predecessors in the paths of literature in her own neighbourhood, namely, Thomas Day, who, exactly a hundred years ago, wrote "Sandford and Merton," at the little village of Aybridge, within half a dozen miles of Cranbrooke; Anne and Jane Taylor, whose "Original Poems" were, according to Sir Walter Scott, "known to four continents."

Before leaving, you ask to see your hostess's own special portrait gallery of her seven children. First comes "Desborough," then the eldest daughter, in her *débutante's* drawing-room dress of last season; next, two young girls yet in the schoolroom,

> Standing with reluctant feet
> Where the brook and river meet,

and then the three "nursery" children, one of whom is taken in her mother's arms. Lastly, you are shown a faded portrait of the famous author herself, taken at the age of fourteen, and called "A Yellow-haired Lassie," and, in the bright, radiant smile, you recognise the appropriateness of her childish cognomen of "The Laughing Girl."

RHODA BROUGHTON

RHODA BROUGHTON.

THE ancient and historic village of Richmond is too well known to need much description. It is thronged with kingly memories. Entering the old park by Kew Bridge, you drive past the large and beautiful Royal Gardens, extending along the banks of the Thames to Richmond, which were cultivated under the immediate superintendence of King George III. The old manor garden became Crown property in the reign of Edward I., when it was known as Shene, and was converted into a palace by Edward III.; but, being destroyed by fire in 1498, it was rebuilt with great splendour by Henry VII., who changed the name to Richmond, after his title of Earl of Richmond, ere he ascended the throne. Here was Philip I. of Spain right regally entertained. Here was the Princess Elizabeth shut up by her sister Mary, and here occasionally resided Charles I. On the right stands the Observatory, built by Sir William Chambers two centuries ago. When the road turns into the New Park south of Richmond, the coach-man points out the massive brick wall encompassing the eight miles of its circumference, and remarks that in the reign of George II. an attempt was made to exclude the public, which was frustrated however by an enterprising inhabitant, who, pluckily going to law, recovered the right of way, and thus secured the ever-lasting gratitude of later generations.

It is for this picturesque and attractive place Miss Rhoda Broughton has deserted her quiet little home at Oxford, where she had lived for twelve years. On the high ground overlooking the Terrace Gardens, she and her sister, Mrs. Newcome, have established themselves in the quiet and peace they both love, in a comfortable house, standing back from the road, which commands an extensive view of the river, winding serpent-like through a forest of trees. Ushered upstairs into the drawing-room, where the author receives you with much cordiality, the first thing which strikes you is the sweet rich voice in which her welcome is uttered. Standing facing the setting sun, with its golden light reflected on her, you observe that she is above the middle height, and graceful in figure; the hair, rolled back from the low broad strong-looking forehead, is becomingly tinged with grey over the right temple, harmonizing well with the darker shades on the neat, well-shaped head. The mouth and chin indicate firmness and resolution. In repose, the expression might almost be called sad, but as she speaks, the frankness in the grey eyes, set well apart, at once dispels the idea, and the pleasant musical laugh betrays the vein of fun and wit—entirely of an original kind—which runs through her books. She is dressed in some fabric of dark green, with velvet sleeves and bodice; the latter relieved at the upper part with a paler shade of embroidered vest. The windows open on to a broad trellised verandah, which runs the whole length of the house; and, stepping out to it, Miss Broughton bids you look at the exquisite view. It is a lovely day in latest autumn, the trees, turned to every shade of gold, copper, and brown, are shedding their leaves profusely. The sinking sun is leaving the sky deeply tinged with waves of pink and purple, and the river looks like a silver stream, with here and there a tinge of reflected colour, unbroken by a single boat. The air is pure and still, with a faint suspicion of a coming frost. For a few moments you both stand in rapt silence admiring the beautiful prospect, yet sighing to think that the winter is so near at hand; then your hostess leads the way back into the drawing-room, where tea is served, and as you settle comfortably in a luxurious couch covered with tapestry of the first Empire, and sip the fragrant beverage out of a cup of old Spode, the eye travels round the quiet restful room, and notices the many little knick-knacks that fill it.

On the right stands an antique writing table, with pigeon-hole drawers, and old blue china grouped over the top. The two ancient oak cabinets are covered with pretty "bits"; growing in a cunningly-concealed basket is an immense pyramid of ferns and palms, which are Miss Broughton's particular delight. On the little plush-covered table by the side of a delicately wrought iron Italian stand—whereof the copper bowl is filled with autumnal flowers—lies a business-like work-bag, filled to overflowing, which gives a home-like look to the room and indicates that it is useful as well as orna-

mental. On asking Miss Broughton for a peep into
her sanctuary, she smiles indulgently, and begs you
to descend. The white-painted fresh-looking staircase
is partially covered with Persian carpet of warm
colour, and, throughout, the dado is composed of
Indian matting, above which hang many engravings
and photographs. The large black-and-white lozenge-
shape tiles give the hall an indescribably bright
appearance, which here and there the long Indian
rugs subdue, yet throw up into relief. You enter the
room sacred to the gifted authoress, and look round.
Where are the manuscripts, the "copy," the "proofs,"
which might reasonably have been expected? There
is no indication of her work on the old oak knee-
hole writing-table beyond a single blank sheet of
paper reposing on a large wooden portfolio, exquisitely
painted on both sides by her friend Mrs. Andrew
Spottiswoode at Dresden. A solitary penholder lies
on a china inkstand, flanked by a pair of large green
jars from Hyères. She half guesses your look of inter-
rogation, and remarks that she is "resting" awhile,
now that her latest book "Alas!" is published, before
launching another, entitled "Mrs. Bligh." *Elle recule
pour mieux sauter*, but at the present moment, as
she kindly causes it to be understood that no
encroachment is being made on her valuable time,
you do not hesitate to ask for some details of her
literary life.

Rhoda Broughton was born at Segrwyd Hall,
Denbighshire. Her father was a clergyman, and held
the family living in Cheshire, where her childish
days were passed, varied by visits to her grandfather,

Sir Henry Broughton, at Broughton Hall, Staffordshire. Her father was a student, and himself grounded
her in Shakespeare and the English classics, and
imparted also the rudiments of Latin and Greek. She
was brought up strictly, and the hours of study were
long, but made interesting by her scholarly instructor.
Asking Miss Broughton if her father had been an
author, she replies, "only of his sermons, and I do
not believe any of my relations wrote a line in their
lives." It is a surprise to hear that her great gifts,
her originality of style, her wonderful descriptions
of scenery, her subtle humour, are not hereditary.
Keenly interested, you ask her how then the idea
of writing occurred to her.

She says she remembers a certain wet Sunday
afternoon when she was about twenty-two; she was
distinctly bored by a stupid book which she was
trying to read, when "the spirit moved her to write."
It was on the leaves of an old copy-book lying at
hand that she delivered her soul of the ideas which
poured in on her brain. Day after day, night after
night, she wrote swiftly and in secret, until at the
end of six weeks she found a vast heap of manuscript accumulated, to which she gave the title of
"Not Wisely, but Too Well." Miss Broughton kept
it by her until January, 1865, when she crossed
over to Ireland on a visit to her uncle-in-law, Mr.
Joseph Sheridan Le Fanu, then editor of the *Dublin
University Magazine;* she selected two chapters at
random and read them aloud to him. He at once
prognosticated the success of the book; accepted it
as a serial, and later on, suggested to Mr Bentley

that he should bring it out in three volume form.
Here, however, a check occurred. The reader pronounced so unfavourably of its merits, that Mr.
Bentley held off. But the inspiration, once set in
motion, could not be stopped, and soon found vent
in a new work, "Cometh up as a Flower." This
was well received. A couple of columns of favourable
criticism in the *Times*, and various eulogistic notices
in other papers, soon caused it to become such a
marked success that Mr. Bentley reconsidered the
matter. His deliberation happily ended in the
purchase of "Not Wisely but Too Well" from
Tinsley, so that the two books were actually brought
out in the same year. The home of Miss Broughton's ancestors, Broughton Hall, built in the reign
of one of the old Tudors, is so well depicted in
"Cometh up as a Flower," that none who have read
the book and seen the place can fail to observe
the absolute truthfulness of the description.

A propos of this novel, Miss Broughton tells an
amusing anecdote :—"It was claimed by other
people," she says; "a lady told an acquaintance of
mine that her son had written it, which diverted
me much."

The fame of these books went far afield. Some
years ago a graceful tribute was paid to the author.
Captain Markham, of H.M. ship *Alert*, begged to be
introduced, and told her that in a remote Arctic
region they had by common consent christened an
icebound mountain, "Mount Rhoda," in grateful
acknowledgment of the pleasure which her books had
given the officers of the ship on their perilous voyage.

Temple Bar secured her next two novels, "Red as a Rose is she" and "Goodbye, Sweetheart." About once in two years Miss Broughton delights the world with a new book. "Nancy," "Twilight Stories," "Joan," "Second Thoughts," "Dr. Cupid," "Belinda," followed at about these intervals, but her latest work, "Alas!" must take a high stand, if only for her faithful delineation of life in Florence, her intimate knowledge of all things artistic, her scenes laid in Algeria, which place she visited last year, and her vivid and graphic descriptions of those lovely countries, which are an education in themselves. And the humorous touches! How much everyone sympathises with the meek, but excellent "Amelia," whom no one thoroughly appreciates until after her death. Uneducated in art, she appeals pitifully in the following words to her lover, who finds out her worth too late.

"And now, where shall we go? that is the next thing—not to any gallery or church, I think, if you don't mind. I say such stupid things about art, and the more I try the stupider they are; let us go somewhere into the country. I can understand the country, I am not afraid of saying stupid things about it."

You tell her later of an observation made to you quite lately by her sister author, Miss Braddon, ever keenly appreciative of the gifts of another, on reading a striking description in "Alas" of the sea after a storm, which runs thus:—"A sea even more wonderful than radiant; no servile copy of the sky and clouds to-day, but with astonishing colours of its own; a faint yet glorious green for a part of its

watery breadth; then what our poverty compels us
to call blue; and then a great tablecloth of inky
purple, which looks so solid, that the tiny white
boats which are crossing it seem to be sailing on
dry land." Miss Braddon remarked, "Rhoda Broughton is a genius and a prose poet." Your hostess is
charmed with the kindly speech.

No solitary copy can be seen, in the well-filled
book-cases, of the author's works. She says that
she sells them out and out at once, and then has
"done with them"; but "Come," she adds, "we
have talked long enough about my books: let me
show you a few of my treasures," and she points
out a small sketch by Hamilton Aidé, two busts of
Lord Wolseley and Mr. Carlyle, presented to her by
Sir Edgar Boehm; presentation copies from Matthew
Arnold, Lord Lytton, Henry James, Andrew Lang,
etc., etc., and an ornamental plate rack, by which
she sets great store, from Adelaide Kemble (Mrs.
Sartoris); a very ancient engraving of Titian's
"Danaë" hangs over the mantelpiece opposite three
lovely photographs of "Garrick between Tragedy
and Comedy." The floor of this delightful room is
covered with peacock-blue felt and a few rugs of
Eastern manufacture; a small aviary of birds stands
by the window, which is open, for your hostess is a
"great believer in plenty of fresh air and a good
fire." Ere taking leave, you ask if the two fine
pugs basking on the rugs are especial pets. "Yes,"
says Miss Broughton, "but," mournfully, "they are
a degenerate race; and not the dear dog heroes of
my books. *They* are all dead and gone!"

MRS ARTHUR STANNARD

("JOHN STRANGE WINTER")

MRS. ARTHUR STANNARD

("JOHN STRANGE WINTER").

EMERGING from the Earl's Court Station, where once
stood the old manor house of the De Veres, and
glancing at the noble row of buildings across the road
which until quite lately was the site of a *maison de
santé*, it seems impossible to realise that it was at the
end of the last century a miniature private zoological
garden. Yet here the great anatomist and surgeon,
John Hunter, kept a collection of rare and foreign
animals ; here, too, was the kitchen and the great
cauldron in which he performed the gruesome opera-
tion of boiling down the giant O'Brien, whose skeleton
can be seen in the museum of the College of Surgeons.
It is to be hoped that the ghost of the big Irishman
was safely laid when the work of destruction was
carried on ! Turning to the left, you go down
Trebovir-road, past the great red-stepped house of
the well-known and successful "crammer" and army
coach, Captain Pinhey, which leads out into Nevern-
square. Perhaps in nothing more than in the present
style of building does the growing artistic spirit of the
day assert itself. Although the houses are not erected
with the solid masonry of other days, which seemed

to defy the hand of time, they rejoice in more picturesque effects, and certainly the handsome, spacious Nevern-square, with its large gardens, its three well-kept tennis courts, and its fine red-brick dwellings, is a striking instance of the fact. It is barely a decade and a half of years since this site was occupied by large nursery gardens, through which a winding country lane led to St. Mathias' Church yonder; now it is surrounded by stately mansions, broad roads, and pleasant gardens. On the south-side a ruddy gleam of fire-light through the red window-blinds marks the residence of the popular author, John Strange Winter. Passing through the outer and inner entrance doors, with mounted antlers, and Swiss carvings hung between them, you reach the long, narrow hall, where the tesselated black-and-white paving is covered for the most part with heavy Wilton carpets; the rich, deep-red walls are profusely decorated with quaint old prints, whose sombreness is relieved by Nankin and Spode china. A later inspection shows these to include some choice engravings by Morland, a few miniatures, and a group of family silhouettes. ("Had we any more black relations?" Mrs. Stannard, when a child, once asked her mother on being told which members of her family they protrayed.)

Entering the dining-room on the right, your hostess is discovered, deeply engaged in dressing dolls for an approaching juvenile festivity, when each little guest is to receive some gift. Clouds of filmy muslin, embroidery, lace, and silk lie before her, and several of those already attired repose in a row on the sofa. She extends a firm, white hand in cordial greeting, and as there is only one more doll to complete the set, you settle down beside her to watch the process, and notice the deft and nimble fingers, as they swiftly run up a flounce or adjust a tiny trimming. She is dressed in a black and grey tea-gown, which looks like fine tapestry, with grey satin sleeves, panels, and front.

Mrs. Arthur Stannard is a tall, handsome young woman. She has fine, dark brown eyes, which sparkle with intellect and humour, level eyebrows, and dark hair curling over her low forehead, and well-shaped head; she has a pretty but firm little mouth, and clear-cut chin, indicative of strength of will. Her face has settled somewhat into gravity as she pursues her occupation, for she has put into this apparently trivial matter, just as she does in greater things, her very best efforts with that thoroughness which characterises her; but as she suddenly looks up, and catches you intently watching her, she smiles a sweet, bright smile, and laughs a low, rippling laugh, as she seems to guess exactly what are your thoughts. "It is for the children," she says softly, and in those few words she betrays at once the sympathy of her nature, that sympathy with these little ones which has caused the children of her pen to live so vividly in the hearts of her readers.

It is a large lofty room, pale green in colour, with carved oak dado. A bright, clear fire blazing in the wide, tiled hearth makes the heavy, polished brass fender and "dogs" glisten like gold. On the high, black, carved "chimney shelf," as Mrs. Stannard calls it, stand three valuable old blue jars, and the low, broad overmantel is composed of genuine Dutch tiles,

three hundred years in age, framed in wood. Over
this is grouped a collection of ancient blue Delft;
the walls are hung with a few good proof engravings;
at night the room is amply lighted by the huge
hanging, crimson-shaded lamp, which casts a soft,
becoming glow over every corner; the floor is covered
with a thick Axminster carpet of subdued colouring,
and with the exception of a handsome old carved oak
dower-chest, and grandfather clock, with loud and
sonorous strike, which both date back into the last
century, the rest of the furniture is mahogany;
pieces picked up here and there, restored, modernised,
and chosen with an eye to effect as well as to comfort.

Mrs. Stannard is the only daughter of the late
Rev. Henry Vaughan Palmer, Rector of St. Margaret's,
York. For some time Mr. Palmer had been an officer
in the Royal Artillery before his convictions led him
to lay down his sword and enter the church militant ;
he had come of several generations of soldiers, and
to the last day of his life found his greatest pleasure
in the society of military men; this perhaps accounts
for Mrs. Stannard's almost instinctive knowledge of
army men and army ways.   Asking her if, when
a child, she loved books, and gave promise of her
brilliant gift, she says, smiling, " Well, as regards
my lessons, most emphatically no !   I was a restless,
impatient sort of child, who tired of everything before
it was half done.   I think, like all very enthusiastic
people, that I was never as happy as with books,
that is to say, novels.   I was just eleven when I went
to my first school, but I had read Thackeray, Dickens,
Charles Reade, and Whyte Melville up to date, besides

many others, and I was never restricted in my reading; I never remember in my life my father or mother telling me not to read any particular book, and," speaking very impressively, " I am all the better for it. Years afterwards, when my father died—I was twenty-one then—I felt that the few stories I had written and sold up to that time, were but child's play. Then I began to work in real earnest, studying certain authors that I might clearly realise the difference of their method and style." But the thought at once arises, that the touching and simple pathos of her style is entirely original, and born of no earthly model.

And then, as ofttime happens when two women are sitting together in friendly converse, a word is dropped about her married life. Ah ! here, though much could be said, in deference to your hostess's wishes the pen must be stayed. All who know Mr. and Mrs. Stannard know how complete and perfect is their union. Mr. Stannard is a civil engineer, and at one time served under the late General Gordon. He is very pardonably proud of his clever wife, and efficiently transacts all her business arrangements, the two—so perfect an one—working, as it were, hand in hand.

Her *nom de guerre*, " John Strange Winter," was adopted by the advice of the publishers of her first books, because they thought it wiser that works so military as " Cavalry Life " and " Regimental Legends " should be assumed by the world to be written by a man, and that they would stand a better chance of mercy at the hands of the critics than if they went forth as the acknowledged writing of a woman, and for

a time it was so assumed; but when "Bootles' Baby"
made such a success, and people wanted to know
who the author was, and where he lived, it soon
became known that "he" was a woman, although,
as she did not add her name to the title-page, it
was a good while before it was generally believed.
It may here be remarked that Mrs. Stannard holds
very strongly the opinion that there should be "no
sex in art," and whilst never desiring to conceal her
identity, deprecates the idea of receiving indulgence
or blame on the ground of her work being that of
a woman, as both unjust and absurd. In private
life she carries out her ideas on this point so effectually
that few acquaintances would gather from her conversation (unless it were necessary to "talk shop")
that she was a literary woman at all, as, except to
a fellow worker, she would rather talk on any subject
under the sun than literature.

"The author to whom," according to Ruskin, "we
owe the most finished and faithful rendering ever
yet given of the character of the British soldier" can
portray, too, in a wonderful degree the beauty of
child-life. Of modern creations there can be none
better known to the public, or which have excited
more sympathy, than "Mignon" and "Houp-là."

Correct in detail, as those can prove who were in
India at the time of the terrible mutiny of 1857,
she might have written "A Siege Baby" on the spot
had it not been that she was only born on the thirteenth of January in the previous year, and at that
time was an infant in arms. Fertile in imagination,
acute in observation, sprightly and wholesome in style,

there is a freshness and life in her books which charm
alike old and young, rich and poor, at home and
abroad; and that her popularity is fully maintained
is testified by the gratifying fact that a late story,
"He went for a Soldier," one of the slightest of her
efforts, had a larger sale during the first month after
publication than any previous work from her pen in
the same period. One practical result of this book
must be mentioned. The scene is laid at Doverscourt,
a few miles from Mr. and Mrs. Stannard's pretty
summer home at Wix. She had been greatly distressed, when visiting that seaside place, by the sight
of the overloaded hackney-carriages, with their poor,
broken-down horses. Immediately after her indignant
comments on this fact in her story, bye-laws were
passed bringing these vehicles under effective police
supervision.

Besides those already named, amongst some two
or three and twenty novels, which are all so well
known as not to need description—for are they not
to be found in every library and on every railway
bookstall in the United Kingdom?—"Beautiful Jim,"
"Harvest," "Dinna Forget," and a most pathetic story
called "My Poor Dick," remain fixed on the memory.
This last is perhaps the author's own favourite.
"Bootles' Baby," as all the play-going world knows,
was dramatised and brought out four years ago at
the Globe Theatre in London. It has been on tour
ever since, and there seems no intention of terminating
its long run, dates having been booked far into the
year. A late story, entitled "The Other Man's Wife,"
has been running in a serial in various newspapers,

and is now issued in two-volume form. One great element in the author's success and world-wide literary reputation is undoubtedly to be found in her creations of the children of her military heroes, alike among the officers' quarters and those " on the strength." She has the happy knack of depicting them at once simple, natural, and lovable.

" I never begin a novel," says Mrs. Stannard, " until I have got a certain scene in my mind. I cannot write any kind of story without having one dramatic scene clearly before me; when I have got it, I work up to that ; then the story arranges itself. But this is only the germ, the first conception of the tale. As I write one thread after another spins itself out, to be taken up afterwards to form a consecutive, concise whole. Some-times I lose my original story altogether, but never any dramatic situation towards which I am working, and the end is often quite different to what I had intended. When this happens I very seldom try to fight against fate. I think all stories ought more or less to write themselves, and it seems to me that this must make a tale more like real life than if it were all carefully mapped out beforehand, and then simply padded up to some requisite length."

By this time the last doll is finished and added to the row on the sofa. They all look as if they had been turned out of a first-class milliners' establishment. Mrs. Stannard suggests a move to her study, and leads the way up the wide staircase, the handrail of which is protected by a broad and heavy brass guard, put there for the sake of the little children of the house. A broad settee on the wide conservatory landing invites

you to rest awhile and look at all the odds and ends
which your hostess says are so precious to her. Here
are two handsome Chippendale chairs picked up in
Essex, many photographs of the house at Wix, a dozen
pieces of Lancashire Delph porcelain, made specially as
a wedding present for Mrs. Stannard's grandmother in
1810, some Staffordshire hunting jugs, and some quaint
little figures, "all rubbish," she says, smiling, " but
precious to me." There is, however, a Spode dinner
service in blue which is emphatically not rubbish, and
a set of Oriental dishes, blue and red, which are very
effective. The landing is richly carpeted; the windows and the doors of the conservatory are all of
stained glass, while above hangs an old Empire lamp
of beautiful design filled in with small cathedral glass.
The first door on the left leads into the author's
study. It is a charming room, small but lofty, with
pale blue walls hung with many little pictures, plates,
old looking-glasses, and chenille curtains of terra-cotta
and pale blue softly blended. A pretty inlaid bookcase stands opposite the window, filled with a few
well-selected books. The horseshoe hanging yonder
was cast in the Balaclava charge. She has indeed a
goodly collection of these, and owns to a weakness to
them, declaring that her first great success was
achieved on the day that she picked one up at Harro-
gate. There must be many hundreds of photographs
scattered about in this room, and it would be a day's
occupation to look through them all; but each has its
own interest for her, and most of them are of people
well known in the literary, scientific, artistic, and
fashionable world. " I never sit here," she says. " It

is my work-room, pure and simple. Sometimes my husband comes up, and then I read to him all my newly-written stuff, but this I do every day."

The next door opens into the drawing-room, where there is a rich harmony in the details of the decoration and furniture, which suggests the presence of good and cultivated taste, combined with a general sense of luxury and comfort. The entire colouring is blended, from old gold to terra-cotta, from Indian red to golden brown. On the left stands a cabinet crowded with choicest bits of china, in the middle of which is placed the bouquet, carefully preserved, presented to the author by Mr. Ruskin on her birthday. A lovely Dutch marqueterie table contains a goodly collection of antique silver, and among the pictures on the walls are a painting by Lawrence Phillips, Batley's etching of Irving and Ellen Terry, also one of Mrs. Stannard, and a series of all the original and clever pen-and-ink sketches in " Bootles' Children," by Bernard Partridge, drawn as illustrations to the story in the *Lady's Pictorial.*

After lingering long over afternoon tea, you express a wish to see the children before they sleep. Mrs. Stannard leads the way first to a room next her own, which is occupied by a fair little maiden, seven years of age, with grey-blue eyes, sunny hair, and a wild-rose complexion, who asks you to "go and see the twins." Accordingly their mother takes you on to a large night-nursery, where the two little ones, boy and girl, are being prepared for bed. They are just turned four, and are called Eliot and Violet Mignon, after two of the characters in Mrs. Stannard's books. They are perfectly friendly, and as you bend to kiss the baby girl last, she looks reproachfully out of her great dark eyes, and sternly commands you to "kiss Gertie, too." (Gertie is the under nurse.) This raises a hearty laugh, under cover of which you hastily retreat.

Above all things, Mrs. Stannard is a thoroughly domestic woman. Popular in society, constantly entertaining with great hospitality, she yet contrives to attend to every detail of her large household, which consequently goes like clockwork. She writes for about two hours every morning, and keeps a neat record book, in which she duly enters the number of pages written each day.

Presently Mr. Stannard comes in, and soon suggests an adjournment to his study downstairs, a snug, business-like room, half filled with despatch-boxes, books, and MSS. On a table stands a large folio-like volume, which is Mrs. Stannard's visiting book, containing many hundreds of names. She looks rue-fully at a clip containing some sixty unanswered letters, and candidly confesses that she finds considerable difficulty with her private correspondence and her calls, both of which accumulate faster than she can respond to; though, as she says, her many friends are very indulgent to her on those scores, and are "quite willing to make allowance for a poor woman who has the bulk of her literary work cut out for a year or two in advance, three little children, and a houseful of servants to manage; but, happily," she adds, "good servants. I have been so lucky in that way."

Just now, indeed, she claims especial indulgence in

respect to social observances, for, as though so busy
a life were not enough to exhaust her energies, early
in 1891 she added a new burden to her indefatigable pen, by starting a penny weekly magazine
under the title of *Golden Gates*, subsequently altered
to *Winter's Weekly* in deference to the opinion of
those who objected to the somewhat religious sound
of the former name. The little paper was the first
weekly periodical that was ever exclusively owned,
edited, and published by a popular novelist, and its
fortunes have been watched with vivid interest by
all who know how treacherous and adventuresome
are such enterprises. The fresh, frank individuality
of *Winter's Weekly* has, however, made friends for
the journal wherever it has gone, and if John Strange
Winter can keep it at its present point of uncon-
ventional interest, it may consolidate into a valuable property. Already it seems to have suggested
the publication of new journals on similar lines,
though no other woman novelist has yet had the
courage to follow suit.

Later works of this favourite writer are "Mere
Luck," "My Geoff," "Lumley, the Painter," also a
powerful and pathetic novel, in two volumes, entitled
"Only Human." Her last is a story called "A
Soldier's Children," which she has given for the
benefit of the Victoria Hospital for Children, Chelsea.

But with all this accumulation of business, these
domestic cares, and social claims, somehow Mrs.
Stannard never seems in a hurry. The kind and
hospitable young couple are always ready to do an
act of kindness, and to welcome with help and

counsel a new aspirant to fame in the thorny paths of literature. Small wonder that they are so much sought after in society, and so heartily welcomed wherever they go—and one is seldom seen without the other. You go on your way with every hearty good wish that each year may bring them ever-increasing prosperity and success, for in such union there is strength.

MRS. ALEXANDER.

ABOUT three miles north-west of St. Paul's lies a
comparatively new suburb of the great metropolis,
which but forty years ago was described as " a hamlet
in the parish of Marylebone," and through which
passes the Grand Junction Canal, almost reaching to
Kilburn. London, with her ever-grasping clutch, has
seized on the vast tract of ground, which erstwhile
grew potatoes and cabbages for the multitude, and,
abolishing the nursery and market-gardens, has transformed them into broad streets, of which one of the
longest is Portsdown-road.

Not altogether inartistic is the row of substantially
built houses where Mrs. Alexander Hector has been
for some years located. It is far enough away to
enable the popular authoress to pursue her literary
vocation in peace and quiet, yet sufficiently near to
keep her in touch with the busy world of literature
and art, wherein she is deservedly so great a favourite.
The blue fan, serving as a screen for the window, is a
sort of land-mark distinguishing the house from its
fellows. You are shown into the library, where Mrs.
Alexander is seated at a handsome oak writing-table,
busily engaged in finishing the last words of a chapter

MRS ALEXANDER

in her new story. She looks up with a smile of welcome, and is about to discontinue her occupation; but you hastily beg her to go on with her work, which will give you time to look around; and as she complies with the request, she says pleasantly, " Well, then, just for three minutes only."

Your glance lights again on the gentle author herself, and you watch the pen gliding easily over the page, which rests on a diminutive shred of well-worn blotting-paper. The face is fair and smooth, the hair, slightly grey, is simply parted back from the forehead, and the three-quarter profile, which presents itself to your gaze, is straight and well-cut. She wears a little white cap, and a long black gown, trimmed with jet, and close by her side lies an enormous Persian tabby cat of great age.

The study is divided from the adjoining room by heavy curtains drawn aside and a Japanese screen. It is all perfectly simple and unpretending, but the rooms are thoroughly comfortable and home-like.

The chapter being finished, your hostess rises, declares herself entirely at your service, and mentions that she is now engaged on a new three volume novel, which is to come out early next year in America, and is as yet unnamed.

Mrs. Alexander was born in Ireland, though no touch of accent can be detected. She never left that country until after her nineteenth birthday. Her father belonged to an old squirearchal family, the Frenches of Roscommon. He was a keen sportsman, and a member of the famous Kildare Hunt. The few old pictures which hang on the wall are all family portraits. One represents a paternal ancestor, Lord Annaly, painted in his peer's robes. He was one of the Gore family, of whom no less than nine members sat at the same time in parliament shortly before the Union. Another picture of a comfortable-looking old gentleman in a powdered wig is the portrait of a high legal dignitary, well known in his day as Theobald Wolfe, a great-uncle of Mrs. Alexander. A third is a seventeenth-century portrait of Colonel Dominic French, who looks manly and resolute, in spite of his yellow satin coat, flowing wig, and lace cravat, drawn through his buttonhole. This gentleman was the first Protestant of the family, and is credited with having given up his faith for love of his wife, who simpers beside him in an alarmingly *décolletée* blue dress, suggestive of the courtly style in the time of the Merry Monarch. Her husband, with the ardour of a convert—or a pervert—raised a regiment of dragoons among his tenantry, and fought on the winning side at the Battle of the Boyne.

Mrs. Alexander remarks that her "kinsfolk and acquaintance in early life, were, if not illiterate, certainly unliterary." "I always loved books," she adds, "and was fortunate, when a very young girl, barely out of the schoolroom, in winning the favour of a dear old blind Scotchman, whose wife was a family friend. He was a profound thinker, and an earnest student before he lost his sight. My happiest and most profitable hours were spent in reading aloud to him books, no doubt a good deal beyond my grasp, but which, thanks to his kind and patient explanations, proved the most valuable part of my very irregular education. In reading the newspapers to him, I also gathered some idea of politics, probably very vague ideas, but so liberal in their tendency that my relatives, who were 'bitter Protestants' and the highest of high Tories, looked on me, if not as a 'black sheep,' certainly as a 'lost mutton.' The tendency has remained with me, though my consciousness of the many-sided immensity of the subject, has kept me from forming any decided opinions."

The only bits of ancestry she values, Mrs. Alexander says, are her descent from Jeremy Taylor, the celebrated Bishop of Down and Connor, and the near cousinship of her grandmother to Lord Kilwarden, who was the first victim in Emmet's rising; that high-minded judge, whose last words, as he yielded up his life to the cruel pikes of his assailants, were, "Let them have a fair trial."

The above-mentioned Jeremy Taylor, and the Rev. Charles Wolfe—whose well-known poem, "The Burial of Sir John Moore," was so greatly appreciated by Lord Byron—were the only literary members of the family on her father's side ; on her mother's, she can claim kindred with Edmund Malone, the well-known annotator of Shakespeare.

On leaving Ireland, Mrs. Alexander, with her parents, travelled a good deal, both at home and abroad, occasionally sojourning in London, where, while still young, she began to write. Her first attempts were made in the *Family Herald* and *Household Words*, beginning with a sketch called " Billeted in Boulogne." This is an account of their own personal experience,

when they endured the inconvenience of having
French soldiers quartered on them.

It was about this time that she was introduced
to Mrs. Lynn Linton, by the late Adelaide Proctor,
with whose family she was on terms of some intimacy,
and with whose charming grandmother, the once well-
known and admired Mrs. Basil Montague, she was a
prime favourite. From this introduction arose the
long, close friendship with the brilliant author of
"Joshua Davidson," which Mrs. Alexander values so
highly, and of which she is so justly proud.

In 1858 she married Mr. Hector, and wrote no more
until she became a widow.

Mr. Hector was a great explorer and traveller. He
had been a member of Landor's expedition to seek
the sources of the Niger, and immediately after his
return to England he joined General Chesney in his
attempt to steam down the Euphrates to the Persian
Gulf. He was also with Layard during his discoveries
in Nineveh, and spent many years in Turkish Arabia.
A man of great enterprise and ability, he was the
pioneer of commerce, and was the first who sent from
London a ship and cargo direct to the Persian Gulf, thereby opening up the trade between the two countries.

It was after her husband's long illness, which ter-
minated fatally, that Mrs. Alexander again turned
her thoughts to literature, to seek distraction from
her bereavement. It was then she wrote "The
Wooing o't." The book was a great success; it ran
first through the pages of *Temple Bar*; it was then
published in three volumes, passed through many
editions, and has a world-wide reputation.

" I always write leisurely," says Mrs. Alexander; "I never will hurry, or write against time. No, I have not much method," she answers, in reply to your question, " nor am I quite without it. My stories are generally suggested to me by some trait of character or disposition, which I have adapted rather than produced. My people are rarely portraits, they are rather mosaics; and, I *must* say, I am exceedingly shy of dealing with my men. Women I *do* understand. Character to me is all-important. If I can but place the workings of heart and mind before my readers, the incidents which put them in motion are of small importance comparatively. Of course, a strong, clear, logical plot is a treasure not to be found every day! I am not a rapid writer; I like to live with my characters, to get thoroughly acquainted with them; and I am always sorry to part with the companions who have brought me many a pleasant hour of oblivion— oblivion from the carking cares that crowd outside my study door."

There is one point on which you would fain differ from the author. An intimate knowledge of her books convinces you that her power of dealing with her " men " is very great, and that her habits of observation have stood her in good stead, whilst depicting with ready wit and considerable skill the characters of her heroes. As you follow step by step the career of the fascinating Trafford, in " The Wooing o't," and watch the workings of his mind, the struggles between his natural cynicism and pride, and his love for the humbly-born but high-souled little heroine Maggie; his graceful rejection of the hand and fortune of the proud heiress, and the final triumph of love over pedi-gree, you can with truth echo the author's words, and feel that you too are "sorry to part" with him and his wife, and would gladly welcome a sequel to their histories.

Mrs. Alexander observes that there *is* one character in that book drawn from life, but adds, with a laugh, she "will not tell you which it is." You have, how-ever, a suspicion of your own.

"Her Dearest Foe" was the author's next work. It is constructed on entirely different lines, but it is equally absorbing. The varied fortunes of the brave heroine of the "Berlin Bazaar," of the masterful Sir Hugh Galbraith, and the faithful cousin Tom, keep up an engrossing interest from the first line to the last.

Her husband's Christian name being Alexander, she elected to write under that appellation, fearing that her first book might be a failure. Having begun with it, she has ever since kept the same *nom de plume*, and she remarks, "It does just as well as any other."

The great success which attended these two books justified Mrs. Alexander's further efforts. "Maid, Wife, or Widow," a clever little story, is an "Episode of the '66 War in Germany", "Which Shall it Be?" "Look Before You Leap," and "Ralph Wilton's Weird" were brought out during the next few years. They were all favourably reviewed, and many of them passed into several editions. These were followed at intervals by "Second Life," "At Bay," "A Life Interest," "The Admiral's Ward," "By Woman's Wit." Mrs. Alexander wrote "The Freres" during a long residence in Ger-many, whither she went for the education of her children. The fact that she was on intimate terms with many of the good old German families enabled her to write graphically from her personal knowledge of the country.

In "The Executors" Mrs. Alexander broke new ground. The life-like delineation of Karapet is drawn from her own observation and experience of Syrian Christians, but the incidents are, of course, imaginary.

"Blind Fate," "A Woman's Heart," "Mammon," "The Snare of the Fowler," followed in due course, also some clever little shilling stories. The author's latest published work in three volumes is called "For His Sake," a pleasant and interesting novel, well worthy of the writer of "The Wooing o't."

Mrs. Alexander's great ambition originally was to write a play; indeed, her first few stories were planned with that object in view, but she soon abandoned the idea, and says she "turned them into novels instead." That there was some dramatic power in a few of her earlier efforts is evident, as she was applied to for permission to dramatise "Her Dearest Foe" and "By Woman's Wit." "Though," she adds, "it seems to me that the latter is not suited to the stage."

Mrs. Alexander writes best in England. She says that London "inspires her." She holds strong views upon education, and maintains that girls, as well as boys, should be trained to follow some definite line in life. She would have any special talent, whereby its possessor could, if necessary, earn her own living cultivated to the utmost; and, consistently following out her principles, she has sent her youngest daughter,

E

who has a decided genius for painting, to work in
one of the best-known studios in Paris, where she
takes a fairly good place, and by her diligence and
ardour for her art at least deserves success. Another
daughter fulfils the onerous task of being "mother's
right hand." But she has yet a third, who has found
a happy career in the bonds of wedlock, and has made
her home at Versailles. She is now on a visit to her
mother, and whilst you are conversing, the door opens,
the young wife comes in with a lovely infant in her
arms, and the "first grandchild" is introduced with
pride. He is a perfect cherub, and makes friends
instantly.

Asking Mrs. Alexander about her early friends in
literature, she mentions with grateful warmth the
name of Mrs. S. C. Hall, "whose ready kindness
never failed." "To her," she says, "I owe the most
valuable introduction I ever had. It was to the
late Mr. W. H. Wills, editor of *Household Words*.
To his advice and encouragement I am deeply
indebted. His skill and discrimination as an editor
were most remarkable, whilst his knowledge and
wide experience were always placed generously at
the service of the young and earnest wanderer in the
paths of literature, numbers of whom have had reason
to bless the day when they first knew Harry Wills."

Mrs. Alexander is pre-eminently a lovable woman.
In the large society where she is so well known, and
so much respected, to mention her name is to draw
forth affectionate encomiums on all sides. You venture
to make some allusion to this fact; a faint smile comes
over the placid countenance, as she says inquiringly,

" Yes ? I believe I have made many friends. You
see, I never rub people the wrong way if I can help
it, and I think I have some correct ideas respecting
the true value of trifles. Yet I believe I have a
backbone; at least I hope so, for mere softness and
compliance will not bear the friction of life."

HELEN MATHERS.

(MRS. REEVES.)

ALTHOUGH it is but two o'clock in the afternoon, the streets are black as night. With the delightful variety of an English climate, the temperature has suddenly fallen, and a rapid thaw has set in, converting the heavy fall of snow, which but two days before threatened to cover the whole of London, into a slough of mud. It is a pleasant change to turn from these outer discomforts into the warm and well-lighted house which Mrs. Reeves has made so bright and comfortable.

You have judiciously managed to arrive five minutes earlier than the hour appointed, in the hope of being able to make a few mental notes before Helen Mathers comes in, and your perspicacity is rewarded, for a bird's-eye glance around assures you that she possesses a refined and artistic taste, which is displayed in the general arrangement of the room. Lighted from above by a glass dome, another room is visible and again a glimpse of a third beyond. The quaint originality of their shape and build suggests the idea, of what indeed is the fact, that the house was built more than a century and a half ago.

HELEN MATHERS

(MRS REEVES)

The first room is very long, and its soft Axminster carpet of amber colour shaded up to brown gives the key-note to the decorations, which from the heavily embossed gold leather paper on the walls to the orange-coloured Indian scarves that drape the exquisite white overmantels (now wreathed with long sprays of ivy, grasses, and red leaves), would delight the heart of a sun-worshipper as Helen Mathers declares herself to be.

As she now comes in, she seems to bring an additional sense of the fitness of things. She carries a big basket of China tea-roses, which she has just received from a friend in the country, and the long white cachemire and silk tea-gown which she wears looks thoroughly appropriate, despite the inclement season. It is her favourite colour for house wear in summer or winter, and certainly nothing could be more becoming to her soft, creamy complexion, and the natural tints of the thick, bright copper-coloured hair, which, curling over her brow, is twisted loosely into a great knot, lying low on the back of her head.

The conversation turning upon the peculiar structure of the rooms, Mrs. Reeves proposes to take you into the one innermost which is truly a curiosity. A very old cathedral glass partition opens on to a square and lofty room, used as an inner hall, with great velvet shields of china and brasses on its gold leather walls, and quaint old oak chairs, cabinets, and high old-fashioned clock. A portrait in sepia of Mrs. Reeves, done by Alfred Ward, hangs over a paneled door on the left. It was to this picture that Mr. Frederick Locker wrote the following lines:—

"Not mine to praise your eyes and wit,
　Although your portrait here I view,
　So what I may not say to you
　I've said to it."

Opposite is a very wide, high door that opens
into the oak-panelled room, which may well have
been a banqueting hall of the last century. It is
lighted from above, and each pane of glass has in its
centre, in vivid colours, the initials of the royal per-
sonage who, if the coats of arms abounding everywhere are to be trusted, may have occupied this room
over a hundred years ago. By the way, the harp is
absent from these armorial bearings.

One entire side of the room is filled by a vast
mirror, set in a magnificently carved oak frame, and
supported on either side by colossal winged female
figures, that are matched (and in the glass reflected)
by the caryatides who appear to hold up the massive
carvings above the door, which is itself covered entirely
by superb carvings of beast and bird, and laughing
boys playing at Bacchus with great clusters of grapes.
Round this unique room runs an oak paneling of
about five feet in height, surmounted by a ledge,
now decorated with trails of ivy, and above the oak
cupboards are panels representing a boar hunt, and
worth, it is said, a fabulous sum. But the glory of
the room is the mantelpiece, reaching to the roof.
It was probably once an altar piece, as the centre
panel represents the Crucifixion. Two busts—one of
Queen Elizabeth, the other of the Earl of Leicester—
frown down on you from a great height, and do not
please you half as well as a bronze Venus of Milo

below. The hearth itself (of an incredibly old pattern, with heavy iron fender, which suggests a prison) has on either side two odd-looking figures, that are supposed to represent Joan of Arc and her keeper. He carries a knotted whip in one hand, and seems to look ferociously on poor Joan in her half-manly, half-feminine garb.

"I am very fond of these two," says Mrs. Reeves, looking affectionately at them, "and often dust their faces, but I am not at all fond of sitting in this room. I much prefer my sunny quarters upstairs, and these high carved oak chairs are uncomfortable to sit in, especially at dinner!"

But pleasant as it is, there is other business on hand, and you cannot linger over these beautiful antiquities; the afternoon is wearing on, and Mrs. Reeves leads the way to the drawing-rooms, which are also oddly shaped, and open one out of the other, like those downstairs; but those rooms are very different to look upon, and are, in your hostess's opinion, "much more cheery." You can step from the long windows on to a flower-filled balcony that looks up and down Grosvenor Street. The hangings of the first room are of yellow satin, of the second room pink; the furniture is merely of basket work, but made beautiful and comfortable by many soft cushions; and a long glass set in a frame of white woodwork, its low shelf covered with rare old yellow china and flowers, reflects the gold and cream leather walls, and the overmantel crammed with a lovely litter of china, pictures, and odds and ends, in the centre of which is a horseshoe. "Picked up by my boy, Phil," says Mrs. Reeves, as you examine it, "and we always say it has brought us luck."

But when you ask to see her writing-room—for there is not a sign of pen, ink, and paper to be seen on a modest white escritoire behind the door—she shakes her head and laughs.

"I have no writing-room and no particular table," she says, "indeed I can't say in the least how my books get written. I jot down anything that I especially observe, or think of, on a bit of paper, and when I have a great many pieces I sort them out, and usually pin them together in some sort of a sequence. At home, where I had an immense room to write in over the library, the boys used to say no one must speak to me if my 'authoress lock' were standing up over my forehead, but if I ever display it nowadays, nobody," she adds, ruefully, "is deterred by it! Often, just as I have settled down to do a good morning's work, and have perhaps finished a page, someone comes in and puts letters or account books on it, or my boy Phil rushes up and lays his air gun or his banjo on the table, or my husband brings in some little commission or a heap of notes to be answered for him. I always tell them," laughing, "that everyone combines to put out of sight the story which is being written, and often it is not touched again for a week; but my composition, when really begun, is very rapid, and my ideas seem to run out of my pen. At my old home they used to say I wrote the things that they thought, which was a good, lazy way of getting out of it."

This leads to the subject of her "old home," and

Mrs. Reeves imparts some interesting details of her youthful days. She was born at Misterton, Somersetshire, in the house described in "Comin' thro' the Rye," and she has always most passionately loved it. Mrs. Reeves was one of twelve children, who spent the greater part of their time in outdoor sports and amusements, in which the girls were almost as proficient as the boys. Their father was a great martinet, and never permitted any encroachment on the regular lesson hours with their governess. "When I was only eight years old," says your hostess, "our grandmamma Buckingham (after whom I take my second Christian name) sent us a biography of famous persons, arranged alphabetically. I looked down the list to see if a Mathers were amongst them. It was not, and I took a pencil, and made a bracket, writing in my name, Helen Mathers, novelist; so the ruling idea must have been in me early."

The colour of her hair was Helen Mathers's greatest trouble in her childhood. It was a rich red, and in the familiar home circle she was called "Carrots," to her great annoyance, until she was sixteen. She says:—"It gave me such genuine distress that before I was nine years old, I had written a story depicting the sufferings of a red-haired girl who wanted to marry a man who was in love with her golden-haired sister. I inscribed this in an old pocket-book, looking out the names and places in the *Times* each day, and afterwards, in agonies of shyness, I read it aloud to the assembled family, who received it with shouts of mirth!"

At the age of thirteen, she was sent to Chantry School, and, unfortunately for her, she was placed at once in the first class, consisting of girls many years older than herself. Always ardent and ambitious, she worked so hard that quite suddenly her health broke down, and she became deaf—an affliction which has partially remained to this day. No doubt this trouble drove her more into herself, and helped her to concentrate her thoughts on literature. She wrote and wrote incessantly for pure love of it, and before she was sixteen had completed her poem, "The Token of the Silver Lily." This she gave to a friend of her family who was acquainted with Dante Gabriel Rossetti. The great man read it, and sent her a message to the effect that, if she persevered, she bid fair at some future day to succeed. This highly delighted the girl, who was always working while the others played in the beautiful place to which her parents had removed when they left Misterton. This later home is described as "Penroses" in her late novel, "Adieu!" which previously ran as a serial in a monthly magazine.

Her first appearance in print is thus described :— "It was hay-making time, and everybody, boys and girls, children, servants, and all, were down in the hayfield, when someone brought me a shabby little halfpenny wrapper with the magic word 'Jersey' at the top. I gave a sort of whoop, and fled down the lawn and across the orchards, and into the bosom of my family like one possessed. 'Boys, girls!' I cried ; 'it's *accepted*—it's here in *print!*

Look at it!' And never did a prouder heart beat
than the heart under my white frock that day for
my first-born bantling of the pen. I had been
yachting with my brother-in-law, Mr. Hamborough,
a short time previously, with this result, that I
wrote a sketch of him and his wife and the place,
and, signing it 'N.'—short for 'Nell'—I took counsel with Mr. George Augustus Sala, whom I did not
know in those days, but who was very kind in
replying to me, and he despatched it to *Belgravia*.
When it *did* appear Jersey was very angry, and
declared it was libelled, and I should not have ventured to go over there again for a long while!"

About three years later she produced her first
novel, "Comin' thro' the Rye." It proved a great
success, and was rapidly translated into many
languages; indeed, a copy in Sanscrit was sent to
her. This work was written unknown to her family.
"My poor father," says Mrs. Reeves, sadly, "I got
him into the story, and though I did not mean to
be unkind or disrespectful, I could not get him out
again. I hardly drew a free breath for months
afterwards, fearing someone would tell him I had
written it, and that he would be grievously offended;
but I was young and foolish, too young a great deal
I often think to succeed, but it makes me feel a
sort of Methuselah now."

A story is told that many years ago a very youthful writer supplemented a story of her own with
several pages of this book, and wrote to Messrs.
Tillotson, saying she had written the twin novel
to "Comin' thro' the Rye," and would they buy it?

The publishers told Mrs. Reeves of this application. She was much amused, and in high good humour wrote back to say that she had always understood twins appeared about the same time, and that she had never heard before of one arriving seven years after the other.

In 1876 Helen Mathers married Mr. Henry Reeves, the well-known surgeon and specialist on Orthopædics. He has been on the staff of the London Hospital for nearly twenty years, and he, too, is an author, but his works bear more stupendous and alarming names than those of his wife, such as "Human Morphology," "Bodily Deformities"—sad, significant title! But not only as the skilful surgeon, the renowned specialist, the student, and author, is Henry Reeves known. There is another section of the world—amongst the poor and suffering, the over-worked clerk, the under-paid governess, the struggling artist, where his name like many another in his noble profession, is loved and revered, and where the word "fee" is never heard of, and the "left hand knoweth not what the right hand doeth." Did you not know all this from personal experience, it is almost to be read in the kind, bene-volent face. His wife says, laughing, that "he is so unselfish, he never thinks of himself, and I have always to be looking after him to see that he gets even a meal in peace"; and she adds, in a low and tender tone, "but he is the kindest and best of husbands." They have but one child—"Phil"—a bright, handsome boy of fourteen. He is the idol of their hearts, and like quicksilver in his brightness. His mother says when he was only three, he was found sitting at her desk, wielding a pen with great vigour, and throwing much ink about, as he dipped his golden curls in the blots he was making. "What are you doing?" his mother asked. "Writing ''Tory of a Sin,'" he said, with great dignity; and now that he is older he composes with great rapidity.

"He is at school now," says Mrs. Reeves, "and the house is like a tomb without him. If it were not for my needlework (my especial vanity) I could not get through the long weeks between his holidays. Children, flowers, needlework—these are my chief delights; and as I often have to do without the first two, my needle is often a great comfort to me."

Shortly after her marriage, Mrs. Reeves again took up her pen, and during the next few years she wrote several novels and novelettes, selecting peculiarly attractive titles. Amongst these books are "Cherry Ripe," "As He Comes up the Stair," "The Story of a Sin," "The Land of the Leal," "My Lady Greensleeves," "Eyre's Acquittal," etc., etc. Referring to a character in the last of these, you ask to see the book; but there is not a single volume visible; they are all conspicuous by their absence.

Mrs. Reeves remarks that she "has done nothing to speak of lately, feeling she has had nothing to say." Some months ago the inclination to begin a new story came back to her, and she set diligently to work while it lasted. A great catastrophe occurred. The first volume was finished when, having occasion to go on other business to her publisher, she had the manuscript put into the hansom which was to convey her to his office. After a long conversation, she suddenly remembered that the parcel had been left in the cab, and from that day to this she has never recovered it. At the time she did not take the matter seriously, feeling sure the precious packet would be found at Scotland Yard; but, though rewards were offered and handbills circulated by the thousand, all was of no avail. Mrs. Reeves adds, "the Press most kindly assisted me in every possible way. Either the cabman threw it away, in total ignorance of its value, and then was afraid to come forward and confess it, or some dishonest person who next got into the cab may have sold, or used the story, in America probably, or elsewhere. *Nous verrons!* I have written it over again. It took me a few weeks only, without notes, without a scrap of anything to help me, save my memory, and never in my life did I sit down to a harder task."

The author is very modest in her own opinion of this last book, and adds ruefully, "I feel miserable over it, but I never *am* at all satisfied with my work, and when I sent it to my publishers, I told them that they had much better put it into the fire—it fell so entirely short of what I had intended." They however, happily took quite a different view of its merits, and the novel will shortly be brought out in three volumes.

Helen Mathers is a great needlewoman. Not only are the long satin curtains, the pillows, cushions, and dainty lamp shades all made by her own hands; but she can cut out and sew any article of feminine apparel. She has, indeed, a very pretty taste in dress, and many of her friends are in the habit of consulting her in that line—from the designing of their smartest gowns to the little economies of "doing up the old ones to look like new." "And yet," says Mrs. Reeves plaintively, "people call me extravagant. Why! I have not even got a fashionable dressmaker. All my makings and mendings and turnings are done at home by a clever little workwoman, under my own superintendance, and I am most careful and economical. When a child, I was never taught the value of money, but I learnt it later by experience, and experience, after all, is the best teacher. I look upon myself as a sort of 'Aunt Sally,' at whom Fate is always having a 'shy,' chipping off a bit here, and a bit there, but never really knocking me off my perch."

A great solid silver donkey with panniers which must hold a pint of ink, stands on a table close to an oval Venetian glass framed in gold and silver. Mrs. Reeves observes that though she has no writing-table, that is her especial ink-stand, which is carried about from room to room. It was given to her when very young, and, she laughingly adds, "You can imagine all the complimentary remarks the boys at home made to me about it." She goes on to say, "I always loved a good laugh, even though it were against myself. We were such a happy united family in the big old house. We are all scattered now," she remarks sadly; "some are dead, some are abroad, and one sister, who married a son of Dr. Russell, of *Times* renown, is in China with her husband."

Mrs. Reeves is essentially a domestic woman. She cares comparatively but little for society, and is never as happy as when at home, with her husband sitting on the other side of the fire-place, like "Darby and Joan." She is excellent company, and a brilliant conversationalist. She possesses that good gift, a low, sweet voice, which glides on from topic to topic—now gay, with flashes of wit and mirth, now subdued to gravity or pathos. Albeit, she is a good listener, and has the happy knack of drawing out talk. Yet, though constantly conversing on people and social matters, not one unkindly word or suspicion of scandal escapes her lips. She has a good word to say for all, and speaks with affectionate gratitude of many. She prefers the company of woman, and says that her best friends have been those of her own sex. But the charm of her society has beguiled you into a long visit, and whilst bidding her good-bye the feeling arises that if a friend in need were wanted, a friend indeed would be found in "Helen Mathers."

FLORENCE MARRYAT

FLORENCE MARRYAT.

BATTLING with a fierce snowstorm, and a keen east wind, which drives the flakes straight into your face like repeated stings of a small sharp whip, a welcome shelter is presently found in Florence Marryat's pretty, picturesque little house in St. Andrew's Road, West Kensington. Two bright red pots filled with evergreens mark the house, which is built in the Elizabethan style of architecture, with a covered verandah running along the upper part. By a strange coincidence, the famous author has settled down within a stone's throw of the place where her distinguished father—the late Captain Marryat, R.N. —once lived. Until three months ago, there stood in the Fulham Palace Road, a large, handsome building enclosed in ten acres of ground, which was first called " Brandenburg Villa," and was inhabited by the celebrated singer Madame Sontag. It next fell into the hands of the Duke of Sussex, who changed its name to Sussex House, and finally sold it to his equerry Captain Marryat, who exchanged it with Mrs. Alexander Copeland for the Manor of Langham, in Norfolk, where he died. For some years past Sussex House has been in Chancery, but now it is pulled down; the land is sold out in building plots, and the pleasure grounds will be turned into the usual streets and rows of houses for the needs of the ever-increasing population. The study—or as Florence Marryat calls it, her "literary workshop"—is very small, but so well arranged that it seems a sort of *multum in parvo*, everything a writer can want being at hand. It has a look of thorough snugness and comfort. The large and well-worn writing table is loaded with books of reference and a vast heap of tidily-arranged manuscript, betokening the fact that yet another new novel is under weigh. A massive brass inkstand, bright as gold, is flanked on each side by a fierce-looking dragon. Two of the walls are lined with bookshelves from floor to ceiling, filled with books which must number many hundreds of volumes. Over the fireplace hangs an old-fashioned round mirror set in a dull yellow frame, mounted on plush, around whose broad margin is displayed a variety of china plates, picked up in the many foreign countries which Miss Marryat has visited, and the effect is particularly good. The room is lighted at the further corner by glass doors opening into an aviary and conservatory, which is bright with many red-berried winter plants; this little glass-house opens on to the big kennels where Miss Marryat's canine pets are made so comfortable.

But the door opens. Enters your hostess with two ringdoves perched familiarly on her shoulder. She is tall in stature, erect in carriage, fair in complexion: she has large blue eyes—set well apart—straight, well-formed eyebrows, and an abundance of soft, fair, fluffy hair. She is dressed very simply in a long black tea-gown with Watteau pleat, very plainly made, but perfect in cut and fit, and looking quite unstudied in its becoming graceful simplicity.

Florence Marryat is the youngest of the eleven children of the late well-known author, Captain Marryat, R.N., C.B., F.R.S. Her mother, who died at the good old age of ninety—in full possession of all her faculties—was a daughter of Sir Stephen Shairp, of Houston, Linlithgow, who was for many years H.B.M. Consul-General and *Chargé d'Affaires* at the Court of Russia. One side of the little study is dedicated to the relics of her father, and in the centre hangs his portrait, surrounded by trophies and memories. The picture is painted by the sculptor Behnes, in water-colours, and represents a tall, fair, slight, though muscular-looking man leaning against the mast of his ship, *Ariadne*, dressed in the full uniform of those days, a long-tailed coat, white duck trousers, and cocked hat held under his arm. Two smaller pictures of him are pen-and-ink drawings by Count D'Orsay and Sir Edward Belcher respectively.

Entering the service at a very early age, and in troublous times, Captain Marryat gained rapid promotion, and had been in no less than fifty-nine naval engagements before he was twenty-one, and with the single exception of Lord Nelson he was the youngest Post Captain ever known, having indeed attained that rank at the age of twenty-four. After the first Burmese war, in which he took so distinguished a part, he was offered a baronetcy as a reward for his services, but refused it, choosing instead a crest and arms to commemorate the circumstance, with the stipulation that the arms should be such as his daughters might carry. This was accordingly done, and at the present moment there are only eleven women in England who possess the same right, of which number Miss Marryat and her sisters make five. The crest, with arms (a fleur-de-lis and a Burmese boat with sixteen rowers on an azure ground, with three bars argent and three bars sable) is framed, and hangs close to what she calls her "Marryat Museum." Just below the portrait is an oval ebony frame containing an etching of a beaver done on a piece of ship's copper by her father, a morocco case close by holds all his medals, which were bequeathed to her, including the Legion of Honour bestowed on him by the Emperor Napoleon, and the picture of the dead Emperor, sketched by the gallant sailor, and published by Colnaghi, which is considered the best portrait of him ever taken. His daughter remarks: —"It was always said of my father that he ever displayed to perfection that courage, energy, and presence of mind which were natural to his lion-hearted character. Unlike the veteran who 'shouldered his crutch to show how fields were won,' he never voluntarily referred to exploits of which any man might have been proud. He was content to *do,* and know that he had *done,* and left to others the pride which he might justly have felt for himself."

Independent of his nautical career, Captain Marryat had other great talents. His writings will never be forgotten, from "Peter Simple" and "Midshipman Easy" down to "Masterman Ready," the much-beloved books of children. His "Code of Signals" is so celebrated that reference must just be made to it. Shortly before he was elected a Fellow of the Royal Society, he invented and brought to perfection the code which was at once adopted in the Merchant Service, and is now generally used by the British and French navies, in India, at the Cape of Good Hope, and other English settlements, and by the Mercantile Marine of North America. It is also published in the Dutch and Italian languages, and, by an order of the French Government, no merchant vessel can be insured without these signals being on board. Rising, Miss Marryat puts the original work into your hands, and you observe, with something like awe, that it is all written in the deceased sailor's own hand; the penmanship is like copper-plate, the flags and signals are painted, and each page is neatly indexed. Needless to say, it is regarded as a priceless treasure by his daughter.

Born of such a gifted father, it is small wonder that the child should have inherited brilliant talents. She was never sent to school, but was taught under a succession of governesses. "On looking back," she says with compunction, "I regret to remember that I treated them all very badly, for I was a downright troublesome child. I was an omnivorous reader, and as no restriction was placed on my choice of books, I read everything I could find, lying for hours full length on the rug, face downwards, arms propping up my head, with fingers in ears

to shut out every disturbing sound, the while per-
petually summoned to come to my lessons. I may
be said to have educated myself, and probably I
got more real learning out of this mode of procedure
than if I had gone through the regular routine of
the schoolroom, with the cut-and-dried conventional
system of the education of that day."

Florence Marryat has been twice married : first
at the age of sixteen to Captain Ross Church, of
the Madras Staff Corps, and secondly to Colonel
Francis Lean of the Royal Marines. By the first
marriage she had eight children, of whom six survive.

The first three-volume novel she published was
called "Love's Conflict." It was written under
sad circumstances. Her children were ill of scarlet
fever; most of the servants, terror-stricken, had
deserted her, and it was in the intervals of nursing
these little ones that, to divert her sad thoughts,
she took to her pen. From that time she wrote
steadily and rapidly, and up to the present date
she has actually turned out fifty-seven novels besides
an enormous quantity of journalistic work, about
one hundred short stories, and numerous essays,
poems, and recitations. She says of herself, that
from earliest youth she had always determined on
being a novelist, and at the age of ten she wrote a
story for the amusement of her playfellows, and
illustrated it with her own pen-and-ink sketches
(for be it known, the accomplished author has
likewise inherited this talent from her father, and
to this day she will decorate many a letter to her
favourite friends with funny and clever little illus-

trations and caricatures). But she wisely formed
the determination that she would never publish
anything until her judgment was more matured, so
as to ensure success, that she "would study people,
nature, nature's ways, and character, and then she
would let the world know what she thought"; and
in this piece of self-denial she has shown extreme
wisdom, and reaped her reward in the long record
of successes that she has scored and the large fortune she has made, but which, alas! she no longer
possesses. "Others have spent it for me," she says
plaintively; but she adds generously, "and I do
not grudge it to them." Part of it enabled her,
at any rate, to give each and all of her children a
thoroughly good education, and she is proud to think
that they owe it all to her own hard work. Miss
Marryat is always especially flattered to hear that
her novels are favourites with women, and she had
a gratifying proof of this when visiting Canada in
1885. She was waited on by a deputation of
ladies, armed with bouquets and presents, to thank
her for having written that charming story called
"My Own Child."

"Gup," which had an extensive sale, is entirely
an Anglo-Indian book, not so much of a novel as a
collection of character sketches and tales, which her
powers of observation enabled her to form out of
the life in Indian stations. For the benefit of the
uninitiated, the word "Gup" shall be translated
from Hindustanee into English: "Gossip." "Woman
Against Woman," "Veronique," "Petronel," "Nelly
Brooke," "Fighting the Air," were amongst the

earliest of the eighteen novels that she brought out
in the first eleven years of her literary career. These,
together with her "Girls of Feversham," have been
republished in Germany and America, and translated into Russian, German, Swedish, and French.
Miss Marryat says : "I never sit down deliberately
to compose or think out a plot. The most ordinary
remark or anecdote may supply the motive, and the
rest comes by itself. Sometimes I have as many
as a dozen plots, in different stages of completion,
floating in my brain. They appear to me like a set
of houses, the first of which is fully furnished ; the
second finished, but empty ; the third in course of
building; till the furthest in the distance is nothing
but an outline. As soon as one is complete, I feel
I *must* write it down ; but I never think of the
one I am writing, always of the next one that
is to be, and sometimes of three or four at a time,
till I drive them forcibly away. I never feel at
home with a plot till I have settled the names of
the characters to my satisfaction. As soon as I
have done that they become sentient beings in my
eyes, and seem to dictate what I shall write. I
lose myself so completely whilst writing, that I
have no idea, till I take it up to correct, what I
have written." Judging by the great heap of MSS.
alluded to on her writing-table, there seems but
little for the writer to correct. At your request,
she hands you half a dozen pages, and you notice
but three alterations amongst them ; the facile pen,
the medium of her thoughts, seems to have known
exactly what it had to write. The novel is called

"How like a Woman," and will shortly make its appearance.

Her latest published works are "On Circumstantial Evidence," "A Scarlet Sin," "Mount Eden," "Blindfold," "Brave Heart and True," "The Risen Dead," "There is no Death," and "The Nobler Sex." With respect to Miss Marryat's book, "There is no Death," many people have pronounced it to be, not only the most remarkable book that she has ever written, but the most remarkable publication of the time. To the public it is so full of marvels as to appear almost incredible, but to her friends, who know that everything related there happened, under the author's eyes, it is more wonderful still. The amount of correspondence that she has received on the subject ever since the book appeared in June, 1891, is incalculable. Even to this date she has seven or eight letters daily, all containing the same demand, "Tell us how we can see our Dead." This book has done more to convince many people of the truth of Spiritualism than any yet written. Florence Marryat numbers her converts by the hundred and they are all gathered from educated people; men of letters and of science have written to her from every part of the world, and many clergymen have succumbed to her courageous assertions. It is curious and interesting to know that Miss Marryat's experiences are not only those of the past, but that she passes through just as wonderful things every day of her life, and the spirit world is quite as familiar to her as the natural one, and far more interesting. Whether her readers sympathise with her or not, or whether they believe that she really saw and heard all the marvels related in "There is no Death," the book must remain as a remarkable record of the experiences of a woman whose friends know her to be incapable of telling a lie and especially on a subject which she holds to be sacred. " I really do not care much," says Miss Marryat with a smile, " if my readers believe me or not. If they do not it is their loss, not mine. I have done what I considered to be my duty in trying to convince the world of what *I* know to be true, and to which I shall continue to testify as long as I have breath."

"Tom Tiddler's Ground " is the history of her own adventures while in America. Many of her books have been dramatised, and at one time nine of these plays were running simultaneously in the provinces. She says, " The most successful of my works are transcripts of my own experience. I have been accused of caricaturing my acquaintances, but it is untrue. The majority of them are not worth the trouble, and it is far easier for me to draw a picture from my own imagination, than to endure the society of a disagreeable person for the sake of copying him or her."

But Miss Marryat's talents are versatile. After a long illness when her physicians recommended rest from literature, believing an entire change of occupation would be the best tonic for her, she went upon the stage—a pursuit which she had always dearly loved—and possessing a fine voice, and great musical gifts, with considerable dramatic power, she has been successful, both as an actress and an entertainer. She wrote a play called " Her World Against a Lie " (from her own novel), which was produced at the

Prince of Wales' Theatre, and in which she played the chief comedy part, Mrs. Hephzibah Horton, with so much skill and *aplomb*, that the *Era, Figaro, Morning Post,* and other papers, criticised her performances most favourably. She also wrote "Miss Chester" and "Charmyon" in conjunction with Sir Charles Young. She was engaged for the opening of the Prince of Wales' (then the Princes') Theatre when she played "Queen Altemire" in *The Palace of Truth.* She has toured with D'Oyly Carte's *Patience* companies, with George Grossmith in *Entre Nous,* and finally with her own company in *The Golden Goblet* (written by her son Frank). Altogether Miss Marryat has pursued her dramatic life for fifteen years, and has given hundreds of recitations and musical entertainments which she has written for herself. One of these last, called "Love Letters," she has taken through the provinces three times, and once through America. It lasts two hours; she accompanies herself on the piano, and the music was written by George Grossmith. Another is a comic lecture entitled, "Women of the future (1991); or, what shall we do with our men?" She has also made many tours throughout the United Kingdom, giving recitals and readings from her father's works, and other pieces by Albery and Grossmith.

For the last seven years Miss Marryat has never looked at a criticism on her books. She says her publishers are her best friends, and their purses are her assessors, and she is quite satisfied with the result. She has an intense love of animals, and asks if you would object to the presence of her dogs, as this is the hour for their admittance. On the contrary, it is what

you have been longing for, and two magnificent bull-
dogs of long pedigree are let in.   Ferocious as is their
appearance, their manners are perfect, and their great
brown eyes seem human in their intelligence as each
comes up to make acquaintance.   Meantime the two
doves have gone peacefully to sleep, each perched
on a brass dragon, and the dogs eye them respectfully,
as if they were all members of " a happy family."

A neat little maid comes in with a tea-tray, but ere
she is permitted to lay the prettily embroidered cloth,
Miss Marryat directs attention to the table, which is a
curiosity.   It is a small round table, made from the oak
planks of the quarter deck of H.M.S. *Ariadne*.   This
was sent to her by a gentleman who never saw her,
with a letter saying that she would prize the wood
over which her father's feet had so often trod.   It
bears in the centre a brass inscription, as follows :—
" Made from the timbers of H.M.S. Ariadne, com-
manded by Captain Marryat, R.N., C.B., 1828."

Miss Marryat, probably wishing to pay you a
peculiar honour, pushes forward her own special revolving writing chair ; but no, you had surreptitiously
tried it whilst waiting for her, and unhesitatingly
pronounce it to be the most uncomfortable piece of
furniture ever made.   It is constructed of wood, is
highly polished, and has a hard seat, hard elbow rests,
and a hard unyielding back.   She laughs heartily, and
declares she will hear no word against her "old arm-
chair" ; she says she has got used to it ; it has been,
like herself, a great traveller ; she has written in it for
twenty years, and it is a particular favourite.   Miss
Marryat wears a diamond ring, which has a peculiar

history, and is very old. During the first Burmese war in which her father was engaged, the natives were in the habit of making little slits in their skin, and inserting therein any particular stone of value they wished to conceal. One of these men was taken prisoner, and on being searched, or felt over—for there was not much clothing to search—a small hard lump was found on his leg, which at once revealed the presence of some valuable. A slight incision produced a diamond, which was confiscated, set, and presented by the good old sailor to his sister-in-law, Mrs. Horace Marryat, whose only son, Colonel Fitzroy Marryat, gave it to his cousin, the author.

She takes you into the adjoining room to see two oil-paintings of wrecks, *chef d'œuvres* of the great Flemish seascape painter, Louis Boeckhaussen, and valued at a high figure. There is a story attached to these also. They belonged originally to the Marryat collection at Wimbledon House, and were given to her brother Frederick by his grandmother on his being promoted to be first lieutenant of the *Sphynx*, and were hanging in his cabin when that ship was wrecked off the Needles, Isle of Wight. They remained fourteen days under water, and when rescued were sent to a Plymouth dealer to be cleaned. Lieutenant Marryat, for his bravery on that occasion, was immediately appointed to the *Sphynx's* twin vessel, the ill-fated *Avenger*, who went down with 380 souls on the Sorelli rocks.

After this catastrophe, the dealer sent the paintings to the young officer's mother, saying it was by his instructions, and that he had refused to take them to sea again, as he declared that they were "much too good to go overboard." Miss Marryat also possesses a painting by Cawno, from "Japhet in search of a Father," which was left to her by the will of the late Mr. Richard Bently, the publisher, and this she prizes highly. She has several presentation pens, one of porcupine quill and silver, with which her father wrote his last five novels; another of ivory, coral, and gold, inscribed with her name and presented by Messrs. Macniven and Cameron; a third of silver, and a fourth of gold and ivory, given by admirers of her writings; fifthly, and the one she values most and chiefly uses, a penholder of solid gold with amethysts, which belonged to an American ancestress of the family, for Miss Marryat's paternal grandmother was a Boston belle. This was a tribute from her American relations when she crossed the Atlantic, with the words that she was "the most worthy member to retain it." A noise of barking and scratching at the door is heard outside. Florence Marryat opens it, and many tiny, rough, prize terriers rush in. She laughs at your exclamation of surprise at the number of her dog friends and answers, "They are not all kept entirely for amusement. I sell the puppies, and they fetch large prices. It is quite the fashion to be in trade now-a-days, you know. One lady runs a boarding-house, another, her emporium for furniture, a third, her bonnet shop, a fourth, her dress-making establishment, so why not I, my kennels? I love dogs better than bonnets, or chairs, or people, and so I derive pleasure as well as profit from my particular fancy, and I should be lonely without these pets."

But, as though talking of old reminiscences had changed her mood from gay to grave, she asks you to look at a few very special treasures in her writing room. " I call this my room of home memories," she says with exceeding softness and pathos. " There are my children's pictures ; those," pointing to a small shelf, " are my best friend's books." " *Here* are portraits of all whom I love best, my living, and my dead !"

MRS. LOVETT CAMERON.

NESTLING between Knightsbridge on the north, and Brompton Road on the south, lies a quiet, old-fashioned square, which the organ-grinder and brass band are no longer permitted to disturb. Everything is so still that it is difficult to realise that it is within a few minutes' walk from a busy, noisy thoroughfare. So near and yet so far from London's "madding crowd." In summer time when the ancient trees, which are said never to have been disturbed for generations, are in full leaf, the little square might indeed be a slice out of the country itself; and even now, with bare and leafless branches, it presents a peaceful, rural appearance, for the hoar frost has covered every bough and shrub with a million of glittering particles, which sparkle like diamonds in the wintry sunshine. In the centre of the north side of Montpelier Square is Mrs. Lovett Cameron's home, a cheerful-looking little house, gay with window boxes, and fleecy muslin curtains draped with bright coloured ribbons. An application at the brass horse-shoe knocker is promptly responded to, and you are admitted into the hall and vociferously greeted by "Nancy," a handsome fox-terrier, the pet of the house, a treasure-trove from the Dogs' Home

MRS LOVETT CAMERON

The first object which attracts the eye, and, as it were, overshadows you, is the head of a gigantic Indian buffalo, so sleek and life-like in appearance, with its huge horns, that you involuntarily shudder to think what a formidable opponent the savage monster must have proved in the flesh ere he became the trophy of that gallant sportsman, the late Hector Cameron.

Ascending the staircase, the walls of which are hung with a series of Colonel Crealock's spirited hunting sketches, you are ushered into the drawing-room, which is divided midway by a carved white wood archway of Moorish design. Large palms, tall arum lilies, and graceful ferns, are grouped here and there about the room; no sound is heard save the song of caged birds. The Oriental bowls and jars are filled with great double chrysanthemums of golden brown, and other winter flowers; but a light step approaches; the door softly opens, and the author enters : seeing her framed in the doorway, clad in the soft folds of a simply-made violet velvet tea-gown, the first glance conveys to the mind an immediate impression that she is in thorough harmony with her surroundings.

Mrs. Lovett Cameron is a fair, slight woman, a little below the middle height; her large blue eyes have a very thoughtful, gentle expression; her broad low brow is crowned with bright chestnut coloured hair. Her habitually serious look changes, however, when having settled you into a corner of the couch, with a cup of steaming coffee, she enters into friendly conversation. Meanwhile you cast furtive glances around the room. A bright fire blazes cheerfully

G

on the blue and brown tiled hearth.   The carved
white mantelpiece, with side recesses, is covered with
delicate specimens of old Dresden china, and surmounted by a broad shelf, on which stand five exquisite
antique Japanese jars, the *bleu poudré* and deep
crimson being thrown into relief by the soft tints of
the "buttercup" coloured wall paper.

Amongst the pictures which adorn the walls is a
portrait, after Sir Godfrey Kneller, of Sir Edmund
Verney, an ancestor of the family, bearing the inscription "Standard Bearer to Charles I., who lost his life
in the Battle of Edghill." The original painting is at
Liscombe, Buckinghamshire, a property which still
belongs to the Lovett family. Further on is a lovely
copy of the Madonna Caracci, in the Dresden Gallery.
Several pieces of valuable old blue china, quaint bits
of Oriental flat figures, together with a plate or two of
old Dutch ware decorate the walls, and an ancient
convex mirror of great antiquity. Two antique corner cupboards (Dutch) with flat glass doors disclose
many little treasures of enamel, old Worcester and
Nankin, which Mrs. Cameron says that she prizes
as much from association as for their own intrinsic
value. An Italian cabinet inlaid with ebony and
ivory occupies one side of the wall, and, unlocking
its doors, she takes out some priceless scraps of
old lace of cobweb-looking fabric, which she inherited from a maternal ancestress, together with a
few pieces of the Queen Anne silver which are
scattered on the tiny marqueterie table yonder.
Amongst these there is a richly-chased tankard, on
which is the inscription, "Oration Prize adjudged to

Verney Lovett, of Trinity College, Cambridge, in the year 1774." There is an amusing story told of another of Mrs. Cameron's ancestresses. She was a Huguenot, a Mademoiselle de Bosquet, and, at the time of the persecution of the French Protestants, when only a little girl, she was packed up in a basket, smuggled out of France and sent over to England to ensure her safety.

The long, dwarf bookcase on the right is filled with literary treasures, inherited from the "Oration Prize" winner. Mrs. Cameron takes out several, and mentions that they are valuable editions of "Montaigne," "Chesterfield's Letters," the "Tattler," the "Spectator," etc., but the gem of the collection, and one that she greatly values, is a complete set of the poems of Edmund Waller, dated 1729, in good preservation, each poem headed with engravings by Vertue, chiefly portraits of the Stuart family. The bookcase opposite contains several presentation copies from brother and sister writers. Amongst them you look in vain for the author's own works, but she says that they shall all be seen presently in her own study below, and as she leads the way thither, past the conservatory, you pause to admire the picturesque grouping of the flowers and palms, some so high that the cages of the feathered songsters are half concealed. Your hostess remarks that she "delights in flowers, and is always lucky with them."

Turning to the right, she opens the door of her cosy little writing-room. The dark red walls, with a frieze of large Japanese flowers, are hung with etchings, photographs, and pictures, all of which

have their own story. Here is a complete series
of Aitken's "First Point to Point Race"; there
portraits of the "Prize Fox-terriers of England,"
presented to her by the late Sir John Reid. Also
sundry winners of the Derby, and many a pet dog
and horse. Mrs. Cameron points out her husband's
favourite hunter, "Roscommon," and his wonderful
pony, "Tommy Dod," who "jumped like a cat,"
and carried him for many seasons in Leicestershire,
and who, with his master, was often mentioned with
honour in *Baily's Magazine*. A few sketches of
the Thames indicate her favourite resort for leisure
hours, many summer days and autumn holidays
being spent on the river, in quiet nooks and corners, where, under the able tuition of her barrister
brother, Norman Pearson, late of Balliol, and coach
of the "Kingston Eight," Mrs. Lovett Cameron has
achieved considerable dexterity in sculling and
canoeing.

Antlers and deers' heads, ranged high near the
ceiling, testify further to the sporting proclivities of
the family. Over a quaint little corner cupboard
a big stuffed hawk looks down with an absurdly
wise expression. A high, three-cornered, and somewhat ascetic-looking chair is pushed aside from a
proportionately high and business-like writing table
—a handsome old English piece of furniture, which
is loaded with manuscript and books of reference,
denoting the occupation in which Mrs. Cameron was
probably engaged when summoned to receive you,
and you hastily begin a word of apology; but she
turns it aside and observes that she was "quite glad

to be interrupted, as she had been working beyond her usual hour."

Over the table hangs a venerable canary, *ætat.* fourteen, who has learnt to be mute in business hours. Opposite the window stands a large antique Chippendale bookcase with glass doors, filled with books of history, travel, biography, English poets, and old dramatists. One shelf is reserved for another purpose, and here can be read the names of fourteen three-volume novels, well known to the world, written by Mrs. Lovett Cameron. Her husband has had them all bound alike in Russian leather, and looks on them as his own especial property. This shelf is now nearly full, and Mrs. Cameron remarks laughingly that "by rights she ought to die when it *is* full, as there will be no room for any more in the cupboard." Of these novels, the first, "Juliet's Guardian," made its bow to the public in 1876, having previously appeared in the pages of *Belgravia.* "Jack's Secret" ran as a serial through the same magazine, having been applied for, when *Belgravia* changed hands, by the present owner "to bring him luck." Taking out one after another of these daintily-bound volumes—"Deceivers Ever," "Vera Nevill," "Pure Gold," "A North Country Maid," "A Dead Past," "In a Grass Country," "A Devout Lover," "This Wicked World," "Worth Winning," "The Cost of a Lie," "Neck or Nothing," and other short stories—you see that most of them have passed through several editions, and in "In a Grass Country," "ninth edition," proving the special popularity of that particular book, which chiefly made

Mrs. Lovett Cameron's literary reputation. Her latest additions to these entertaining works of fiction are "A Lost Wife," "Weak Woman," and "A Daughter's Heart."

It is always deeply interesting to hear about the early days of such a well-known writer. Explaining to Mrs. Cameron that not only in Europe, but also in the Colonies where her books are as largely circulated, that she has many friends and admirers who will love to hear all about her first literary efforts, she kindly consents to gratify you, and says, that "to begin at the beginning," she was sent at the early age of six to Paris, to acquire the language; she was placed in the family of the late M. Nizard, an academician, and a man of some literary repute, who later on became a member of the Senate. She has a vivid recollection of the house—since demolished —surrounded by a large garden in the Rue de Conscelles, where her childish days were spent. Amongst such surroundings, it was natural that the girl should become imbued with a love of reading, which, though carefully guided, was stimulated to the utmost, and when, later on, after some further years at a school in England, she returned home, she found herself in constant disgrace, because she was always reading and hated needlework. As her mother and sister were enthusiastic in this feminine accomplishment, and were constantly engrossed in the embroidering of church altar-cloths and linen, they were inclined to look on books as an excuse for idleness.

It was at this time that the young girl-student

secretly wrote several short stories, and, although
very shy of these efforts, she one day confided to
her elder sister that she "felt certain she could
write a novel." With the honest candour of a
family circle towards each other, she was promptly
extinguished with the remark, " That is nonsense.
If you had any talent for writing, it would have
shown itself before this." Thus discouraged, she
laid aside the idea, and never resumed it until after
her marriage, when the talent which had lain dormant could no longer be hidden. The story of the
launching of her first novel is most interesting, as
showing the courage and perseverance of the young
author.

She had no acquaintance with a single member
of the literary profession—no interest with any
editor or publisher ; nevertheless, on the completion
of "Juliet's Guardian," she took up, by chance, the
nearest book at hand; reading therein the names
of Chatto and Windus, she then and there packed
up her MS., and without any introduction, but
with many qualms, made her way to their office.
She was courteously received, and informed that she
might leave it, and after a brief period of anxious
waiting, the good news came that it was accepted.
Shortly after, it was brought out, and the young
author's first step to fame was accomplished.

Rising to replace this volume, you inadvertently
press against a panel in the lower cupboard, which
falling open, dislodges a large and somewhat dis-
coloured roll of newspapers, and hastening to gather
them up with a murmured word of regret for the

accident, Mrs. Cameron remarks with a laugh that
they are copies of a paper, the *City Advertiser*, which
she and her two brothers started, and actually kept
going for six months, the three meeting once a week
to carry it on. It was a source of endless amusement
to them, until the scattering of the family caused it
to die a natural death.

The easel yonder holds a large framed photograph
of the head of an Apollo, discovered when digging
under the streets of Athens; and opposite stands a
portfolio full of sketches and maps, descriptive of
the route taken by her brother-in-law, Commander
Lovett Cameron, the well-known African traveller,
who nearly seventeen years ago went on foot across
Africa with a small party of friends, but, alas! came
back alone. He was the only survivor of the
intrepid band, the rest all succumbed to the perils
of the expedition. He it was who surveyed the
southern portion of Lake Tanganyika, proving it to
be a lake, and discovered the river Lukuga, which
is the outlet thereof. Pursuing his travels further,
he also proved Lualaba and Congo to be one river,
and later discovered Lake Kassali and the sources
of the Zambesi.

But whilst following out the route on a well-worn
map, and listening to these interesting details, youthful voices are heard outside, which recall the fact that
it is the first day of the holidays, and a tap at the
door is followed by the entrance of Mrs. Cameron's
two fine, bright boys, accompanied by their father.

The elder lad, "Verney" is at Winchester, the
"school for scholars," and he has already evinced a

distinct talent for composition, combined with a fund
of humour, which has found vent in one or two
clever, though childish stories, which betoken the
probability that he has inherited his mother's gift
of writing, but the younger boy, "Hector," bravely
tells you he "likes play better than lessons, and
he means to go abroad and shoot elephants." As
he is, however, only twelve years old his parents
feel no immediate anxiety on *that* score.

Mrs. Lovett Cameron seldom writes after two
o'clock. She uses a pen placed in a funny little
stump of a broken mother-of-pearl holder, and, hand-
ing it to you, she says, "I have a superstition about
it. Every one of my novels has been mainly
written with it, and I often say that if I use
another penholder, I write badly. I have told my
husband to put it into my coffin."

She is a capital woman of business, and remarks
that she "bought all her experience for herself."

Those who do not know Mrs. Cameron well, think
that she is cold and proud. Truly, she does not
wear her heart on her sleeve; but not to all is
revealed the true nature of the woman. Do you
go to consult her on a tiresome bit of business,
to take a tale of deserving charity, to confide a
personal grief? Though in the midst of writing a
sentence, the busy pen is thrown aside, as she
straightens the tangled web, opens her purse to the
pitiful story, or, with tender sympathy, enters into
the sorrow.

The good old "grandfather" clock in the corner is
a very ancient and much-treasured relic; its hands,

however, mark that it is time to go; but Mrs. Lovett Cameron asks you to "stay a moment." She runs lightly upstairs and returns with a bunch of the gold and brown chrysanthemums, which she puts into your hands; then, casting a last look at the fierce buffalo, you pass out into the quiet little square, and in less than five minutes find yourself again in the noisy region of cabs and omnibuses.

MRS HUNGERFORD

MRS. HUNGERFORD.

It is well worth encountering the perils of the sea, even in the middle of winter, and in the teeth of a north-east wind, if only to experience the absolute comfort and ease with which, in these space-annihilating days, the once-dreaded journey from England to the Emerald Isle can be made. You have resolved to accept a hospitable invitation from Mrs. Hungerford, the well-known author of "Molly Bawn," etc., to visit her at her lovely home, St. Brenda's, Bandon, co. Cork, where a "hearty Irish welcome" is promised, and though circumstances prevent your availing yourself of the "month's holiday" so kindly offered, and limit an absence from home to but four days, it is delightful to find that, travelling by the best of all possible routes—the Irish Mail—it is to be accomplished easily and without any fatiguing haste.

Having given due notice of your intentions, you arrive at Euston just in time for the 7.15 a.m. express, and find that by the kindness of the station-master a compartment is reserved, and every arrangement, including an excellent meal, is made for your comfort. The carriages are lighted by electricity, and run so smoothly that it is possible to get a couple of hours' good sleep, which the very early start has made so desirable. On reaching Holyhead at 1.30 p.m. to the minute, you are met by the courteous and attentive marine superintendent, Captain Cay, R.N., who takes you straight on board the *Ireland,* the newest addition to the fleet of fine ships, owned by the City of Dublin Steam Packet Company. She is a magnificent vessel, 380 feet long, 38 feet in beam, 2,589 tons, and 6,000 horse-power; her fine, broad bridge, handsome deck-houses, and brass work glisten in the bright sunlight. She carries electric light; and the many airy private cabins indicate that, though built for speed, the comfort of her passengers has been a matter of much consideration. She is well captained, well officered, well manned, and well navigated. The good-looking, weather-beaten Captain Kendall is indeed the commodore of the company, and has made the passage for nearly thirty years. There is an unusually large number of passengers to-day, for it is the first week of the accelerated speed, and it is amusing to notice the rapidity with which the mails are shipped, on men's backs, which plan is found quicker than any appliance. Captain Cay remarks that it is no uncommon thing to ship seven hundred sacks on foreign mail days; he says, too, that never since these vessels were started has there been a single accident to life or limb. But the last bag is on board, steam is up, and away goes the ship past the South Stack lighthouse, built on an island under precipitous cliffs, from which a gun is fired when foggy, and in about an hour the Irish coast becomes visible, Howth and Bray Head. The sea gets pretty rough, but luckily does not interfere with your excellent appetite for the first-class refreshments supplied. The swift-revolving paddles churn the big waves into a thick foam as the good ship *Ireland* ploughs her way through at the rate of twenty knots an hour, "making good weather of it," and actually accomplishes the voyage in three hours and fifteen minutes—one of the shortest runs on record. The punctuality with which these mail packets make the passage in all weathers is indeed truly wonderful—a fact which is experienced a few days later on the return journey. Kingstown is reached at 6.10 p.m. (Irish time), where the mail train is waiting to convey passengers by the new loop line that runs in a curve right through "dear dirty Dublin," as it is popularly called, to Kingsbridge, and so on to Cork, where you put up for the night at the Imperial Hotel.

Another bright sunshiny morning opens, and shows old Cork at her best. Cork! the old city of Father Prout's poem, "The Bells of Shandon," which begins thus :—

> With deep affection and recollection
> I often think of Shandon bells,
> Whose sounds so wild would in days of childhood
> Fling round my cradle their magic spells,
> On this I ponder where'er I wander,
> And thus grow fonder, sweet Cork, of thee ;
> With the bells of Shandon
> That sound so grand on, etc., etc.

The river Lee runs through the handsome little city, and has often been favourably compared with the Rhine. But Bandon must be reached, which is easily managed in an hour by rail, and there you are met by your host with a neat dog-cart, and good

grey mare ; being in light marching order, your kit is
quickly stowed away by a smart-looking groom, and
soon you find yourself tearing along at a spanking pace
through the "most Protestant" town of Bandon, where
Mr. Hungerford pulls up for a moment to point out the
spot where once the old gates stood, whereon was
written the legend, "Let no Papist enter here." Years
after, a priest in the dead of night added to it. He
wrote :—

> Whoever wrote this, wrote it *well*,
> The same is written on the gates of *Hell.*

Then up the hill past Ballymoden Church, in through
the gates of Castle Bernard, past Lord Bandon's beautiful old castle covered with exquisite ivy, out through a
second gate, over the railway, a drive of twenty minutes
in all, and so up to the gates of St. Brenda's. A private
road of about half a mile long, hedged on either side
by privet and hawthorn and golden furze, leads to the
avenue proper, the entrance gate of which is flanked
by two handsome deodars. It takes a few minutes
more to arrive at a large, square, ivy-clad house, and
ere there is time to take in an idea of its gardens and
surroundings, the great hall door is flung open, a little
form trips down the stone steps, and almost before the
horse has come to a standstill, Mrs. Hungerford gives
you indeed the "hearty Irish welcome" she promised.

It is now about four o'clock, and the day is growing
dark. Your hostess draws you in hastily out of the
cold, into a spacious hall lighted by a hanging Eastern
lamp, and by two other lamps let into the wide circular
staircase at the lower end of it. The drawing-room door

is open, and a stream of ruddy light from half-a-dozen crimson shaded lamps, rushing out, seems to welcome you too. It is a large, handsome room, very lofty, and charmingly furnished, with a Persian carpet, tiny tables, low lounging chairs, innumerable knick-knacks of all kinds, ferns, winter flowers of every sort, screens and palms. A great fire of pine-logs is roaring up the chimney. The piano is draped with Bokhara plush, and everywhere the latest magazines, novels, and papers are scattered.

Mrs. Hungerford is a very tiny woman, but slight and well-proportioned. Her large hazel eyes, sparkling with fun and merriment, are shaded by thick, curly lashes. She has a small, determined mouth, and the chin slightly upturned, gives a *piquante* expression to the intelligent face—so bright and vivacious. Her hair is of a fair-brown colour, a little lighter than her eye-lashes, and is piled up high on the top of her head, breaking away into natural curls over her brow. She is clad in an exquisite tea-gown of dark blue plush, with a soft, hanging, loose front of a lighter shade of silk. Some old lace ruffles finish off the wrists and throat, and she wears a pair of little high-heeled *Louis quinze* shoes, which display her small and pretty feet. She looks the embodiment of good temper, merry wit, and *espièglerie.*

It is difficult to realize that she is the mother of the six children who are grouped in the background. One lovely little fairy, "Vera," aged three and a half, runs clinging up to her skirts, and peeps out shyly. Her delicate colouring suggests a bit of dainty Dresden china. Later on, you discover that this is actually the pet name by which she is known, being indeed quite famous here as a small beauty. " Master Tom," a splendid roly-poly fellow, aged sixteen months, is playing with a heap of toys on the rug near the fire and is carefully watched over by a young brother of five. The three other girls are charming little maidens. The eldest, though but in her early teens, is intellectual and studious; the second has a decided talent for painting, whilst the third, says her mother, laughing, " is a consummate idler, but witty and clever."

By and bye your hostess takes you into what she calls her " den," for a long, undisturbed chat, and this room also bears the stamp of her taste and love of study. A big log fire burns merrily here, too, in the huge grate, and lights up a splendid old oak cabinet, reaching from floor to ceiling, which, with four more bookcases, seems literally crammed with dictionaries, books of reference, novels, and other light literature ; but the picturesque is not wanting, and there are plenty of other decorations, such as paintings, flowers, and valuable old china to be seen. Here the clever little author passes three hours every morning. She is, as usual, over-full of work, sells as fast as she can write, and has at the present time more commissions than she can get through during the next few years. Everything is very or- derly—each big or little bundle of MSS. is neatly tied together and duly labelled. She opens one drawer of a great knee-hole writing table, which discloses hundreds of half sheets of paper. " Yes," she says, with a laugh; " I scribble my notes on these: they

are the backs of my friends' letters; how aston-
ished many of them would be if they knew that
the last half sheet they write me becomes on the
spot a medium for the latest full-blown accounts
of a murder, or a laugh, or a swindle, perhaps, more
frequently, a flirtation! I am a bad sleeper," she
adds, "I think my brain is too active, for I always
plan out my best scenes at night, and write them
out in the morning without any trouble." She finds,
too, that driving has a curious effect upon her; the
action of the air seems to stimulate her. She dislikes
talking, or being talked to, when driving, but loves
to think, and to watch the lovely variations of the
world around her, and often comes home filled with
fresh ideas, scenes, and conversations, which she
scribbles down without even waiting to throw off
her furs. Asking her how she goes to work about
her plot, she answers with a reproachful little
laugh—"That is unkind! You know I never *have*
a plot really, not the *bonâ fide* plot one looks
for in a novel. An idea comes to me, or I to it,"
she says, airily, "a scene—a situation—a young
man, a young woman, and on that mental hint I
begin to build," but the question naturally arises,
she must make a beginning? "Indeed, no," she replies; "it has frequently happened to me that I
have written the last chapter first, and so, as it were,
worked backwards."

"Phyllis" was the young author's first work. It
was written before she was nineteen, and was read
by Mr. James Payn, who accepted it for Messrs. Smith
and Elder.

H

Mrs. Hungerford is the daughter of the late Rev.
Canon Hamilton, rector and vicar choral of St. Faugh-
nan's cathedral in Ross Carberry, co. Cork, one of the
oldest churches in Ireland. Her grandfather was John
Hamilton, of Vesington, Dunboyne, a property thirteen
miles out of Dublin. The family is very old, very
distinguished, and came over from Scotland to Ireland
in the reign of James I.

Most of her family are in the army; but of literary
talent, she remarks, it has but little to boast. Her
principal works are " Phyllis," " Molly Bawn," " Mrs.
Geoffrey," " Portia," " Rossmoyne," " Undercurrents,"
"A Life's Remorse," "A Born Coquette," "A Conquering
Heroine." She has written up to this time thirty-
two novels, besides uncountable articles for home
and American papers. In the latter country she
enjoys an enormous popularity, and everything she
writes is rapidly printed off. First sheets of the
novels in hand are bought from her for American
publications, months before there is any chance of
their being completed. In Australia, too, her books
are eagerly looked for, whilst every story she has
ever written can be found in the Tauchnitz series.

She began to write when very young, at school
taking always the prize in composition. As a mere
child she could always keep other children spell-
bound whilst telling them fairy stories of her own
invention. "I remember," she says, turning round
with a laugh, " when I was about ten years old,
writing a ghost story which so frightened myself,
that when I went to bed that night, I couldn't sleep
till I had tucked my head under the bedclothes.

This," she adds, "I have always considered my *chef d'œuvre*, as I don't believe I have ever succeeded in frightening anyone ever since." At eighteen she gave herself up seriously, or rather, gaily, to literary work. All her books teem with wit and humour. One of her last creations, the delightful old butler, Murphy, in "A Born Coquette," is equal to anything ever written by her compatriot, Charles Lever. Not that she has devoted herself entirely to mirth-moving situations. The delicacy of her love scenes, the light-ness of touch that distinguishes her numerous flirtations can only be equalled by the pathos she has thrown into her work every now and then, as if to temper her brightness with a little shade. Her descriptions of scenery are specially vivid and delightful, and very often full of poetry. She is never didactic or goody-goody, neither does she revel in risky situ-ations, nor give the world stories which, to quote the well-known saying of a popular playwright, "no nice girl would allow her mother to read."

Mrs. Hungerford married first when very young, but her husband died in less than six years, leaving her with three little girls. In 1883 she married Mr. Henry Hungerford. He also is Irish, and his father's place, Cahirmore, of about eleven thousand acres, lies nearly twenty miles to the west of Bandon. "It may interest you," she says, "to hear that my husband was at the same school as Mr. Rider Haggard. I remember when we were all much younger than we are now, the two boys came over for their holidays to Cahirmore, and one day in my old home 'Milleen' we all went down to the kitchen to cast bullets. We little thought then that the quiet, shy schoolboy, was destined to be the author of 'King Solomon's Mines.'"

Nothing less than a genius is Mrs. Hungerford at gardening. Her dress protected by a pretty holland apron, her hands encased in brown leather gloves, she digs and delves. Followed by many children, each armed with one of "mother's own" implements—for she has her own little spade and hoe, and rake, and trowel, and fork—she plants her own seeds, and pricks her own seedlings, prunes, grafts, and watches with the deepest eagerness to see them grow. In springtime, her interest is alike divided between the opening buds of her daffodils, and the breaking of the eggs of the first little chickens, for she has a fine poultry yard too, and is very successful in her management of it. She is full of vitality, and is the pivot on which every member of the house turns. Blessed with an adoring husband, and healthy, handsome, obedient children, who come to her for everything and tell her anything, her life seems idyllic.

"Now and then," she remarks laughing, "I really have great difficulty in securing two quiet hours for my work"; but everything is done in such method and order, the writing included, there is little wonder that so much is got through. It is a full, happy, complete life. "I think," she adds, "my one great dread and anxiety is a review. I never yet have got over my terror of it, and as each one arrives, I tremble and quake afresh ere reading."

"April's Lady" is one of the author's lately published works. It is in three volumes, and ran previously as a serial in *Belgravia*. "Lady Patty," a society sketch drawn from life, had a most favourable reception from the critics and public alike, but in her last novel, very cleverly entitled "Nor Wife, Nor Maid," Mrs. Hungerford is to be seen, or rather read, at her best. This charming book, so full of pathos, so replete with tenderness, ran into a second edition in about ten days. In it the author has taken somewhat of a departure from her usual lively style. Here she has indeed given "sorrow words." The third volume is so especially powerful and dramatic, that it keeps the attention chained. The description indeed of poor Mary's grief and despair are hardly to be outdone. The plot contains a delicate situation, most delicately worked out. Not a word or suspicion of a word jars upon the reader. It is not however all gloom. There is in it a second pair of lovers who help to lift the clouds, and bring a smile to the lips of the reader.

Mrs. Hungerford does not often leave her pretty Irish home. What with her incessant literary work, her manifold domestic occupations, and the cares of her large family, she can seldom be induced to quit what she calls, "an out and out country life," even to pay visits to her English friends. Mr. Hungerford unhesitatingly declares that everything in the house seems wrong, and there is a howl of dismay from the children when the presiding genius even suggests a few days' leave of absence. Last year, however, she determined to go over to London at the pressing invitation of a friend, in order to make the acquaintance of some of her distinguished brothers and sisters of the pen, and she speaks of how thoroughly she enjoyed that visit, with an eager delight. "Everyone

was so kind," she says, " so flattering, far, far too
flattering. They all seemed to have some pretty thing
to say to me. I have felt a little spoilt ever since.
However, I am going to try what a little more flattery
will do for me, so Mr. Hungerford and I hope to accept,
next Spring, a second invitation from the same friend,
who wants us to go to a large ball she is going to
give some time in May for some charitable institution—a Cottage Hospital I believe; but come," she
adds, suddenly springing up, " we have spent quite
too much time over my stupid self. Come back to
the drawing-room and the chicks, I am sure they
must be wondering where we are, and the tea and the
cakes are growing cold."

At this moment the door opens, and her husband,
gun in hand, with muddy boots and gaiters, nods to
you from the threshold; he says he dare not enter the
"den" in this state, and hurries up to change before
joining the tea table. "He is a great athlete," says his
wife, "good at cricket, football, and hockey, and equally
fond of shooting, fishing, and riding." That he is a
capital whip, you have already found out.

In the morning you see from the library window a
flower garden and shrubbery, with rose trees galore,
and after breakfast a stroll round the place is proposed.
A brisk walk down the avenue first, and then back to
the beech trees standing on the lawn, which slopes
away from the house down to a river running at the
bottom of a deep valley, up the long gravelled walk
by the hall door, and you turn into a handsome walled
kitchen garden, where fruit trees abound—apple and
pear trees laden with fruit, a quarter of an acre of

strawberry beds, and currant and raspberry bushes in plenty.

But time and tide, trains and steamers, wait for no man, or woman either. A few hours later you regretfully bid adieu to the charming little author, and watch her until the bend of the road hides her from your sight. Mr. Hungerford sees you through the first stage of the journey, which is all accomplished satisfactorily, and you reach home to find that whilst you have been luxuriating in fresh sea and country air, London has been wrapped in four days of gloom and darkness.

MATÍLDA BETHAM-EDWARDS.

A WINDING road from the top of the old-fashioned High Street of Hastings leads to High Wickham, where, on an elevation of some hundred feet above the level of the main road on the East Hill stands a cottage, which is the abode of a learned and accomplished author, Miss Betham-Edwards. The quaint little " Villa Julia," as she has named it after a friend, is the first of a terrace of picturesque and irregularly-built houses. A tortuous path winds up the steep ascent, and on reaching the summit, one of the finest views in Southern England is obtained.

The vast panorama embraces sea, woodland, streets, and roads, the umbrageous Old London coach-road, above, the grassy slopes reaching to the West and Castle hills. Far beyond may be seen the crumbling ruins of the Conqueror's stronghold (alas ! this historic spot is now defaced by an odiously vulgar and dis-figuring " lift ! "), and further still, the noble headland of Beachy Head and broad expanse of sea, on which the rays of sunshine glitter brightly. Between the East and West hills, a green environment, lies nestled the town, with its fine old churches of All Saints' and St. Clement's. On a clear day, such as the present,

MATILDA BETHAM-EDWARDS

no view can be more exhilarating, and the ridge on which Miss Betham-Edwards's cottage stands is lifted high above the noise of the road below. Behind stretch the gorse-covered downs leading to Fairlight, from whence may be seen the coast of France, forty miles off, as the crow flies. Close under the author's windows are hawthorn trees made merry by robins all through the winter, and at the back of the house may be heard the cuckoo, the thrush, and the blackbird, as in the heart of the country. Truly, it is a unique spot, inviting to repose and inspiring cheerfulness of mind.

The interior of the Villa Julia is in thorough keeping with the exterior. The little study which commands this glorious view is upstairs. It is a charming room, simplicity itself, yet gives evidence of taste and culture. There is nothing here to offend the eye, and no suggestion of the art-decorator, but it is all just an expression of its occupant's taste and character. "I have a fancy," says Miss Betham-Edwards, "to have different shades of gold-colour running through everything. It is an effective background for the pictures and pottery"; accordingly, the handsome Morocco carpet, bought by herself in the Bazaar at Algiers, is of warm hue. The furniture and wall-paper have the prevailing delicate tints; an arched recess on each side of the fireplace displays lovely specimens of brilliant pottery from Athens and Constantinople, with many shelves below, filled with volumes in various foreign languages. On the mantelshelf stand statuettes of Goethe and Schiller, remembrances of Weimar; the walls are hung with water-colour sketches by Mdme. Bodichen and many French artists. Long low dwarf bookcases fill two sides of the room, the top shelves of which are lavishly adorned with more pottery from Germany, Italy, Spain, and Switzerland, the whole collected by the author on her foreign travels. Her choice little library contains first and foremost the great books of the world, and, besides these, a representative selection of modern literature. "It is in a small compass," she remarks, "but I keep it for myself, eliminating and giving away useless volumes which creep in." On a neatly arranged writing table stand a stationery-case and a French schoolboy's desk, which is rather an ornamental contrivance of *papier-maché.* "I invariably use it," says Miss Edwards, "it is a most convenient thing, and has such a good slope. When one is worn out I buy another. I do not like things about me when I write; I keep a clear table, and MSS. in the next room. I rise early, and work for five hours every morning absolutely undisturbed: my maid does not even bring me a telegram."

From the window just below on the left can be seen the house of one of Miss Betham-Edwards's *confrères,* Mr. Coventry Patmore, the poet. A little further on is the picturesque villa which Dr. Elizabeth Blackwell (the first woman doctor) inhabits. "As remarkable and good a woman as ever lived," she adds. "I do not go much into society, for I find the winter is the best time for writing. I lead a completely retired literary life, but I have a few kindred spirits around me, and I occasionally hold little receptions when we all meet."

In person Miss Betham-Edwards is about the

medium height, middle-aged, and slender in figure. She is fair in complexion; has hazel eyes, and a mass of thick, dark hair, grey over the temples, and worn in a twist at the back, the ends dispersed neatly round a small and compact head. She is wearing black for the present, being in mourning, but is fond of warm, cheerful colours for habitual use. " But, indeed," she says, smiling, " I have not much time to think of dress, and I was greatly amused by the remark of a former old landlady who, anxious that I should look my best at some social gathering, remarked austerely to me, 'Really, Madam, you do not dress according to your talents !' Upon which I replied 'My good woman, if all folks dressed according to their talents, two-thirds, I fear, would go but scantily clothed.' "

Matilda Barbara Betham-Edwards is a country-woman of Crabbe, R. Bloomfield, Constable, Gains-borough, and Arthur Young. She was born at Westerfield, Suffolk, and in the fine old Elizabethan Manor House of Westerfield, Ipswich, her childhood and girlhood were spent. There was literature in her family on the maternal side, three Bethams having honourably distinguished themselves, viz., her grandfather, the Rev. W. Betham, the compiler of the "Genealogical Tables of the Sovereigns of the World"; her uncle, Sir W. Betham, Ulster King of Arms, the learned and ingenious author of "Etruria Celtica," "The Gael and the Cymri," etc.; and lastly, her aunt and godmother, Matilda Betham, the author of " A Biographical Dictionary of Celebrated Women," and other works, and the intimate friend of Charles and Mary Lamb, Southey, and Coleridge.

From the paternal side Miss Betham-Edwards inherited whatever mother-wit and humour she displays; her father, for whose memory she entertains the deepest affection, was like Arthur Young, an agriculturist, and possessed a genuine vein of native humour. Left motherless at a very early age, she may be called self-educated, her teachers being plenty of the best books, and with her first story-book arose the desire and fixed intention to become herself a story-teller.

In these early days among the cowslip meadows and bean fields of Westerfield, books were the young girl's constant companions, although she had the happiness of having brothers and sisters. By the time she was twelve, she had read through Shakespeare, Walter Scott, "Don Quixote," "The Spectator," "The Arabian Nights," Johnson's "Lives of the Poets"; then, *inter alia*, Milton was an early favourite. As she grew up, the young student held aloof from the dances and other amusements of her sisters, writing, whilst yet in her teens, her first published romance, "The White House by the Sea," a little story which has had a long life, for it has lately been re-issued and numerous "picture-board" editions have appeared. Amongst new editions, cheaper and revised, are those of "Disarmed," "The Parting of the Ways," and "Pearls." By request, some penny stories will shortly appear from her pen. "John and I" and "Dr. Jacob" were the result of residences in Germany, the former giving a picture of South German life, and dates from this period, and the latter being founded on fact.

"On arriving at Frankfort," says Miss Betham-

Edwards, "to spend some time in an Anglo-German family, my host (the Dr. Paulus of 'Dr. Jacob'), almost the first thing, asked of me, 'Have you heard the story of Dr. J—— which has just scandalized this town ?' He then narrated in vivid language the strange career which forms the *motif* of the work. That novel too has had a long existence. It was re-issued again lately, the first edition having appeared many years ago. The personages were mostly taken from life, "a fact I may aver now," she says, "most, alas ! having vanished from the earthly stage." On the breaking up of her Suffolk home, the author travelled in France, Spain, and Algeria with the late Madame Bodichen—the philanthropist, and friend of Cobden, George Eliot, Dante Rossetti, Dr. Elizabeth Blackwell, and Herbert Spencer—herself a charming artist, and writer of no mean power, but best known, perhaps, as the co-foundress with Miss Emily Davis of Girton College. "To the husband of this noble woman," she continues, "I acknowledge myself hardly less indebted, for to Dr. Bodichen I owe my keen interest in France and French history, past and present, and I may say, indirectly, my vast circle of French friends and acquaintances, the result of which has been several works on French rural life, and the greatest happiness and interest to myself."

"Kitty," which was first published in 1870 in three volumes, later on, in one volume, and which is, perhaps, the most popular of Miss Betham-Edwards's stories, belongs to this period. In Bishop Thirlwall's "Letters to a Friend " occurs the following from the

late Lord Houghton : "'Kitty' is the best novel I
have ever read."

A compliment the author valued hardly less came
from a very different quarter. Messrs. Moody and
Sankey, the American revivalists, wrote to her, and
asked if she could not write for their organ a story
on the lines of "Kitty," but with a distinctly Evangelical bias. The request was regretfully refused.
Each character in this original and delightful book
is drawn to perfection and sustained to the end, which
comes all too soon. The genuine novel-lover, indeed,
feels somewhat cheated, for did not the author almost
promise in the last page a sequel? A new edition
has just been published.

"Kitty" was followed by the "Sylvestres," which
first ran through *Good Words* as a serial. Socialistic
ideas were not so much in evidence then as now, and
many subscribers to this excellent family journal gave
it up, frightened by views which are at the present
moment common property. No story, nevertheless, has
brought Miss Betham-Edwards more flattering testimony than this; especially grateful letters from
working men pleased a writer whose own views,
political, social, and theological, have ever been with
the party of progress. The books already mentioned
are, without doubt, her most important novels, though
some simple domestic stories, "Bridget" for instance,
"Lisabee's Love Story," "The Wild Flower of Ravens-
wood," "Felicia," and "Brother Gabriel," are generally
liked; whilst in America several later works, "Disarmed," and particularly the two German Idylls,
"Exchange no Robbery" and "Love and Mirage"

(which last novel originally appeared as a serial in *Harper's Weekly Magazine* in America), have found much favour. Of this novel, indeed, Miss Betham-Edwards received a gratifying compliment from Mr. John Morley, who wrote to her, saying: "'Love and Mirage' is very graceful, pretty, interesting, and pathetic. I have read it with real pleasure." It has twice been translated into German. Of later years many editions have been reproduced in one volume form. Another American favourite is the French idyllic story, "Half-Way," now re-issued in one volume.

In 1891 Miss Betham-Edwards received a signal honour at the hands of the French Government, viz., the last dignity of "*Officier de l'Instruction Publique de France.*" She is the only English woman who enjoys this distinction, given as a recognition of her numerous studies of rural France. Her last and most important work in this field is in one volume, "France of To-day," written by request and published simultaneously in London, Leipzig, and New York. In fiction her most recent contributions are "The Romance of a French Parsonage" in two volumes, "Two Aunts and a Nephew" in one volume, and a collection of stories, entitled "A Dream of Millions." Of this the late lamented Amelia B. Edwards wrote to her cousin: "It is worthy of Balzac."

Miss Betham-Edwards has devoted herself entirely to literature, and is an excellent linguist. "I have been again and again entreated," she says, "to take part in philanthropy, public work, to accept a place on the School Board, etc., but have stoutly resisted. A worthy following of literature implies nothing less than

the devotion of a life-time.   Literary laziness and
literary 'Liebig,' *i.e.*, second-hand knowledge or cram-
ming, I have ever held in disesteem. If I want to read
a book I master the language in which it is written.
If I want to understand a subject I do not go to a
review or a cyclopædia for a digest, but to the longest,
completest, most comprehensive work to be had thereon.
In odd moments I have attained sufficient Latin and
Greek to enjoy Tacitus and Plato in the original.
French, German, Spanish, and Italian I consider the
necessary, I should say the obligatory, equipments of
a literary calling.   It seems to me that an ordinarily
long life admits of reading the choicest works of the
chief European literatures in the original, and how
much do they lose in translation !"

An early afternoon tea is served in the snug little
dining-room below, in which stands a magnificent inlaid
Spanish oak chest, occupying nearly the whole side of
the wall. This is a treasure heirloom, and is dated 1626,
the time of Charles I.'s accession to the throne. Two
quaint old prints of Ipswich and Bury St. Edmunds are
also old family relics.   On the table is a German bowl
from Ilmennau—Goethe's favourite resort—filled with
lovely purple and white anemones, which have just
arrived from Cannes, and in other little foreign vases are
early primroses and violets, for Hastings has enjoyed a
long continuance of bright sunshine and mild weather.
Whilst at tea, the conversation turns on music, celebrated people whom your hostess has met, and many
social subjects. Miss Betham-Edwards says, " Music
has ever been one of my recreations, the piano being a
friend, a necessity of existence, but, of course, a busy

author has not much time for pianoforte playing. *Vidi tantum!* I have known and heard the great Liszt. I have also spent a week under the same roof as George Eliot and G. H. Lewes. I have watched the great French artist, Daubigny, paint a flotilla of fishing boats from a window at Hastings. I have heard Gambetta deliver an oration, Victor Hugo read a speech, the grandson of Goethe talk of *den Grossvater* in the great poet's house at Weimar. Browning, too, I used to meet at George Eliot's and Lord Houghton's breakfast parties. Tourgenieff, Herbert Spencer, and how many other distinguished men I have met! It is such recollections as these that brace one up to do, or strive to do, one's best, to contribute one's mite to the golden store-house of our national literature, with no thought of money or fame!"

Miss Betham-Edwards is a first cousin of the late Miss Amelia Blandford Edwards, the distinguished Egyptologist, and author of "Barbara's History," etc. The author of "Kitty" is a Nonconformist, and holds advanced opinions. She is an ardent disciple of Herbert Spencer, a keen antagonist of vivisection, and has written on the subject, the only social topic, indeed, which ever occupies her pen. She divides her time between her cottage residence on the hills above Hastings and her beloved France, where she has as many dear friends as in England. Of her own works, the author's favourite characters are the humorous ones. The Rev. Dr. Bacchus in "Next of Kin," Anne Brindle in "Half-way," Polly Cornford in "Kitty" ("Where on earth," Lord Houghton asked her, "did you get the original of that delightful woman!"), and

I

Fräulein Fink in " Dr. Jacob," a study from life. As
works of imagination, perhaps " Love and Mirage " and
" Forestalled " are, in her estimation, the best. " The
Parting of the Ways," " For One and the World," are
also among a long list of Miss Betham-Edwards's works.
She has written a great many short stories, whilst four
charming volumes of travel must not be omitted ; they
are entitled " The Roof of France," " A Winter with the
Swallows," "Through Spain to the Sahara," and "Holidays in Eastern France." These journeys are all
described with much brightness, reality, and graphic
word-painting, and betoken so thorough a knowledge
of the scenes and people that they form most pleasant
and instructive reading. Many of the works above
mentioned have been translated into French—" Kitty "
has just gone into its second editon in that language—
German, and Norwegian, and all are published in
Tauchnitz.

" I am always glad," remarks the author, "to hear of
cheap editions. I should like to see good books brought
out at a penny. I have had various publishers, and
never quarrelled with any of them. I know Mr. George
Bentley well. He is a man of great literary culture,
and is always kindness itself to me. The late Mr.
Blackett, too, was a great friend." Miss Betham-
Edwards holds such decided and sensible views on one
of the great questions of the day that they shall be
given in her own words. " I consider," she says emphatically, " cremation to be an absolute duty towards
those to come, and support it on hygienic and rational-
istic grounds. Each individual should do his or her
best to promote it."

The conversation of this sympathetic and intellectual woman is so fascinating that you are loath to leave without hearing somewhat of her own principal reading. Expressing the wish to her, she smiles pleasantly, and says : " My favourite English novels are ' Villette ' and 'The Scarlet Letter,' both perfect to my thinking, and consummate as stories and works of art. In German, my favourite novelist is Paul Heyse. George Sand I regard as the greatest novelist of the age. George Eliot's sombre realism repels me, whilst I fully admit her enormous power. 'Don Quixote' in Spanish, with some other favourite works, I read over and over again, Lessing's 'Nathan the Wise,' Schiller's ' Æsthetic Letters,' these, and some of Goethe's smaller works I re-read regularly every year ; they are necessary mental pabulum. Spinoza is also a favourite, second only to Plato. Of contemporary writers, Spencer, Harrison, Morley, and Renan stand first in my opinion ; whilst of the living novelists I can only say that I endeavour to appreciate all. For the stories of the late Mrs. Ewing I entertain the highest admiration ; also I delight in the graceful author of ' The Atelier du Lys.' Tolstoi, Ibsen, Zola, and that school, I find repulsive in the extreme. Imaginative literature should, above all things, delight. With the sadness inherent in life should be mingled a hopeful note, a touch of poetry, a glimpse of the beautiful and of the ideal."

Miss Betham-Edwards has one faithful and cherished companion, who always accompanies her in her walks, and who sits quietly beside her when she writes. This is a white Pomeranian dog, very intelligent and affectionate, who will certainly never be lost while he

wears his present "necklace," bearing the following
inscription :—

> My name is Muff,
> That's short enough ;
> My home's Villa Julia,
> That's slightly peculiar ;
> On the east side you'll find it,
> With Fairlight behind it ;
> My missus is a poet,
> By this you should know it.

Ere the train leaves there is a good hour to spare ; so,
taking leave of the gifted author, you employ the
time in sauntering about the town, and first go to see
the fine church of St. Mary Star-of-the-Sea, founded by
Mr. Coventry Patmore ; also some ancient buildings of
quaint architecture, in which the notorious Titus Oates
is said to have lived. The Albert Memorial is the
most prominent object in the town, occupying a central
position at the junction of six roads, and close by
are the renowned Breach's oyster rooms, where the
temptation to taste the Whitstable bivalve in the fresh
white-tiled shop is not to be resisted ; but whilst there
the great clock on the Memorial warns you to be up
and away.   There is much food for meditation on the
return journey to town ; and on reflecting over all that
Miss Betham-Edwards has learnt and achieved, the
poet's lines involuntarily suggest themselves :

> " And still the wonder grew,
> That one small head should carry all ' she ' knew."

EDNA LYALL

EDNA LYALL.

To the befogged Londoner there is perhaps no greater treat than to escape for forty-eight hours to the seaside even in the depths of winter, and whilst spinning along by the London, Brighton, and South Coast express, there is a pleasurable sense of excitement in the feeling that you are going to breathe the fresh sea air of Eastbourne untainted by smuts and smoke. "The Empress of watering-places," as a well-known journalist has named it, is now seen in its best aspect. It presents quite a different phase in August and September, when the residents, almost to a man, desert the town, having previously with great prudence let their houses at a high figure, and the place is given over to the holiday-makers, nigger minstrels, braying bands, and itinerant beach preachers. Now its genial, pleasant society is in full swing, and merry golf parties are the order of the day. Few places have increased with more rapid growth during the last fifteen or twenty years, or become more popular as a residence than Eastbourne, partly owing to the excellent train service, partly to the well-organised supervision over every detail in the whole town, and again probably more to the bright, healthy atmosphere, which registers three hundred days of sunshine as against sixty-nine in London.

In one of the prettiest roads in this pleasant sea-side town stands—a little way back from the red-and-black tiled pavement—a large brown creeper-covered house with red tiled roof built in the Gothic style of architecture. Though it has only been constructed during late years, the gables and points give it an old-fashioned and picturesque look, but beauty and variety of style are studied at Eastbourne, and each house is apparently designed with a view to artistic effect. College Road is bordered on either side by Sussex elms. The approach is by gates right and left which open into a garden filled with shrubs. On seeking admittance you are taken up to a bright, cheerful room which faces the west, and has all the outward and visible signs of being devoted to literary and artistic pursuits. As the young author, Edna Lyall, rises from the type-writer in the corner opposite the door, with kindly greeting, you are at once struck with her extremely youthful appearance. She is about the medium height, pale in complexion, with dark hair rolled back from a broad forehead which betokens a strongly intellectual and logical cast of mind. She has well-defined, arched eyebrows, and very dark blue eyes, which light up softly as she speaks. Her manner is gentle and sympathetic, and her voice is sweet in tone. She wears a simply-made gown of olive-green material, relieved with embroidery of a lighter colour.

The room seems exactly what one would expect

on only looking at her. It is the room of a student who prefers books to society, and every part of it bears evidence of the simplicity, refinement, and quiet comfort of her tastes. It is square and low, with a broad cottage window, commanding a lovely view over the Downs, which have somewhat of an Alpine look, the high hills in the distance, and the furthermost broad belt of trees in the grounds of Compton Place are tipped with snow, as also are those in the foreground, belonging to some private gardens. The whole scene, now flooded in sunshine, is a constant delight to Edna Lyall, who says that she "rejoices in the knowledge that it can never be built out." Over the window hangs a wrought-iron scroll-work fern basket, which looks like Italian manufacture, but is in reality made by the boys of St. John's, Bethnal Green Industry developed by Miss Bromby. Under this is a broad, low shelf, covered with terra-cotta cloth, which is the repository of many little treasures. The floor is covered with Indian matting, strewn about with a few brightly-coloured Indian and Persian rugs; and in the centre is a comfortable couch with a guitar lying on it. The pretty American walnut-wood writing-table against the wall on the right has a raised desk and little cupboards with glass doors, which reveal many good bits of china. On the further side is a handsome revolving table filled with books, and in the corner stands an old grandfather clock of the seventeenth century. There is a neat arrangement for hiding manuscripts out of sight, a tall piece of furniture with little narrow drawers, also a piano opposite, and a variety of quaintly-shaped chairs; but the feature of the room is a large ornamental book-case on the left, filled with a hundred or so of standard volumes. On the mantelshelf, amongst odds and ends of china, stand some favourite portraits, and the author particularly calls attention to a photograph of her great friend, Mrs. Mary Davies, whom she describes as "a woman of most beautiful character." Another is of Captain Burges, R.N., who was killed at Camperdowne, a third is a platinotype head of George Macdonald, a fourth is of Frederick Denison Maurice, the theologian, the others represent some of her principal heroes, Sir Walter Scott, Algernon Sydney, John Hampden, and Mr. Gladstone. There are many good pictures on the walls, a few pretty landscapes in water-colours, a fine photograph of Sant's "Soul's Awakening," and an Irish trout stream in oils; two are especially attractive, the large and beautifully-executed photograph over the fireplace of Hoffman's "The Child Christ in the Temple," and "The Grotto of Posilipo," the grotto described by Edna Lyall in her novel, "The Knight Errant."

Ada Ellen Bayly (Edna Lyall) was born and educated at Brighton. Her father, Mr. Robert Bayly, barrister-at-law, of the Inner Temple, died when she was eleven, and three years later she lost her mother. Always a thoughtful, studious child, at the age of ten she had already written some short stories, which were read and thought promising by her parents, who, however, wisely made her understand that story-writing must stand second to her own training.

From that time forward she was always preparing for her future profession. After losing both her parents the young girl made her home with a sister, who had married Canon Crowfoot, of Lincoln. It was shortly after leaving school that she wrote her first book, " Won by Waiting," a story of home life in France and England. It is a charming story, simple in sketch and style, with some clever bits of character-painting, in which, as her later books show, she excels.

There is a peculiar interest in her second novel, " Donovan." This work was written at intervals during three years. " When beginning it," says the young author, " I had very little notion of what I had undertaken. Sometimes I wrote easily; sometimes I was at a standstill." But the reason is easily explained. It was about that time that she began to experience a great mental conflict. Profoundly religious by nature, she entered deeply into the theological questions of the day, and though the struggle was deep and painful, she never rested until her mind was satisfied. " No one can regret," says Edna Lyall, " having been forced to face the problems which ' Donovan ' had to face, and I am very thankful to have had that struggle. I wished to draw the picture of a perfectly isolated man and his gradual awakening. He had, of course, to begin by professing himself an atheist and a misanthrope ; but very soon he begins to love a child, then a dog, then a woman. By these means he comes to realize his selfishness, and to detest it; he begins to love humanity, to pity and help his worst enemy, and

finally to 'love the highest' when he sees it. Someone made me laugh the other day by saying that
'it was stated on the best authority that Edna
Lyall had cried most bitterly at the thought of
having written "Donovan" and "We Two," and
would give anything to recall them.' I can only tell
you that all that makes life worth living came to
me through writing those books. So much for
gossip! The struggle is one which we have each
to go through. We must think it all out for our-
selves," she goes on to say softly, whilst a bright,
glad smile illumines her face; for light and peace
have come to her, and she describes herself as having
surmounted the storm, and achieved the haven of
rest and happiness in her belief. "Won by Waiting"
and "Donovan" had, according to the author, "fallen
flat."

In 1884 she introduced "We Two" to the world.
This book, which is a distinct story, is yet in a sense
a continuation of the former, and was the outcome
of all that she had lived through in the preceding
years. It was so well reviewed in all the leading
journals, and became so much talked about, that
people began to ask for "Donovan" so extensively,
that it took a new lease of life, and was soon as
popular as or more so than its sequel. These two
works were brought out by Messrs. Hurst and
Blackett.

In September, 1884, Edna Lyall came to Eastbourne, and established herself with her sister, Mrs.
Jameson, whose husband, the Rev. Hampden Jameson,
is attached to the handsome church, St. Saviour's,

standing close by, and she is herself a member of the congregation. Soon after her arrival a new book was begun ; this is a historical novel, and the author gives an interesting account of the facts which suggested the work. " Shortly after I had finished ' We Two,' " she says, " I happened to visit an uncle and aunt of mine, whose charming old house in Suffolk— Badmondisfield Hall—was connected with some of the happiest days of my very happy childhood. The place had always been an ideal place for dream stories and old-world plays. I knew every nook of the quaint old hall and garden and park, and now the spell laid hold of me again, and the characters of Hugo and Randolph, with whom I had had such delightful imaginary games in old days, started into life once more. One morning, pacing to and fro beside the bowling-green between the house and the moat, the thought flashed into my mind that the time of the Rye House plot would best develop the character of my hero—a naturally yielding and submissive boy, whose will was held in bondage by the stronger will of his elder brother. Little by little the outline of the story shaped itself in my mind. Every history of England to be found in the ancient bookcases was pulled down, old papers relating to the old house and its owners looked through, old pictures studied, and the possibility of Hugo's escapade in the musician's gallery at the end of the dining-hall tested by an inch tape and elaborate calculations."

On leaving Suffolk, Edna Lyall went up to London to study the reign of Charles II. in the reading-room of the British Museum. The story was published in

1885 under the title of "In the Golden Days"—"a title which," she says, "some people fancied I had meant seriously, but which, of course, referred to the first line of the 'Vicar of Bray.'" In this work are undoubtedly some of the finest characters of Edna Lyall's creation. The chapter headed "The Seventh of December" contains a most touching account of the patriot Algernon Sydney's death. Whilst still engaged on this book the author spent many weeks yachting in the Mediterranean, and during one visit to Naples and its neighbourhood used some of the experience she had gained during former visits to Italy to begin and think out the plot of "Knight-Errant." "The motive of that book," she remarks, "is, I think, so distinctly expressed that I need not say much about it. The motto I chose for the title-page shows that in its central idea—reconciliation—it is the completion of 'Donovan' and 'We Two,' though, naturally, as a story of stage life, it is quite unlike them in plot and surroundings. I dislike 'novels with a purpose' as much as any one," she adds, "but at the same time it seems to me that each book must have its particular *motive.*"

"Knight-Errant" is a book of thrilling adventure and absorbing interest ; the account of the attack on the hero, Carlo, in the Grotto of Posilipo, is so powerfully drawn that it keeps the reader in breathless suspense. Norway, too, is one of her favourite haunts, and in the land of the mountain and the fjord she is quite at home. Intensely fond of nature, she has depicted, in her latest three-volume novel (Hurst and Blackett), "A Hardy Norseman," in most realistic language, the exquisite scenery that she witnessed during some of her long, solitary carriole drives. She spent many very happy days with her friends, Presten Kielland (brother of the well-known Norwegian author, Alexander Kielland) and his charming wife and children. " He and his eldest daughter," says the young author, " are excellent English scholars, and I owe to them an introduction to Norwegian life which as a mere tourist I could never have gained."

None who read Edna Lyall's books can fail to be struck by her tender and vivid word-painting of animals (the faithful dog, " Waif," is familiar to all) and of little children, but here she can draw from the life, as there are eight little nephews and nieces downstairs whom she adores, and with whom she is a great favourite.

But the mid-day sun is high in the heavens, and your hostess proposes to take you for a stroll round the grand extension parade below the Wish Tower, and as you walk she beguiles the time with pleasant conversation on personal incidents. Referring to a little sketch published in the form of a shilling book by Messrs. Longmans in 1887, called the " Autobiography of a Slander," " Ah ! " she says, smiling, " that *was* written ' with a purpose,' and was suggested by a very disagreeable incident. On returning from one of our delightful Norwegian tours, I was greeted on every side by a persistent report that had been set afloat to the effect that I was in a lunatic asylum ! We found out at this time that an impostor had been going about announcing that she was ' Edna Lyall,' and that in Ceylon, and during her voyage home, she had deceived many people. The only possible explanation of the lunatic asylum slander seems to be that this woman was in reality mad. But the episode was decidedly unpleasant, and set me thinking on the birth and growth of such monstrously untrue reports. During the autumn of 1886 I wrote the little story, taking different types of gossip for each stage in the Slander's growth and baleful power—the gossip of small dull towns, of country life, of cathedral precincts, of London clubs, and the gossip of members of my own profession in search of ' copy.' "

By this time you have reached a spot called by the inhabitants Mentone. The broad tiled walk is sheltered by the great cliff, behind which is a steep embankment prettily planted with shrubs, and traversed here and there by steep little zigzag paths running upwards to the heights, whilst before you rises the grand outline of Beachy Head. The sky is brilliantly blue as far as eye can reach all around. The sun (which you had not seen in town for six weeks) is shining brightly, casting its radiance on the calm sea, the little wavelets are gently breaking over the pebbles below, and the fresh, pure air is most exhilarating. A few invalids in bath chairs are being drawn slowly along, and all the beauty and fashion of Eastbourne are out enjoying a sun-bath. Amongst the *habitués* you recognize many well-known faces. That tall, graceful, Madonna-like woman, with her fair young daughter, surrounded by a group of friends, is Mrs. Royston-Pigott, widow of the eminent scientist. The handsome soldierly man with the benevolent face is General Buchanan, of cavalry renown, and close to him strolls

his youngest daughter, radiant in the beauty of youth.
Edna Lyall observes that Mr. Balfour is occasionally
to be seen on the links enjoying a game of golf.
Everyone seems revelling in the warmth of this
January sunshine, but time presses, and you may
not linger. If aught could compensate for turning
away from such a scene, it is the charm of your
hostess's conversation, as she walks with you and
speaks of her favourite poets—Tennyson, Mrs. Browning, and Whittier, whilst she declares her favourite
characters in prose fiction are " Jeanie Deans " and
Thackeray's " Esmond." Asking her which are her
special pets in her own books, she says, laughing, " As
Anthony Trollope said when asked a similar question,
' I like them all,' but perhaps Carlo the best, so far.
You asked me just now, when we were interrupted,
how my books succeeded. ' Won by Waiting ' had a
very small sale. It was favourably reviewed in several
papers, and cut into mincemeat by a very clever
weekly journal, so wittily, that even a youthful author
could only laugh! Then it ' joined the majority.'
' Donovan,' in spite of many excellent reviews, shared
the same fate ; only 320 copies sold, then he, too, sank
into oblivion temporarily. It was a hard time, and I
could not resist weaving some of my memories of
those literary struggles into my latest story—a little
sketch called ' Derrick Vaughan, Novelist,' published
first in *Murray's Magazine*, later, in one volume form,
by Methuen. Since May, 1889, I have been unable to
write at all, owing to my long attack of rheumatism
and fever, but now that I am growing strong, I hope
to set to work again " ; and as you bid adieu to this

gifted and interesting woman, you heartily re-echo the wish.

Sic transit gloria mundi. A couple of hours later the train has borne you swiftly from the glorious sunlight and sea into the persistent gloom and obscurity of London. The speed slackens, you glide into the station, your brief holiday is at an end.

ROSA NOUCHETTE CAREY

ROSA NOUCHETTE CAREY.

ALTHOUGH a sad change has come over the ancient and historic village of Putney, and it has lost much of its quaint and picturesque environment since the destruction of the toll-house and the dear old bridge of 1729, with its score of narrow openings—at once the delight of artists and the curse of bargees—there is still a bit left which has escaped the hands of the Philistines. Unique and fair is the view from the magnificent, though aggressively modern, granite structure which now spans the river; and how many memories of the past are aroused! The grey old church of St. Mary's, Putney, and the massive tower of All Saints, Fulham, flank either end. This latter edifice, originally built as a chapel of ease to Wimbledon, is of great antiquity, and has been twice rebuilt, once in the reign of Henry VII. and again in 1836, when the grand old tower, which gives such a prominent feature to the landscape, was restored. On one side is the fine terrace of lofty houses known as The Cedars, with their wide breezy gardens overlooking the river, so short a time since the scene of many pleasant garden parties, when a well-known and popular author occupied one of these houses. Now, alas! they are all empty and deserted; cranes

K

and stones and heaps of rubbish have transformed their
time-honoured lawns into desolation. No scheme of
utilization seems to suggest itself, and meanwhile the
noble site is unused, and these handsome tenements
are rapidly solving the question, and, abandoned to all
the ravages of time, are dropping into obtrusive decay.
On the other side of the bridge there is a glimpse of
the shady grounds of Fulham Palace, the leafy foliage
of the Bishop's Moat and Avenue, and a view of a
lovely line of trees on the shore skirting the grounds of
old Ranelagh—now given up to the building fiend—
and Hurlingham, while the broad silvery river itself,
and its slow-moving barges and boats with brown and
red sails, give life and colouring to the scene. At
night, when the lights only of unlovely Hammersmith
are gleaming across the water, the effect is decidedly
picturesque.

In a second the mind involuntarily travels back a
few centuries, and pictures to itself the appearance
of this same spot when the army under Cromwell
made it their head quarters, while the King was a
prisoner in Hampton Court ; when forts were standing
on each side, and a bridge of boats was constructed
across the river, by order of the Earl of Essex, during
the Civil War, on the retreat of the Royalists after the
battle of Brentford. But the imaginary panorama
fades, and your thoughts return to the present age as
you drive a few hundred yards further on, and reach
the top of a long terrace of small but artistically built
red-brick Elizabethan houses, where in one which is
semi-detached, the well-known writer, Miss Rosa
Nouchette Carey, has made her home with her eldest

widowed sister and her family. The author meets you at the threshold of her study at the top of the staircase, and takes you into what she calls her "snuggery," a simple, but tastefully furnished room, looking out into a large garden, where birds of all sorts are encouraged to come; a thrush sings melodiously, and is among many singing birds a daily visitor. An oak knee-hole writing-table, with raised blotting-pad, stands in the corner by the window, and on it is a vase full of bright scarlet geraniums and ferns. Everything is arranged with great neatness, and each spot seems to have its use. Little and big lounging chairs, a low spring couch, one or two small tables, a bookcase filled with well-bound books, and a cabinet covered with photographs and pretty little odds and ends of china, all combine to make a cheerful, comfortable, and attractive whole. A cage is on the floor, and perched on the top is a beautiful cockateel, or Australian Joey bird, of the parrot type, with grey top-knot, yellow tuft and pink feathers on the sides of the head, which give it the odd appearance of a fine healthy colour on the cheeks. This intelligent bird is a great pet of your hostess, and walks up and downstairs in answer to her call.

Miss Rosa Nouchette Carey is tall, slender, and erect in carriage. She has large blue-grey eyes with long lashes, and her soft dark hair, in which a silver thread may be seen here and there, is parted smoothly over her brow, and plaited neatly round her head. She wears a black dress with brocaded velvet sleeves, and is cordial and peculiarly gentle in manner.

" We have lived here six years," she says, in a low,

tuneful voice; "but Putney is getting quite spoilt. They have pulled down and built over the grand old Jacobin House, which stood close by in the Richmond Road, with its seven drawing-rooms, subterranean passages, and lovely gardens which were a joy to us, also Fairfax House, with its pleasant garden and its fine old trees."

There are other, not a few, historical recollections of Putney. Queen Elizabeth used often to stay at the house of Mr. Lacy, the clothier, who also entertained Charles I. It was the birthplace of Edward Gibbon, author of "The Decline and Fall of the Roman Empire"; of Thomas Cromwell, who was made Earl of Essex by Henry VIII.; and of Nicholas West, Bishop of Ely, who originally erected the small chantry chapel in the old church near the bridge ; but though this has been removed from the east end of the south aisle to the east end of the north side, the old style has been carefully preserved. Many eminent people have lived here. Mary Wollstonecraft Godwin, widow of Shelley, had her residence at the White House by the river; Leigh Hunt lived and died in the High Street. Among others, Theodore Hook, Douglas Jerrold, Henry Fuseli, the painter; Toland, the friend of Leibnitz; James Macpherson; and last, but not least, Mrs. Siddons. Putney also witnessed the death of William Pitt, Earl of Chatham.

Rosa Nouchette Carey was born in London, near Old Bow Church, but she has only vague memories of the house and place. She was the youngest but one of a large family of five sisters and two brothers. Her father was a ship-broker, and afterwards had vessels of his own. He was a man of singularly amiable character, and his integrity and many virtues made him universally beloved and respected. Her childhood was passed at Hackney in the old house at Tryons Place, where many happy days were spent in the room called the green-room, overlooking a large old-fashioned garden well filled with shady trees. " It was a simple, happy, uneventful life," says Miss Carey. " Being a delicate child, my education was somewhat desultory. My youngest sister and I were left a good deal alone, and I remember that my chief amusement, besides our regular childish romps, was to select favourite characters from history or fiction, and to try and personify them. I was always the originator of our games, but my sister invariably followed my lead. I used to write little plays which we acted. I began a magazine, and wrote several pieces of poetry, of the most foolish description probably," she adds, smiling, " for I am sure I could not write a line now to save my life ! My greatest pleasure was to relate stories to this same sister over our needlework or under the shade of the old trees."

In this way the whole of " Nellie's Memories " was told verbally, when still in her teens, and was only written down seven years afterwards. " My mother was a strict disciplinarian and was very clever and practical," she continues. " As a girl I was singularly dreamy, and spent all my leisure time in reading and writing poetry ; feeling the impossibility of combining my favourite pursuits with a useful, domestic life, and discouraged by my failures in this respect, I made a deliberate and, as it afterwards proved, a fruitless attempt to quench the longing to write, while at the same time I endeavoured to be more like other girls, but this unnatural repression of a strong instinct could not last, and after some years I gave it up. I am not aware that my mother knew of this strange conflict, but she was the first to rejoice at my literary success. My literary taste is not inherited, except in one solitary case, my father's cousin, Christopher Riethmüller, author of "Teuton," "Legends of the Early Church," "The Adventures of Neville Brooke," and "Aldersleigh."

Later on the family moved to South Hampstead, where Rosa Carey's schooldays began, and it was whilst at school that she formed an enthusiastic friendship with Mathilde Blind, afterwards the clever translator of Marie Bashkirtseff's Journal, and author of "The Descent of Man," and other works. This friendship, which was a source of great interest to both girls, was only interrupted by a divergence of their religious opinions. Mathilde Blind was brought up in the most advanced school of modern freethought, but Rosa Carey, adhering to the simple faith of her childhood, could not follow her there, and the friends drifted apart, sorrowfully, but with warm affection on each side.

The next change in her life was the death of her father, after which terrible bereavement the widowed mother and three daughters lived together, but the gradual breaking-up of the once large family had set in. After their mother's death, the youngest daughter's convictions led her to embrace a conventual life, and she entered the Anglican Sisterhood of St. Thomas of Canterbury. The death of their mother occurred on the same day which three years before had witnessed

their father's end. After this sad event Miss Rosa
Carey says her real vocation in life seemed to spring
up, and she and her remaining home sister went to
Croydon to superintend their widowed brother's
household. Three years later the circle was again
narrowed. Her sister married the Rev. Canon
Simpson, vicar of Kirkby Stephen, Westmoreland, on
the Valley of the Eden, a most lovely spot, where the
author for eleven years regularly paid an annual visit,
and where she laid the scenes depicted in vivid and
eloquent words in her novel "Heriot's Choice." Rising, she points out four pictures, reminiscences of
Westmoreland, which hang over her writing-table.
One is a view of great beauty, a second the exterior
of the church, a third is the handsome interior, which
looks more like a cathedral with its massive pillars
and groined roof, and the fourth represents the
vicarage. Her brother's death soon left the orphan
nieces and nephew to her sole care. "The charge
somewhat tied my hands," said Miss Carey, "and prevented the pursuing of my literary labours as fully as
I could have otherwise done. Interrupted by cares of
house and family, the writing was but fitfully carried
on. Six years after, however, circumstances tended to
break up that home. Three of my charges are married, and one of my nephews is a master at Uppingham.
These six years have been my first leisure for real
work."

The launching of "Nellie's Memories" threatened at
first to cause the young writer some disappointment.
Quite unacquainted with any publishers, and without
any previous introductions, she took the MSS. to Mr.

Tinsley, who at first declined to read it. Some months later she consulted Mrs. Westerton, of Westerton's Library, who good-naturedly undertook to induce him to do so. " I am glad to name her," says Miss Carey. " I shall always remember her with gratitude, for, on hearing that the reader's opinion was highly favourable, she hurriedly drove from some wedding festivity to bring me the good news. I can even recall to mind the dress that she wore on the occasion."

Not to many girl-authors is it given that her first novel shall bring her name and fame, but this simple, domestic story of English home-life speedily became a great favourite. Though free from any mystery or dramatic incidents, the individuality of the characters, the pure wholesome tone, and the interest which is kept up to the end, caused this charming story to be widely known and to be re-issued in many editions up to the present date. The next venture was " Wee Wifie," which Miss Carey pronounces to have been a failure; but as that work has been quite lately demanded by the public, it is possible that she may have taken too modest a view of its merits. On being applied to for permission to bring it out again, she at first refused, thinking that it would not add to her literary reputation; but subsequently, however, she rewrote and lengthened it, though without altering the plot, and it has passed into a new edition.

Her next five novels—entitled respectively "Barbara Heathcote's Trial," "Robert Ord's Atonement," "Wooed and Married," "Heriot's Choice," and "Queenie's Whim" —came out at intervals of two years between each other, and were followed by " Mary St. John." Then

came a delightful book called " Not Like Other Girls,"
which was a great success. This is a spirited and
amusing story of a widowed mother and her three
plucky girls, who, in the days of their prosperity, were
sensibly brought up to make their own frocks, and
who, when plunged into poverty, turned this excellent
talent to such good account that they set up in business
as dressmakers, being employed alike by the squiress
at the Hall and by the village butcher's wife, and there
is as much of quiet humour described in their inter-
view with this worthy dame, and their attempts to
tone down her somewhat florid taste, as there is in
the discussions and opinions of the neighbours and
friends of the family about the venture of these wise
and practical girls. Since Miss Carey came to Putney
she has brought out " Lover or Friend," " Only the
Governess," " The Search for Basil Lyndhurst," and
" Sir Godfrey's Grand-daughters." She is also on
the staff of the *Girl's Own Paper*, and, whenever
she has time, sends short stories, which run as serials
for six months in that journal before being issued
in single volume form. Four of these tales have
already appeared.

It is quite obvious to the readers of Miss Carey's
works that she is fond of young people—she has,
indeed, at the present time a regularly established
class for young girls and servants over fifteen years of
age, which had already been formed in connection with
the Fulham Sunday School, in which she takes a
great interest—and that the distinctive characteristic
throughout all her books is a tendency to elevate to
lofty aspirations, to noble ideas, and to purity of

thought. With great descriptive power, considerable and often quiet fun, there is a delicacy and tenderness, a knowledge and strength of purpose, combined with so much fertility of resource and originality that the interest never flags, and the sensation, on putting down any of her works, is that of having dwelt in a thoroughly healthy atmosphere. "Heriot's Choice" was originally written for Miss Charlotte Yonge, and was brought out as a serial in the *Monthly Packet* before being issued in three-volume form, but all Rosa Nouchette Carey's books are published by Messrs. Bentley.

"My ambition has ever been," says the gentle author, "to try to do good and not harm by my works, and to write books which any mother can give a girl to read. I do not exactly form plots, I think of one character and circle round that. Of course, I like to meditate well on my characters before beginning to write, and I live so entirely in and with them when writing that I feel restless, and experience a sense of loss and blank when a book is finished, and I have to wait until another grows in my mind. I have sometimes rather regretted a tone of sadness running through some of my earlier stories, but they were tinged with many years of sorrow. Now I can write more cheerfully. Like many authors, I only work from breakfast to luncheon, sometimes at the table, more often with my blotting-pad on my knee before the fire, and I cannot do without plenty of air and exercise, and often walk round Putney Heath. More than twenty years ago I was introduced to Mrs. Henry Wood, who used often to come down to the old Jacobin House, of which I spoke just now. Our acquaintance ripened into an intimacy which only ended with her life. She was very quiet, interesting, and unlike anyone else, but no one ever filled the niche left by her death. Some of my favourite books are 'Amiel's Journal,' Currer Bell's works, George Eliot's, and biographies; also psychological works, the study of mind and character, whilst in poetry I prefer Jean Ingelow and Mrs. Browning."

The long-standing friendship with Helen Marion Burnside—the well-known writer of many clever tales for children, booklets, verses, and songs—began when they were in their early womanhood. Eighteen years ago Miss Burnside became an inmate of Miss Carey's house, and ever since they have shared the same home, living in pleasant harmony and affection.

Presently comes an invitation to join the family five o'clock tea-table. Glass doors in the drawing-room lead into the conservatory, whence issues the soft cooing of ring-doves. The pretty marqueterie cabinets disclose a set of Indian carved ivory chessmen and many quaint bits of china, whilst on a sofa, in solitary state, sits a knowing-looking little tame squirrel with a blue ribbon round its neck. After tea, on the arrival of some visitors, you are so lucky as to get a few minutes' private conversation with Miss Burnside, and you learn a few facts concerning your hostess that could never have been gleaned from one of such reticence and modesty as she. "I do not think," says Helen Marion Burnside, "that I have known any author who has to make her writing—the real work of her life—so secondary a matter as has Rosa Carey.

She has so consistently *lived* her religion, so to speak, that family duty and devotion to its many members have always come first. She never hesitates for a moment to give up the most important professional work if she can do anything in the way of nursing or comforting any of them, and she is *the* one to whom each of the family turns in any crisis of life. Having had so much of this, and rather weak health to struggle against, it is the greatest wonder to me that she has been able to write as many books as she has done, and in so bright a spirit as many are written. Of course, real womanly woman's work *is* the highest work, but I think few writers put it so entirely above the professional work as she does. I have often been surprised at her surprise when some little incident has brought her public value home to her. Even now she does not in the least realize that she has her place in the literary world as other contemporary authors have. It is really quite singular and amusing to come across such a simple-minded ' celebrity.' I wonder if you found it out for yourself," she adds quaintly.

Certainly no better words could be found to describe the sympathetic, gifted, and lofty-souled Rosa Nouchette Carey.

ADELINE SERGEANT

ADELINE SERGEANT.

DESPITE the proverb that "comparisons are odious," there is a great fascination to those who love to explore the old quarters of London, and to hunt up the records of people who have lived and died there, leaving their mark whether for good or evil, and then to note the difference that a hundred or so of years have made in its buildings and inhabitants. Take old Bloomsbury for instance—by no means an uninteresting stroll—described by Evelyn in 1665 as "a little towne with good aire." Pope alludes to this once fashionable locality thus:—

> "In Palace Yard at nine, you'll find me there,
> At ten for certain, sir, in Bloomsbury Square."

According to Timbs, in his interesting work on London, this "little towne" was the site of the grand old Domesbury Manor, where the kings of England in ancient days had their stables. Yonder great corner house was built by Isaac Ware, editor of *Palladio*, originally a chimney-sweep, of whom it was said, that "his skin was so ingrained with soot, that to his dying day he bore the marks of his early calling." By the way, that particular trade would appear to have been

extremely lucrative in those days, as it is well known
and authenticated that two great squares—not a hundred miles away—were entirely built by one David
Porter, " who held the appointment of chimney-sweep
to the village of Marylebone."

A few hundred yards further on to the north-west,
and you reach the quiet thoroughfare of Chenies Street,
which connects Gower Street and Tottenham Court
Road, and here, indeed, a transformation has taken
place.   Where are the solid, but dull, old, grey houses
which erstwhile stood on this spot ?   Within the last
few years they have all been swept away, and the
street is vastly improved by the imposing block of red-
brick mansions which has been erected, and which
bears outside a brass plate, inscribed "Ladies' Residential
Chambers."   A long-felt want is here supplied.   In an
age when hundreds of women of culture and of position
are earning their living, and whose respective occupations require that they should dwell in the metropolis,
a necessity has arisen for independent quarters, such
as never can be procured in the ordinary lodgings or
boarding-house, where, without being burdened with
the cares of house-keeping, the maximum of comfort
and privacy with the minimum of domestic worry can
be obtained.   All this is amply provided for within
these walls.   Touching an electric button without, the
door is opened by the porter—the only man in the
house—who wears on his breast the Alma, Balaklava,
Inkerman, and Sebastopol medals, you enter a spacious
hall, which opens on all sides into a number of self-
contained flats.   In the centre is a vast well staircase
running up to the top of the building.

On the present occasion business takes you only to the first floor, where, rounding the great corridor, are separate little vestibules, each containing a complete suite of rooms, and Miss Adeline Sergeant's chambers are reached. They are so exquisitely arranged, and display so much artistic taste and refinement, that a few words must be said in description of them. The outer door is covered inside with a. striped Moorish *portière*, and leads into a little hall faced by the study, and opening into the drawing-room on the right. The blue and white walls, on which hang half-a-dozen pictures, are of conventional floral design, relieved by cream-coloured mouldings, which throw up the rich Oriental draperies of the couch and Japanese screen near the door. The floor is laid down with peacock-blue felt and a few Persian rugs of subdued tints, whilst a white Siberian wolf, mounted on a fine black bearskin forms the rug. The broad bay windows are hung with soft cream-coloured muslin and guipure curtains, peeping out from the folds of oatmeal cloth hangings of the same shade of blue. Three dwarf bookcases are fitted into recesses, and are well filled with all the books necessary to a woman of letters. A clear fire blazes and sparkles in the tiled hearth, and throws out a ruddy glow over the bright brasses. The fireplace is draped with wine-coloured brocaded velvet curtains ; the mantelshelf is high, and the long oblong mirror, in plain black narrow frame, is raised just sufficiently to show off the beautiful Oriental china, Benares brass vases, and Indian jars standing thereon. Over it hangs a single plaque, framed in dark oak, copied by Miss F. Robertson, in *violet de fer* on china,

from the original engraving of "Enid, a Saxon Maiden."
There are flowers everywhere—pots of lilies of the
valley, ferns and palms, alike on the little hexagonal
ebonised table in the windows and the small cabinet,
whilst cut daffodils and anemones are grouped in vases
in other parts of the room. The great Arabian brass
salver, with its mystic scrolls and ebonised stand,
forms a suitable tea-table alongside the comfortable
American rocking-chair. The copper-coloured brocaded
silk gown, with a tinge of red, which Adeline Sergeant
wears, with leaves of darker and flowers of lighter
pattern woven in, is in unison with the prevailing tints
by which she is surrounded. A black fur boa is care-
lessly thrown round her shoulders, she is rather below
the middle height, dark grey eyes, with a mischievous
twinkle in them, can be discerned behind the *pince-nez*
which she habitually wears, her good colouring betokens a healthy constitution her extremely thick
hair, lightly touched with grey, is loosely rolled back
from her forehead, she has a merry, bright smile, and
laughs with silvery sweetness on being told you had
nervously expected, from her pictures, to see a strong-
minded, austere-looking woman; but until a sun-portrait
can produce rich colouring, earnestness of purpose,
combined with an ever-changing, laughing expression,
she will appear to those who have only seen her
photograph as being somewhat severe and stern.

Adeline Sergeant was born at Ashbourne, in Derby-
shire. Her father belonged to an old Lincolnshire
family who had lived since the sixteenth century, at
least, on the same ground, and had inhabited for
many years a long, low, rambling house, of which he

used to delight to tell her stories. When yet but a child she went with her parents to Selby, Easingwold, Weston-super-Mare, Worcester, and Rochester, where, when she was nineteen years of age, her father died, and their wanderings practically ended.

" My mother was a quiet, delicate, refined, sensitive woman," says Miss Sergeant, while a look of sadness comes over her face. "She spent most of her spare time in writing, and from her, I suppose, I inherit some of my taste for writing, though it comes from my father's side too, for a cousin of mine is a literary man, and several of my relations dabbled a little in literature. My mother wrote verses and religious stories chiefly; she had a very high ideal of style, and one of my earliest and latest recollections of her is seeing her covering scraps of paper with her peculiarly beautiful handwriting in pencil, and afterwards copying them most carefully in ink at her desk. She had a long illness; she died of consumption, after eight years of confirmed invalidism and gradually wasting away. I remember it now as a remarkable fact that I never knew her to complain or to have anything but the sweetest, brightest smile. Her sense of the ridiculous was acute to the very last, and she was always ready to enjoy a good story. Her appreciation of literature was very great, and it was from her that I learned to enjoy Browning as well as the older masters of verse. After my father's death we removed to the suburbs of London, and my mother died fifteen months later. We were united heart and soul, and her death was the greatest sorrow of my life, especially as I had been much separated from her by school and college life,

and had been promised that I should live at home and
care for her when my elder sister married, but my
mother died four months before the wedding, and that
dream—hers as well as mine, I think—was never
realized."

Adeline Sergeant began to write at the very youthful
age of eight. Her first published verses appeared when
she was but thirteen, and a volume of verse when she
was sixteen years of age. "It always seems to me,"
she continues, "that I owe a great deal to the influ-
ences of the free country life of my early childhood
when we lived at Eastington, near Stonehouse, for two
years. I believe that modern teachers would say that
I wasted my time, for I went to no school then, but
'did lessons' with my mother in a desultory fashion."
Rambling for hours in the fields and lanes by herself,
sometimes with a book and sometimes without, the
young author used conscientiously to set herself her
own tasks; she wrote innumerable stories, had no
playfellows, and no children's books, but she had the
run of her father's library. Here she read Shakespeare
until she knew him by heart; next to Shakespeare
her favourite book was Addison's "Spectator"; after
these came Byron, Mrs. Hemans, and many earlier
poets, Prior, Gay, Dryden, etc. Here, from the age of
eleven to fifteen, she also studied theological writers
like Chalmers, Butler, and Jeremy Taylor; whilst a set
of Encyclopædias, in twenty-two volumes, gave her
many happy hours. It is no wonder that Adeline
Sergeant declares this to have been one of the most
fructifying periods of her life, and that her impressions
of landscape, cloud scenery, effects of light, shade,

sound, etc., are still coloured by her remembrances of that time.

" I think," she observes, smiling, "that this was better bracing for the mind than the indiscriminate devouring of story-books, which is characteristic of young folks nowadays. But I must also add that at Weston, our next place of residence, I simply gorged myself on novels of all sorts, as I had the command of every circulating library in the place, and no control was ever exercised over my reading."

At sixteen Miss Sergeant went to Laleham, Miss Pipe's well-known school at Clapham ; and at eighteen to Queen's College, Harley Street, where she held a scholarship for some time. The death of her sister two years after her marriage left the young girl very much alone in the world. For some years she lived with very dear and kind friends, whose two daughters she had some share in teaching. Having much time free, she went on with her literary work, which had been suspended for a long while after her bereavements, when she had no heart to write anything. After leaving college, Adeline Sergeant devoted herself entirely to study for the Cambridge and other examinations. After taking her First Class Honours Certificate in the women's examination, she gave up her time to teaching, writing, and parochial work of all sorts; she played the organ in church, held Sunday and week-day classes for village children, trained the choir, and so on. A temporary failure in health made a winter in Egypt a real boon to her about that time, and it was on her return that she gave herself up more to literary work.

"I was not at all successful at first," says Miss
Sergeant in a cheerful tone of voice. "My first novel
has never seen the light to this day. My second was
also refused, but has since been re-written and re-issued,
under the name of 'Seventy Times Seven.' I wrote
little stories for little magazines, and a child's book or
two. But I had no success for many years. In 1880
I competed for a prize of £100 offered by the Dundee
People's Friend for a story, and gained it, to my great
delight. I have kept up my connection with this
paper ever since, and am always grateful to the editor
for the help he gave me at a critical time. This story
was 'Jacobi's Wife.' When I heard the good news I
was in Egypt, where I was spending a winter at the
invitation of my friends, Professor and Mrs. Sheldon
Amos. On my return I wrote 'Beyond Recall,' which
embodies my impressions of Egyptian life. I went on
writing for the next two years, and doing other work
as well, but in 1883 I made up my mind to throw
myself entirely into literature."

Miss Sergeant's next step was to write and consult
the kindly Dundee editor on this subject, and in return
she received a proposition from the proprietors that she
should go to live in Dundee and do certain specified
literary work for them. She did so, and counts it as
one of the most fortunate occurrences of her life, as she
made many friends and led a pleasant and healthful
life, first at Newport, in Fife, and then in Dundee.
Two years later, however, it seemed better to her to
return to London, though without severing her connection with Dundee. Since 1887 Adeline Sergeant
has lived more or less in London, although she spends

a good deal of time at the seaside, in the country, and in Scotland, or in visiting at friends' country houses in different parts of England.

Besides the works already named, Adeline Sergeant has produced several highly interesting novels, notably, "An Open Foe," "No Saint," "Esther Denison," and "Name and Fame"—this last was written in collaboration with A. S. Ewing Lester—"Little Miss Colwyn," "A Life Sentence," "Roy's Repentance," "Under False Pretences." Her later works are "Caspar Brooke's Daughter," "An East London Mystery," and "Sir Anthony." "Esther Denison" and "No Saint" are, perhaps, the author's own favourites, although she frankly says that she thinks that they have not found as much favour with the public as some of her more "sensational" stories, though the critics generally liked them better, and, indeed, compared them with George Eliot and some of Mrs. Oliphant's works. Both these books contain many transcripts from her own personal experiences. "Esther Denison" is, indeed, largely autobiographical. It is evident that Miss Sergeant has put her whole heart in this story. A somewhat caustic wit is pleasantly relieved by the earnest tone which runs through it. Without being a theological novel, the description of the struggles of the high-souled but sympathetic heroine is powerfully and faithfully drawn. Many of these books contain strong dramatic incidents ; they are all full of interest, and are characterized by the exceeding good taste and the excellent English in which they are written. They are all popular in America, where they are published by Messrs. Lowell & Son.

"I have sometimes been misunderstood by critics," Miss Sergeant observes, "on account of the absence of any *data* to my books. Having disposed some years ago of many of the copyrights, I see them issued as if they were freshly written, which is not always the case. A weekly reviewer expressed great surprise at the publication of 'Jacobi's Wife' *after* 'No Saint.' As a matter of fact it had been written and sold some years earlier. My own works seem to me to fall into two classes : the one, of incident, when I simply try to tell an interesting story—a perfectly legitimate aim in art, I believe—and the other, of character, with the minimum of story. I like to analyze a character 'to death,' so to speak, and I look on my stories of this sort as the best I have written."

Of one of Adeline Sergeant's late novels, "An East London Mystery," no single word of the plot shall be hinted at, nor shall the intending reader's interest be discounted beforehand. Suffice it to say that from the first page to the last it is full of deeply-absorbing matter. Each character is drawn with a masterly touch, and is admirably sustained throughout; it may be safely predicted that when taken up it will scarcely be laid down until the last leaf be turned.

A peculiar interest is attached to a book which has lately come prominently before the public, and which has created much sensation, called "The Story of a Penitent Soul" (Bentley & Son), to which Adeline Sergeant's name was not affixed, but of which she now acknowledges herself to be the author. It deals with a sad subject handled in a powerful but most delicate manner, and is quite a new departure from her former works. For some time the critics, whilst mostly praising it warmly and at once recognizing that it was written by no ''prentice hand,' were somewhat puzzled as to the authorship. Gradually the secret leaked out, and Miss Sergeant relates in a few eloquent words her reasons for the concealment of her identity with the story. "Every now and then," she says, "I feel the necessity of escaping from the trammels imposed by publishers, editors, and the supposed taste of the public. I want to say my own say, to express what I really mean and feel, to deliver my soul. Then I like to go away ' into the wilderness ' and write for myself, not for the public, without caring whether anybody reads and understands what I write, or whether it is published or not. That is how and why I wrote ' The Story of a Penitent Soul.' It was written because it *had* to be written ; it wrote itself, so to speak. Work done in this way is the only work that seems worth doing and is in itself a joy, but it cannot be done at will, or every day."

Novel-making, however, does not absorb all this industrious author's time. She is an ardent novel reader in three languages. Her favourite writers in English are Thackeray, George Eliot, and Meredith. As she reads French authors more for style than for subject she is not afraid to avow that she greatly admires Daudet, Pierre Loti, Flaubert, and Georges Sand ; the Russian novelists Tolstoi, Dostorievski, and Tour-guénieff are also much to her liking, and she reads American modern writers such as Howell, Henry James, and Egbert Craddock, with pleasure. "But I read other things besides novels," she says. "Even as a child

I was always of a metaphysical turn, and my delight
in books of that sort is so great that I hardly dare
touch them when I am trying to write fiction. They
fascinate and paralyse me. Economics and some
kinds of theological speculation are also a favourite
study."

Her love for economics and the discussion of social
problems has led Adeline Sergeant to join the Fabian
Society, in which she takes great interest. Her
religious tendencies are all in the direction of what is
called "Broad Church," and she is an ardent believer in
Women's Suffrage. She is a member of the committee
of the Somerville Club for women, and is on two
sub-committees. She is the co-secretary for the
Recreative Evening Schools Association in St. Pancras
District, and an Evening School Manager for north and
south St. Pancras. "I must say that I have a great
deal too much to do," she adds, "and I cannot get
through half as much business as I ought. I have a
rather large circle of friends, and I find it difficult to
keep up with my social duties. I generally write all
the morning, but I like to write and can write all day.
At St. Andrews, for instance, where I have just spent
two months, I wrote and read for quite nine or ten
hours every day. One cannot do that in London." As
a recreation Miss Sergeant prefers music to any other,
and, indeed, used to play a good deal once, but has now
no time to keep up any pretence at *technique*. The
same reason has caused her to discard her old pastime
of pen-and-ink drawing, of which she is passionately
fond, but which she found to be rather too trying to
the eyes to be pursued with advantage. " I have done

some elaborate embroidery in my time," she says, "but now I never use my needle for amusement; only for necessity. Any sort of philanthropic work that I undertake is purely secular. I love foreign travel, though I have not gone abroad very lately. I have been in Holland, Belgium, Germany, Italy, and France, besides in Egypt. Switzerland I reserve for a future occasion. It may interest you to hear my unknown American readers every now and then send me kind letters, with requests for autographs or photographs, and that this last likeness, which misled you to think me 'severe and stern,' was taken chiefly in order to be reproduced for the benefit of American as well as English readers. I wonder if it will have the same effect on them," she adds, laughing.

The little study beyond must be visited, and here are Miss Adeline Sergeant's *secretaire* and library. It contains a fairly good collection of English authors, and much French literature; but she has moved about so constantly from place to place, that she has been unable to collect as many books as she would have liked. The great broad couch by the window is a comfortable lounge for a weary writer, and the rest of the furniture is all snug and suitable. Miss Sergeant imparts some interesting information about this unique establishment, which was founded for gentlewomen only, of different occupations. The number of rooms in each flat varies from two to four or five, according to requirements. The whole concern is conducted entirely upon the principles of a gentleman's club, with the great advantage that the tenants can be as much at home and enjoy as absolute a privacy as they desire.

The *cuisine* and all domestic details are under the management of an experienced housekeeper. Breakfasts, luncheons, and dinners are served in the great club-room below during stated hours, each allowing a good margin for the convenience of the members, whilst an adjoining room is reserved for their private parties. This is a gala day at the "Ladies' Residential Chambers." There is a large afternoon " At Home," which is an annual entertainment. Each lady has sent cards to her friends and the guests are beginning to flock in. The coloured-tiled corridors and window-ledges are gaily decorated with palms, ferns, and flowers. A hospitable custom prevails. Wherever a hall-door is found open it is a signal that visitors to the other residents are permitted to enter and look round the rooms. Should any lady be unable to receive she "sports her oak." Ample refreshments are provided in the club-room, and as many doors are invitingly thrown open, you take advantage of the implied permission, and are kindly received by each hostess. There are members of many professions within these walls. Two sets of chambers are occupied by practising medical women, a third by a busy journalist, a fourth by an artist, a fifth by a young musician, a sixth by a fair and gentle girl, who modestly tells you that she is a high-school mistress, and, with kindling eyes, adds, "there is a glorious independence in earning one's own bread." There is a happy *camaraderie* prevailing in this big hive of scholarly, industrious women. Such things as quarrels or petty jealousies are unknown, and when it is stated that these mansions have only been built for four years, and that all the twenty-two sets of chambers which they contain are inhabited, it will be readily understood how much the comfort and freedom of this cheerful club life is appreciated. But the three or four hundred guests are dispersing, and you take leave of Miss Adeline Sergeant, with a sense of gratitude for an entirely novel and interesting entertainment.

MRS. EDWARD KENNARD.

THERE is great wailing and lamentation at Market
Harboro'. King Frost holds the ground in an iron
grip. Fresh snow falling almost daily spreads yet
another and another layer, and all is encrusted hard
and fast, but far around it sparkles like a sea of
diamonds, emitting the colours of a rainbow in the
radiant sunshine. Horses are eating their heads off
and are ready to jump out of their skins; hounds are
getting fat and lazy; the majority of the sportsmen
have long ago taken themselves off to London, Monte
Carlo, and elsewhere, and the few who remain spend
their days in skating, toboganning, and curling.

While the barometer averages nightly ten to twenty
degrees of frost, perhaps the most favourable moment
has arrived to find one's hunting friends freed from the
daily labour they so cheerfully undergo for the sake of
sport. As in ordinary weather a protracted hunt with
Mr. Fernie's hounds, or a long day with the Pytchley,
would at this season have kept Mrs. Edward Kennard
to a late hour in the saddle, you gladly seize the
opportunity afforded, and accept a kind invitation to
visit her at "The Barn." A two-hours' run from St.
Pancras to Leicestershire, with a change at Kettering,

MRS EDWARD KENNARD

lands you at Market Harboro' station, where a neat
brougham, drawn by a pair of handsome brown horses
(with no bearing reins), waits to convey you to Mr.
Edward Kennard's hunting box, which stands back
between two fields of ridge and furrow in the main
road from Kettering to Market Harboro'. A straight
avenue, bordered on either side by lime and fir trees,
breaks into a circular grass front, where the drive
divides, the right road leading to a substantial, comfortable-looking red-brick house, with sloping roof, tall
gable over the entrance-hall, and sides picturesquely
covered with ivy, whilst the left turns to the stables
(that essential part of a sporting establishment), which,
with the kitchen gardens and paddocks, are in the
rear. In usual circumstances a fine vista of undulating
pasture, and extensive views of the happy hunting-
fields of Northamptonshire and Leicestershire, can be
seen, in which are several historical fox-coverts; but
now, in the snow-bound condition of the earth, everything is white, save for the line of dark intersecting
hedgerows, and the delicate tracery of leafless trees
standing in black silhouette against the sky. As the
afternoon advances, a grey haze creeps over the far-
famed Harboro' Vale, shrouding alike "bullfinches"
and "double-oxers," into which sinks a golden sun
behind a bank of crimson and purple clouds.

But the carriage stops. The broad stone steps lead
into the entrance hall, where, facing you, stands a
black, long-haired, stuffed sloth bear, hugging the
sticks and umbrellas, and an oak case, full of English
game-birds. Glass doors open into the broad, lofty,
central hall, giving outlet to numerous rooms, which

are all draped with heavy *portières* on each side. The first to the right opens, and Mrs. Edward Kennard comes out to bid you welcome to "The Barn," and leads the way into the drawing-room, which is bright with a huge, blazing fire and tall lamps. She is above the middle height, and her slight, well-built figure shows to as much advantage in the neatly-fitting brown homespun costume as it does in her well-cut "Busvine" habit. She has a small head, well set on, with dark hair curling over her brow, and dark eyes which, owing to her being short-sighted, have somewhat of a searching expression as she looks at you, and the kindest of smiles. A woman of peculiar grace, gentleness, and refinement, her pluck and skill which are so prominent in the chase and lead her to delight in all field sports, in no way detract from her womanly characteristics in the home circle and other relations in life.

Mrs. Edward Kennard is the second daughter and fourth child of a well-known public man, Mr. Samuel Laing, late member for the counties of Orkney and Shetland, and formerly Finance Minister of India.

"I believe," says your hostess, as you sit at tea, "that I took to scribbling principally through finding time hang heavy on my hands and seeking occupation. I fancy that any small love of literature which I may possess is hereditary, since my father, who is now chairman of the Brighton Railway, has written several important works, notably, "Modern Science and Modern Thoughts," "Problems of the Future," etc., whilst my grandfather, Mr. S. Laing, was also well known as an author in his day, and wrote a famous book of Nor-

wegian travel, still considered one of the best extant.
In the schoolroom (we lived at Hordle, Hants, then)
I was regarded as the dunce, and my childish recollections are always embittered by thoughts of scoldings,
punishments, and admonitions from our various governesses.

At the age of fifteen the young girl was sent to a
private establishment at St. Germains, when, under a
different system of tuition, she began to take an
interest in her studies, and to work in earnest. Two
or three years later she returned to England, and
shortly after married Mr. Edward Kennard, Deputy-
Lieutenant and Magistrate for the counties of Mon-
mouthshire and Northamptonshire, son of the late Mr.
R. W. Kennard, M.P. He, too, has literary as well as
sporting tastes, and is the author of "Fishing in
Strange Waters" and "Sixty Days in America,"
besides being a contributor to the *Illustrated London
News*, *Graphic*, and *The Chase*. He is also an artist,
and every part of the house is decorated with his
clever, spirited sketches in oils and water-colours.

Mrs. Edward Kennard's first literary efforts were a
series of short stories, which she wrote for her two
boys. These were afterwards collected and published
in one volume called "Twilight Tales." Subsequently,
when the little fellows had to be sent to school, and
she describes herself as "having felt lost without
them," during a long period of indifferent health, she
turned her attention to authorship. Her first novel,
"The Right Sort," was produced in 1883, and was
followed by "Straight as a Die," "Twilight Tales,"
and "Killed in the Open." Next came "The Girl in

the Brown Habit," " A Real Good Thing," " A Glorious
Gallop," " A Crack County," " Our Friends in the
Hunting Field," " Matron or Maid," etc., etc. These
are all sporting novels, as most of their names indicate,
and contain the graphic account of many a stirring and
exciting run depicted with the vividness and fidelity
born of accurate knowledge of hounds, horses, and
huntsmen, and long experience in the field. All these
works are very popular at home and in the colonies,
and most of them have passed into many editions.
" Landing a Prize " is the result of several seasons
spent in Norway on the Sandem, Stryn, Etne, Aurland,
Gule, Förde, and Aäro rivers. This book relates to
quite another kind of sport, for the author who can
so successfully negotiate a real Leicestershire flyer—a
high blackthorn fence with a ditch on either side of it
—with such ease and grace, and has ridden first flight
in this county and in Northamptonshire since her marriage, is equally at home in salmon-fishing, and last
year, with considerable dexterity and skill, wielded
her seventeen-foot rod of split cane to such good purpose that she landed a thirty-six pounder, a feat of
which her husband and sons are justly proud ; but you
must go to Mr. Kennard to get details of his wife's
prowess, for she says, modestly, " It is so very difficult
to say anything much of oneself. I like hunting, of
course, but look upon it purely as an agreeable
physical amusement, and not the *one* business of life,
as it is considered in this neighbourhood, a thing to
which all other interests must be sacrificed. Marrying
very young, it has since been my fate to reside in a
hunting county, and therefore I have had few oppor-

tunities for gratifying my love for travel and seeing
fresh scenes. For the last few years, however, we have
spent our summers in Norway, and I have become
almost as fond of salmon-fishing as of riding."

The scene of the author's late work is laid in Germany, and in "A Homburg Beauty" she gives a
vigorous narrative of a steeplechase which she witnessed in that place. The last two novels she produced
are entitled "That Pretty Little Horse-Breaker," and
"Wedded to Sport."

Mrs. Edward Kennard is as clever with her needle
as is her husband with his paint-brush, and many are
the evidences of her capacity in this feminine accomplishment in the room. The curtains, cornices, mantel-
cloths, together with several screens and cushions—
even the window blinds—are all exquisitely embroidered by her industrious fingers. There are many
priceless pieces of very old Japanese bronze, china, and
ancient lacquer work scattered about the room. On
one table is a perfect model in soapstone of an Indian
burying-ground, and above the dado is a narrow terry
velvet ledge on which are strewn lovely bits of
Japanese ivories and other ornaments. The walls are
hung with water-colour paintings of scenes in Egypt,
by Mr. Kennard, and the whole room looks cosy and
comfortable in the glow of warm firelight and coloured
lamp-shades.

An hour or so later you are all sitting at a large
round dinner-table, which is artistically decorated with
quaint dried sea weeds and shells of delicate tints and
shades, grouped on an arrangement of " Liberty " silks,
and the effect is as original as it is pretty.   There are

M

only the family party present : your kind, genial hosts
and their two sons—Lionel, a handsome young Militia
officer reading for a cavalry commission ; and Malcolm,
a naval cadet, who has just passed out of the *Britannia*
with eight months' sea time.   Both are promising
youngsters, the pride and joy of their parents, and
either can hold his own against the "grown-ups" in
the hunting field.   The silver bowl yonder is a prize
gained by "Rainbow" and "Ransom," two fox-hound
puppies walked by Mr. Kennard ; and a large painting
hanging opposite attracting your attention, Mrs. Kennard explains that it was executed by Bassieti, and
was exhibited amongst the Old Masters at Burling-
ton House, and that the original study was purchased
out of the Hamilton collection by the National Gallery,
where it now hangs.   Dinner over, an adjournment to
the billiard-room is proposed.   The walls are hung
with trophies of sport, a forest of stags' horns, including
wild fallow, wapiti, red-deer, chamois, and roebuck.
Your eye is first caught by the monster salmon, painted
on canvas and stretched over the model of the great
fish on the spot where Mrs. Kennard landed it, and
above it hangs a picture of the scene at Tower Sloholen
where the feat was accomplished.   The principal painting in this room is of the author on "Rhoda," long
since defunct, a celebrated mare by Zouave, who carried her several seasons without a fall.   Near this is
Lionel when a child, on his first pony, "Judy," who is
still alive, and spending a happy old age in the paddock.
This pony and the handsome fox-terrier following his
mistress round the room, both figure in "Twilight
Tales."   But old "Skylark" must not be forgotten, and

here hangs his portrait, representing his wonderful
jump—owner up—over water, a distance of twenty-
eight feet from take-off to land.   A curious object lies
on the side table, a British officer's sword, with crest,
monogram, Queen's crown, and V.R. on it, which has
been turned into a barbaric weapon, and is encased in
a rude leather scabbard with silk tassels.   On the
mantelpiece stands a great bronze six-armed monster,
with open mouth, and on a lighted match being
secretly applied behind its back to a tiny gas tube
within, you turn round to find a long thin flame issuing
therefrom, at which the gentlemen light their cigars.
Below this is a border, beautifully embroidered in silks
by Mrs. Kennard, representing hounds in full chase after
a fox. A pleasant game of billiards finishes the evening.

On the morrow Mr. Kennard suggests a further
inspection of other interesting parts of the house, and
promises that at noon, when the horses are dressed, his
wife shall act as cicerone, and do the honours of the
stables.   Accordingly, first Mrs. Edward Kennard's
summer study is visited. It lies between the dining
and drawing rooms, and looks bright and cheerful, with
its amply-filled bookcases, comfortable lounging-chairs,
and little tables.   The writing-table stands in front of
the window, from whence there is a fine view, which in
summer inspires the author to write some of her happy
bits of scenery; but the peculiarity of this room is the
extraordinarily large collection of china ranged in tiers
round the walls.   It is, indeed, a complete dinner service of fifteen dozen plates, designed and painted by
Mr. Kennard, and brought out by Mortlock, and is
quite unique.

On the other side of the hall is a glass case containing a splendid silver-grey fox, stuffed, and carrying a dead pheasant in its mouth. This was a tame fox, reared from a cub. Just at the foot of the great open staircase is the weighing chair and book recording the weights of all the hunting people in these parts. The broad, lofty staircase walls are laden with an *olla podrida* of curiosities, notably some barbaric necklaces and armlets studded with uncut gems, and several full-dress suits of Arab and Nubian ladies, made of grasses and strips of leather, which on breezy days might be considered somewhat too scanty to please the British matron. There are fine old paintings here by Albert Bierstadt, Maes, and Van der Helst, and higher up hangs a more modern one of a hunt in the early days of the author's married life, when dogs supplied the place of children. Amongst a museum of stuffed crocodiles, catamarans, a parrot fish from the Dead Sea, sundry Egyptian warlike implements, musical instruments, and mediæval deities painted on glass, there hangs a solitary broken stirrup leather which has a story. It is the one by which the famous horsewoman was dragged at a gallop over a ridge-and-furrow field, breaking her arm in two places, the horse she rode failing to jump a stiff stile out of a wood. This, and another bad fall—when she was lost to sight in a ditch beneath the heavy body of a fifteen-stone weight-carrier—Mr. Kennard declares to be the two worst accidents he ever witnessed in the hunting-field, "but," he adds, "they have in no way shaken her nerve."

There is just time before keeping tryst with your

hostess to peep into her second writing room, formerly
the nursery, but now devoted to literature and fine art.
From the window, which looks out to the south-east,
can be seen the rifle range and tobogganing ground.
The next is the large photographing room (in which
art the whole family are deeply interested), but noticing a negative plate lying buried under two inches of
ice in a dish, you prudently and promptly beat a
retreat, though not before noticing the lovely effect of
the hoar-frost on the deep ruby-coloured windows
lighted up by the sun. Noon strikes, and descending
the staircase you find your hostess in the hall (both
her hands are full of lumps of sugar for her pets), and
en passant pause to examine a splendid old Italian
cassonè over seven feet long, supported on two ani-
mated-looking griffins. This is one of the finest sixteenth century walnutwood carvings, or rather
sculptures in high relief, in Europe, and is complete
and uninjured.

The long passage at the back of the lower rooms of
the great house opens out into a large square red-brick
courtyard, with coach-house, forge, and two stables
on the right and left, where the good stud-groom
Butlin is waiting. This faithful and trusted retainer
is greatly valued by his employers. He has been in
their service for a great many years, adores his horses,
and is as proud of Mrs. Kennard's riding as are her
husband and boys. He opens the door on the left,
where there are four stalls and two loose boxes, in
which stand "Roulette," a fine bay mare; "Bridget," a
dun pony who goes in harness, and carries the younger
boy to hounds; "Leicester" and "Blackfox," who are

both harness horses and hunters. The magnificent black-brown animal yonder is "Quickstep," a gift from Mrs. Kennard's father; she says, " He does not know what it is to refuse or turn his head, and is one of the boldest and freest horses that ever crossed Leicestershire. I rode him twenty-seven times last season, and he never had a filled leg." In the stable on the right you find "Diana," a handsome bay mare with black points, standing 16·1, and "Grayling," both fine bold fencers; " Grasshopper," and " Magic," a bay mare by "Berserker," and a marvellous hunter. Lastly, "Bobbie," by " Forerunner," who is a great pet, and inherits his natural jumping qualities from his dam, Rhoda. Out of this fine collection " Bobbie" and " Quickstep" are Mrs. Kennard's favourite mounts, though she often rides most of the others. But you are particularly enjoined to see old " Skylark," who occupies a summering box in the smaller yard. This grand old hunter, though twenty years old, can still hold his own after hounds, indeed, Butlin observes that " there is not a horse in the country who can jump or gallop against him for a four mile run." Returning by the side of the field, he points out old " Judy," and a promising filly, " Rosie," who come trotting up to their mistress, in anticipation of their daily sugar.

There is a large and merry party of frozen-out foxhunters at luncheon, after which everyone goes off to the tobogganing ground. Mrs. Edward Kennard is to the fore here too. She seats herself daintily in the little vehicle, and glides down the great hill swiftly and gracefully, though many of the party get an awkward spill, or land ignominiously in a hedge full of

twigs. By and by comes the news that a thaw is
imminent, which sends up all the spirits of the hunting
community delightfully, and great are the preparations
and arrangements. If this state of things continue, ere
many days have elapsed the brave and fearless writer
will once more be in the saddle doing three, and
occasionally four, days a week, mounted alternately on
her good little " Bobbie " or the equally gallant
" Quickstep." Then, although skating and curling
may have kept the sportsmen and women, who did not
forsake Market Harboro', fairly amused, there will be
great jubilation, and once more the delights of the chase
will come as a fresh sensation after a stoppage of so
many weeks. Before long the shires will again be in
their glory, hounds will race over the purified pastures,
foxes will run straight and true, in that best of all
hunting months February, and it is just possible that
the end of the season may yet atone for the disappoint-
ments, inaction, and last, but not least, the expense
which for so long characterised it, and to the " music
of hound and ring of horn " you leave the gentle and
clever author.

JESSIE FOTHERGILL.[1]

WITH a vivid recollection of the comforts enjoyed on a recent trip to Ireland to visit Mrs. Hungerford, you again trust yourself to the tender mercies of the London and North-Western line with the intention of calling on Miss Jessie Fothergill, author of " The First Violin," etc., in her own home.   Starting at 10.10 a.m. from Euston, and having prudently taken another of the young writer's works, " Kith and Kin," to beguile the time during the long journey, you arrive punctually at 2.20 p.m. at the busy, bustling town of Manchester, having found that with the fascinating novel, combined with the smoothly-running and comfortable carriages and a good luncheon basket, four hours have passed like one; so deeply absorbing is the story that you have lost all count of time, and utterly neglected to notice the scenery through which you have been so rapidly carried.   Proposing, however, to repair this omission on the return journey, you select a tidy hansom, with a good-looking bay horse and an intelligent-faced Jehu, desiring him to point out the principal objects of interest to be seen.   Having an

[1] Since the serial publication of these sketches the death of the gifted writer has taken place.

JESSIE FOTHERGILL

hour to spare, there is time to make a *détour*, and drive round the exterior of the great Cheetham Hospital, which, with its college and library, are famous relics of old Manchester, and are in the immediate neighbourhood of the Cathedral, and in a moment you seem to be transported from the ˙bustle and roar of life into the quiet and peace of the old world cloisters.

Presently, driving past St. Peter's Church, the open door invites a peep at the famous painting of the "Descent from the Cross," by Annibal Carracci, which adorns the altar, and, finally, passing on the left Owens College, the principal branch of the Victoria University, the cab pulls up at Miss Fothergill's door.

It is a quiet street lying off Oxford-street, one of the main thoroughfares of Manchester ; and the house, one of a modest little row, is small and ordinary. The rooms are larger than might have been expected from its exterior, notably Miss Fothergill's own "den," as she calls the place where she spends nearly all her time. It is upstairs, and has two windows facing south ; between them stands a large writing table, from which the author rises to welcome you. It is literally covered with papers and manuscripts. "You think it looks extremely untidy," she says with a bright smile, after the first greetings are over. " It is not untidy for me, because I can put my hand on everything that I want. I am much cramped for space, too, in which to arrange my books as I would have them. I have a great many more than these, and they are scattered about in different other rooms in the house, which is only my temporary home, and everything is in disorder now, as I am on the eve of departure for sunnier climes."

The furniture is arranged with the greatest simplicity, but it is all very comfortable ; there are several easy chairs, a good resting couch, and plenty of tables, heaped up with the books, papers, and magazines of her daily reading. Over the fireplace is a large and very good autotype of Leonardo da Vinci's " Monna Lisa," with her mysterious smile and exquisite hands. There are likewise many photographs of Rome, and the art treasures of Rome. On another wall are two of Melozzo da Forti's angels, after those in the Sagrestia dei Canonici at St. Peter's, Rome, and a drawing of Watts' " Love and Death," made by a friend.

" It is all extremely simple and rather shabby," Miss Fothergill remarks placidly, " but it suits me. I rarely enter the downstair rooms except at the stated hour for meals, and, though I detest the dirt and gloom of Manchester, and am always ill in this climate, yet for luxury I do not care. Sumptuous rooms, gorgeous furniture, and an accumulation of 'the pride of life' and 'the lust of the eye' would simply oppress me, and make me feel very uncomfortable."

It is only fair to remark that on this occasion Manchester has put on a bright and smiling appearance. Though the fogs and rain can be as persistent as they are in London, the latter indeed much more frequent, the sun to-day shines brilliantly over the great city, and " dirt and gloom " are conspicuous by their absence.

In person the author is moderately tall and slight in figure. She is pale and delicate-looking, with dark

brown curly hair brushed back from her forehead, and
fine grey eyes, which have a sparkle of mirth in them,
and indicate a keen sense of humour. "I have a keen
sense of fun," she replies in answer to your remark,
"and see the ridiculous side of things, if they have one.
It is a blessed assistance in wending one's way through
life. My mother and all her family possessed it, and
we inherit it from her." She wears a soft black
dress, trimmed with lace and jet embroidery, and she
is so youthful in her appearance that she looks like a
mere girl.

Jessie Fothergill was born at Cheetham Hall, Manchester, and is of mixed Lancashire and Yorkshire
descent. Her father came of an old Yorkshire yeoman
and Quaker family, whose original home—still standing
—was a lonely house called Tarn House, in a lonely
dale—Ravenstonedale, Westmoreland. From there, in
1668, the family, having joined the Society of Friends,
removed to a farmhouse, which some member of it
built for himself in Wensleydale, Yorkshire, a district
which until lately has been quite remote and little
known, but which is now beginning to be sadly spoiled
by the number of visitors from afar, who have found it
out, and who are corrupting the primitive simplicity of
the inhabitants of the dale. This old-world farmstead
was called Carr End. It is still in existence, but has
passed out of the possession of its former owners.

"My father spent his childhood there," says Miss
Fothergill, "and used to keep us entranced, as children,
living in a stiff Manchester suburb, with accounts of
the things to be seen and done there—of the wild
moors, the running waterfalls, the little lake of Semir-

water hard by filled with fish, haunted by birds to us unknown, and bordered by grass and flowers, pleasant woods and rough boulders. I never saw it till I was a grown woman, and, standing in the old-fashioned garden with the remembrance of my dead father in my heart, I formed the intention of making it the scene of a story, and did so." But ere she has finished speaking you recognize the whole description in the volume of "Kith and Kin" which you had been reading in the train.

Miss Fothergill's father spent his early manhood in Rochdale, learning the ins and outs of the cotton trade, the great Lancashire industry, settling with a friend as his partner in business in Manchester. He was a Quaker, and on marrying her mother, who was a member of the Church of England, he was turned out of the Society of Friends for choosing a wife outside the pale of that body. His Nonconformist blood is strong in all his children, and not one of them now belongs to the Established Church. Mrs. Fothergill was the daughter of a medical man at Burnley, in North-East Lancashire, another busy, grimy, manufacturing town.

"I, however," says your young hostess, "knew very little of these northern towns, or the characteristics of their people, the love of which afterwards became part of my life, for, though my father's business was in Manchester, our home was at Bowdon, a popular suburb some eight or ten miles on the Cheshire side of the great city, and as utterly different from its northern outskirts and surroundings as if it belonged to another world."

Misfortune soon brought the young girl in contact with other scenes. When she was a mere child at school, and all her brothers and sisters very young, her father died. Much reduced in circumstances, the family went to live (because it appeared best, most suitable, and convenient) at an out-of-the-way house appertaining to a cotton mill, in an out-of-the-way part of Lancashire, in which her father and his partner had had a business interest.

"There must have been something of the artist," continues Jessie Fothergill, "and something also of the vagabond in me, for I quite well remember going home to this place for the first Christmas holidays after my father's death and being enchanted and delighted—despite the sorrow that overshadowed us—with the rough roads, the wild sweeping moors and fells, the dark stone walls, the strange, uncouth people, the out-of-the-worldness of it all. And the better I knew it the more I loved it, in its winter bleakness and its tempered but delightful summer warmth. I loved its gloom, its grey skies and green fields, the energy and the desperate earnestness of the people, who lived and worked there. I photographed this place minutely under the name of Homerton in a novel called 'Healey.' Here I passed a good many years after that turning-point in a 'young lady's' career—leaving school. Alas! there was little of the 'young lady' about me. I hated company, except exactly that in which I felt myself at home. I loved books, and read all that I could get hold of, and have had many a rebuke for 'poring over those books' instead of qualifying myself as a useful member of society. Almost better, I loved

my wild rambles over the moors, along the rough roads,
into every nook and corner of what would have been
a beautiful vale—the Tadmorden Valley—if man had
but left it as God had made it. But I liked the life
that was around me too, the routine of the great cotton
and flannel mills, the odd habits, the queer sayings and
doings of the workpeople. It was only when compass-
ionate friends or relations, wishing to be kind and to
introduce me to the world, insisted upon appearing in
carriages, presenting me with ball-dresses, and taking
me to entertainments that I was unhappy. I wove
romances, wrote them down, in an attic at the top of
the house, dreamed dreams, and lived, I can conscientiously say, far more intensely in the lives and loves
of my imaginary characters, than even in the ambition
of some day having name and fame."

Both of Jessie Fothergill's two first books " Healey "
and " Aldyth," according to her own account " fell flat
and dead to the ground." Nothing daunted, however,
by their failure, she paused for a while before writing
anything more. Soon after their publication, she paid
two visits to the Continent as the guest of friends,
delighting much in all the new and wonderful things
she saw. But the real enjoyment of foreign life came
on a subsequent journey, when, with a sister and two
young friends, she found herself established in a
German boarding-house at Dusseldorf, on the Rhine,
utterly without any of the luxurious hotels, drives,
dinners, or any correct sight-seeing which she had enjoyed on her former visits, but with a thousand
interests brought by the opening of a new life, the
wonderful discovery of German music, the actual

hearing of all the delightful things she had previously only heard of, which naturally inspired her imagination and fancy. At Dusseldorf she began to write "The First Violin," weaving into the scenes which passed every day before her eyes a series of imaginary adventures of imaginary beings. It was written "in spasms," she says—often altered, again completely changed in plot and incident several times, and it was not actually finished for a very long time after it was begun.

During the fifteen months spent at Dusseldorf she took every opportunity of studying the German language and life, and at the expiration of that time she went back to England—"to the house at the end of the world," she says, smiling; "and soon after my return I took a secretaryship, my heart in my books, making several efforts to get some enterprising publisher to take 'The First Violin.' I went to the firm who had brought out my two first unlucky efforts, but they kindly and parentally advised me, for the sake of whatever literary reputation I might have obtained, not to publish the novel I submitted to them. Much nettled at this, I replied, somewhat petulantly, that I acknowledged their right to refuse it, but not to advise me in the matter, and I *would* publish it. Next I took it to another firm who made it a rule never to bring out any novels except those of some promise. If it were possible to grant the premises of my story, the action itself was consistent enough, but it was up in the clouds and (though so elevated) was below their mark. Finally Mr. Bentley took pity on it, and brought it out in three-volume form, first running it through the pages of *Temple Bar*. Since that time I have not experienced any difficulty in disposing of my wares, though continuous and severe ill-health has been a constant restraint on their rapid production, and has also kept me quiet and obliged me to seek rest and avoid excitement at the expense of many an acquaintance and many a pleasure I should have been glad to enjoy."

On looking back, Jessie Fothergill cannot remember anything which caused her to write beyond the desire to do it. Her first attempts began when she was a mere child. Passionately fond of fairy tales, or any other, good, bad, or indifferent, she read them all, literally living in them when doing so. Then at school she used to instigate the other girls to write stories, because she wished to do so herself. She would tell them marvellous romances, which she had either read or invented. Her talent for writing fiction cannot be called hereditary, since the only family literary productions of which she is aware are a volume or two of sermons preached by some Fothergill who was a Friend, a missionary, and a man of note in his time. "Then, long ago," says the author, "there was a celebrated Dr. John Fothergill in London. I came across his name in one of the volumes of Horace Walpole's letters. He not only made a fortune, but wrote books—purely professional ones, I imagine. My father's people were brought up narrowly as regards literature and accomplishments, as was the fashion in his sect in that day, but he himself was an insatiable devourer of novels

and poetry, and introduced me to the works of Dickens
and Walter Scott, exacting a promise that I should
not read more than three chapters of any given book
in one day, a promise which was faithfully kept, but
with great agony of mind."

Jessie Fothergill forms her plots as follows: She
imagines some given situation, and works round it,
as it were, till she gets the story, all the characters
except the two or three principal ones coming gradually. Next she writes them out, first in a rough draft,
the end of which often contradicts the beginning, but
she knows what she means by that time. Then it
is all copied out and arranged, as she has settled it
clearly in her mind. She is quick in composing,
but slow in deciding which course the story shall
take, as all the people are very real to her, and
sometimes unkindly refuse to be disposed of according
to her original intentions. "I write much more
slowly," says Miss Fothergill, "and much less frequently now that my health is so indifferent. As a
child I learnt very quickly, and sometimes forgot
equally quickly, but never anything that really interested me. I remember winning one prize only
at a very early age, and choosing the most brightly
bound of the books from which I had to select. It
has always been my great regret that I did not
receive a classical education. If I had, I would have
turned it to some purpose; but when I was a child,
music, for which I had absolutely no gift, was
drummed into me, and a little French. German and
Italian I have learnt for myself since. "The Lasses
of Leverhouse" was her third book, but "The First

N

Violin" scored her first success. It went through
several editions, and was followed by "Probation,"
"Kith and Kin," "The Wellfields," "Borderland,"
"Peril," and "From Moor Isles." Most of these
passed first through *Temple Bar* before being issued
in book form, and each has been warmly welcomed
and favourably reviewed. Some have appeared in
Indian and Australian journals, and nearly all her
works are to be found in the *Tauchnitz* edition. " A
March in the Ranks" is the author's latest book.
Besides these, she has written numerous short stories,
among them, "Made or Marred," "One of Three," and
a great many articles and essays for newspapers and
magazines.

Full of interest and incident, carefully and conscientiously worked out, there is one prevailing characteristic
running through all Miss Fothergill's novels. She is
thoroughly straightforward and honest. Hating shams
of all kinds, she pictures what seem to be things that
happen, with due license for arranging the circumstances and catastrophes artistically and dramatically.
"The First Violin" is a book for all time; "Probation,"
"Kith and Kin," "Peril" and "The Wellfields," are
decidedly nineteenth century stories, as many of the
interesting questions of the day appear in them, and
it is evident that the said questions occupied the
gifted writer's mind not a little. " I have absolutely
no sympathy," she says, " with what is often called
realism now, the apotheosis of all that is ugly in
man's life, feelings, and career, told in a minute,
laborious way, and put forth as if it were a discovery.
Life is as full of romance as Italy is full of roses.

It is as full of prose as Lancashire is full of factory
chimneys. I have always tried to be impartial in
my writings, and to let the pendulum swing from
good to bad, from bad to good ; that has been my
aim when I could detach myself enough from my
characters." Here Miss Fothergill draws off a seal
ring which she long ago had engraved with the motto
she chose to guide her through life. "Good fight,
good rest," she adds. "It embodies all I have of
religious creed. It means a good deal when you
come to think of it."

Miss Fothergill is a great reader. She delights
especially in Ruskin, Darwin, Georges Sand, and
George Eliot's works, which she says have solaced
many an hour of pain and illness. In lighter literature
she prefers some of Anthony Trollope's novels, and
considers Mrs. Gaskell's " Sylvia's Lovers " one of the
masterpieces of English fiction, and " Wuthering
Heights" as absolutely unique and unapproachable.
Herbert Spencer and Freeman are great favourites,
whilst in poetry Browning stands first of all in her
affections, and next to him, Morris, Goethe, and bits
of Walt Whitman. Of her own works she remarks
modestly, "It seems to me that I have not much
to say of them. What little I have done has been
done entirely by my own efforts, unassisted by friends
at court, or favour of any kind. It has been a regret
that owing to my having never lived in London I
have not mixed more with scientific or literary people,
and that I only know them through their books."

The author having studied her "Lewis' Topographical
Dictionary " to such good purpose, is thoroughly con-

versant with her own native city, and its doings past
and present, she has therefore much interesting information to impart about its ancient history, the
sources of its wealth, and the origin of the place,
which is so remarkable for the importance of its
manufactures and the great extent of its trade. Manchester may be traced back to a very remote period
of antiquity. It was once distinguished as a principal station of the Druid priests, and was for four
centuries occupied by the Romans, being amply provided with everything requisite for the subsistence
and accommodation of the garrison established in it.
It was as long ago as 1352 that the manufacture
of " Manchester cottons " was introduced, and the
material was in reality a kind of woollen cloth made
from the fleece in an unprepared state. In that period
Flemish artisans settled in the town, where, finding
so many natural advantages, they laid the foundations
of the trade and brought the woollen manufacture to a
great degree of perfection. Nor is the industrious city
without later historical reminiscences. In 1744 Prince
Charles Edward visited Manchester, where he was
hospitably entertained for several weeks at Ancoat's
Hall, the house of Sir Edward Moseley, Bart., returning the following year at the head of an army
of 6000 men, when he took up his quarters at the
house of Mr. Dickenson in Market Place. In 1768
Christian, King of Denmark, lodged with his suite
at the ancient Bull Inn. Early in the present century
the Archdukes John and Lewis of Austria, accompanied by a retinue of scientific men, spent some time
in the place, and in 1817 the late Emperor of Russia,

then the Grand Duke Nicholas, visited Manchester to inspect the aqueducts and excavations at Worsley, and was escorted all over the principal factories.

But the shades of evening draw on; London must be reached to-night, and having likewise been "hospitably entertained," you bid Jessie Fothergill good-bye, with an earnest hope that under southern skies, and in warmer latitudes, she may soon regain her lost health and strength.

LADY DUFFUS HARDY.

IZA DUFFUS HARDY.

At the uppermost end of the long Portsdown Road, which stretches from near St. Saviour's Church away up to Carlton Road, and runs almost parallel with Maida Vale, there stands a large and lofty block of flats known as Portsdown Mansions. In one of these, a cosy suite of rooms on the parlour floor, arranged so as to form a complete maisonette, an industrious mother, Lady Duffus Hardy, and her only child, Iza, tread hand in hand along the paths of literature.

Whilst mounting the broad stone steps which lead to the entrance door, and ere pressing the electric bell, a fierce barking is heard within, but it is only the big good-natured black dog "Sam," keeping faithful watch over his mistresses. The hall door opens, and displays a half-bred pointer whose well-groomed, satin-like coat gives evidence of the care and attention lavished upon him. He is a great pet, and is generally known as the "Household Treasure" or "Family Joy." He inspects you, is apparently satisfied with his scrutiny, wags his tail, and solemnly precedes you into the pleasant home-like drawing-room, where he first keeps a furtive eye on you as you glance around, and presently, in the

LADY DUFFUS HARDY

most comical way, brings up his favourite playmate, an equally jet-black cat, to be stroked and petted, and then departs as if to fetch his mistress. It is all very bright and cheerful : a fair-sized, lofty room, the prevailing tints of pale sage green, with heavy damask curtains, which do not, however, exclude the brilliant glow of sunlight streaming in through an unusually broad window, for Lady Duffus Hardy likes plenty of light, and wisely maintains that people, like plants, thrive best in sunshine.

She certainly justifies her belief. The door opens, and, duly escorted by " Sam," a tall, portly gentlewoman of commanding and dignified presence, with cordial and hearty manner, enters. Her gown of violet velvet harmonizes well with her nearly white hair, which contrasts so favourably with her dark eyebrows and brown eyes. These last have a sparkle of merriment and fun in them, for Lady Hardy is of that pleasant and genial disposition, which loves to look on the best side of people and things, and she is consequently popular with old and young alike. She tells you that she is a Londoner *pur et simple ;* that she was born in Fitzroy Square, when that part of town was in its zenith, and was a favourite locality for great artists, Sir W. Ross, R.A., the celebrated miniature painter, and Sir Charles Eastlake, late President of the Royal Academy, being among their number.

With the exception of a few years spent at Addlestone, where her daughter was born, Lady Hardy has passed all her life in London, residing for many years in the pretty house, standing in the midst of a large and well-wooded garden in St. John's Wood, where she

used to give delightful Saturday evening parties, which
are still pleasantly remembered by her friends.[1]

Lady Hardy was an only child. Her father, Mr. T.
C. McDowell, died five months before her birth, at the
untimely age of twenty-six, when on the threshold of
a promising career, and her early-widowed mother,
resolving that she should never be sent to school, had
her educated entirely at home under her own eye, and
only parted with her on her marriage with Mr., afterwards Sir Thomas Duffus Hardy, D.C.L., Deputy
Keeper of Her Majesty's Records (first at the Tower
and later at the Rolls House), who died in 1879.
" Rarely," says Lady Hardy, " has there been a man at
once so learned and so good." Whilst wading in the
deep fields of historic research, he did not disdain some
of the lighter portions of literature ; indeed, the
prefaces to many of his historical collections were
written in such an entertaining and pleasant vein, that
they by themselves would make delightful essays in
any magazine of the present day. With all his
laborious occupation—for which he used to declare the
year was so short that he must make it into fourteen
months by stealing the balance out of the night—Sir
Thomas Duffus Hardy maintained that the busiest
people have ever the most leisure, and he always had
time to spare to enjoy the society of his friends. It
may be truly said of him that seldom did twenty-four
hours pass without his showing some act of kindness
to one or other of them. This sympathetic and amiable
trait of character has caused his name to be remembered

[1] Since the serial publication of these sketches the death of the
much beloved and respected writer has taken place.

with lasting affection and respect, not only by the erudite scholar, but among his personal friends.

Though always fond of writing, Lady Hardy did not actually set to work seriously at story-making until after her marriage. Then, living in an atmosphere of literature, she began to occupy her leisure hours with her pen, and, having taken much trouble to collect her materials, she wrote "Two Catherines" (Macmillan) and "Paul Wynter's Sacrifice," which went well, and was soon translated into French. This success encouraged her to write "Lizzie," "Madge," "Beryl Fortescue," and "A Hero's Work," all of which were published in three volumes by Messrs. Hurst and Blackett. "Daisy Nicholl" was brought out first by Sampson Low and Co., and then in America, where it was received with much favour, and had a large sale. Her latest novel, "A Dangerous Experiment" (Mr. F. V. White), came out in 1888. During the last two or three years Lady Hardy has written many short stories for high-class magazines and Christmas numbers, which are all bright in dialogue and vigorous in design.

Full of indomitable energy, the author has lately turned her attention to journalism, and is writing a series of articles on social subjects, "which interest me so deeply," she says, laughing, "that I sometimes think of leaving novel-making entirely to Iza." Two of these papers recall themselves particularly to mind at the moment as possessing singular merit—one called "The Morality of Mercy" and the other "Free Pardon." The former was quoted and much complimented in Mr. Donald Nichol's book, "Man's Revenge," an interesting work on the reform of administration of the criminal law, a subject in which Lady Hardy and her daughter take a keen interest.

At this juncture Miss Iza Duffus Hardy comes into the room. She is dressed in a flowered "Liberty" silk tea-gown, with black facings. She bears a striking likeness to her late distinguished father. She, too, is tall, but slight and fragile-looking, pale in complexion, with soft hazel eyes, and brown hair worn in coils round her head. Whilst she does the honours of the tea-tray, you have leisure to look around. Lady Hardy's Chippendale writing-table stands in the window, and her ink-stand is a beautiful bronze model of Titian's own, and was sent to her from Venice. There is a carved Venetian bracket on each side of the fireplace ; on one stands some fancy glass work, and on the other a lovely Cyprus vase, a perfect *replica* of the third century model. The richly-carved jar, flanked on either side by terra-cotta statuettes, is handsome in itself and is treasured because it was a gift from the late Mr. S. C. Hall, who, together with his wife, was an intimate and valued friend of your hostesses. Yonder, on a cabinet, is a large bust of Clytie, also in terra-cotta. Amongst the pictures are, notably, a little gem in oils by Ernest Parton, and a fine water-colour drawing of Durham by Mr. W. H. Brewer. The bookcase is filled with autograph copies by many of their friends, principally Julian Hawthorne, the late Mr. Hepworth Dixon, Mr. and Mrs. S. C. Hall, Mr. P. B. Marston, and Mr. Cordy Jeaffreson. It also contains a goodly collection of Lady and Miss Hardy's favourite poets which are evidently often used. There are volumes of Rossetti, Browning, Morris, Swinburne,

and some by Philip Bourke Marston, the blind poet,
son of Dr. Westland Marston. Over the couch is
spread a large patchwork coverlet, which was made
and embroidered by Miss Hardy, who is as much at
home with the needle as with the pen.

A year after their bereavement, the mother and
daughter having long entertained a desire to visit
America, determined to make a trip across the Atlantic
in 1880. After passing several pleasant weeks in
Canada, enjoying delightful glimpses of the social life
in Ottawa and Toronto, they visited Niagara Falls,
stayed awhile in New York, and then travelled over
the Rocky Mountains to San Francisco, " where," says
Miss Hardy, " we spent a thoroughly pleasant winter,
and received so much genuine kindness and hospitality
that it has endeared the name of the country to us
ever since," and she goes on to tell you that, amongst
many acts of courtesy shown to them—the courtesy
which is so freely displayed to women travelling alone
in America—there was one from a fellow-traveller, who
did not even know their name, until by chance it trans-
pired, when the discovery was made that he had been
intimately acquainted in his youth with Sir Thomas
Hardy, who had given him his first start in life forty
years before, and of whose letters he possessed a large
packet. On their return journey they visited Boston,
where they made the acquaintance of Oliver Wendell
Holmes, and spent a delightful day with the poet
Longfellow at his country residence at Nahant.

In the following spring Lady and Miss Duffus
Hardy returned home, but a year later the restless
spirit of travel again took hold of them, and they

decided to make a second tour in America, this time
embracing the Southern States, and visiting the chief
cities of Virginia, South Carolina, Georgia, and Florida,
on their way to New Orleans, where they met General
Beauregard, the renowned Confederate leader, whose
thrilling reminiscences of the great struggle of 1863-5
Miss Hardy says they can "never forget, any more
than they can forget his unfailing kindness and attention." The experiences of all these expeditions were
embodied by Lady Hardy in her books "Through
Cities and Prairie Lands," and "Down South," both of
which were successful and well received.

Inheriting talent from both parents, and reared
among literary surroundings, Iza Duffus Hardy naturally turned to writing at a very early age. Before she
was fifteen she had planned and begun a novel.
Always of a retiring and studious nature, she describes
her lessons as having been no trouble to her, and her
greatest punishment would have been to deprive her of
them. Being an only and delicate child, her parents
did not like her to be much away from home, so she
was only sent to school for about two years, receiving
all the rest of her education at home. "But I think,"
says Miss Hardy, "that I learned more from my father
than from all my teachers put together."

Her choice of reading was carefully guided, and an
early determination was made that before all things
she would be thorough and conscientious in her work.

Her two first novels, "Not Easily Jealous" and
"Glencairn," were followed in rapid succession by "A
Broken Faith," "Only a Love Story," and "Love,
Honour, and Obey." These two last were originally

IZA DUFFUS HARDY

brought out by Hurst and Blackett, but have been
since published by Mr. F. V. White in a single volume.
Then came a short rest, after which the young author
wrote "The Girl He Did Not Marry," of which Messrs.
Hutchinson are about to produce a new edition in
their "Popular Series." Then the first journey to San
Francisco gave Miss Hardy fresh ground to break, and
suggested the leading ideas of the incidents and
graphic description of the life in the beautiful Cali-
fornian valleys, so charmingly depicted in "Hearts
and Diamonds" and "The Love that He Passed By"
(F. V. White).

"The nucleus of this plot," says Iza Duffus Hardy,
"was a story told to me by a fellow-passenger on the
cars, who had been governor of the gaol at the time of
the attack by the Vigilantes. I connected that with
certain incidents in a celebrated murder trial which
was going on about that time, and built up all the rest
of the story around those scenes."

"Love in Idleness" is a picture drawn from the life,
of a winter spent among the orange groves of South
Florida, a happy and peaceful time of which Lady
Hardy and her daughter speak most enthusiastically,
and declare to have been quite idyllic, the days gliding
away in dream-like fashion, boating on the lakes,
driving through the open woods of the rolling pine
lands, and lounging on the piazzas, enjoying the
exquisite effects of the morning sunshine, the sunset
hazes, or the glorious tropical moonlight. Besides
these books, Iza Duffus Hardy has also embodied
her American experiences in two interesting volumes,
"Oranges and Alligators" (Ward and Downey) and

"Between Two Oceans." The former in particular made such a decided hit that the first edition was exhausted in two or three weeks. This work, widely noticed and quoted, was strongly recommended by many papers to the attention of parents about to send their sons abroad, as giving a fair and true picture, showing both sides of life in Florida.

Asking Miss Hardy for a peep at her study, she leads the way to a comfortable little room at the back of the house, which she calls her "cabin." Here she works from 10 a.m. to 1 p.m. daily, though she confesses to taking occasionally an extra hour or two late in the afternoon, and, the conversation turning on plots, she tells you how she constructs her own. "I always," she observes, "have the story completely planned out before I begin to write it. I often alter details as I go on, but never depart from the main lines. My usual way of making a plot is to build up on and around the principal situation. I get the picture of the strongest scene—the crisis of the story—well into my mind. I see that this situation necessitates a certain group of characters standing in given situations towards each other. Then I let these characters speak for themselves in my mind, and if they do not individualize themselves, I never feel that I can portray them satisfactorily. Having got the characters formed, and the foundation of the story laid, I build up the superstructure just as an artist would first get in the outline of his central group in the foreground, and then sketch out the background and the details."

Miss Hardy's later work, "A New Othello," ran first as a serial through *London Society*, and was afterwards

published by Mr. F. V. White in three volumes.   It
deals largely with hypnotism, and not only to those
readers who are interested in this subject, but also to
the genuine fiction-lover, it is evident that she has
handled the matter in a masterly and skilful style, and
has put excellent work into it.   Before beginning this
book she fully read up the details of hypnotism, studying all the accounts of Dr. Charcot's experiments, whilst
Dr. Morton, of New York, personally related to her the
interesting episodes from his own experience, which
are so ably worked into the story.   The author is also
an occasional contributor of a biographical article, or
a fugitive poem, or a short sketch, to various magazines, and she has just finished another book, called
" Woman's Loyalty," now running through the pages
of *Belgravia*, which she says has been somewhat
delayed, owing to a sharp attack of inflammation of
the eyes, from which she has now happily recovered.

And so the busy days glide on, in peaceful content-
ment; not that these interesting, amiable gentlewomen
shut themselves from society.   On the contrary, their
receptions are crowded with friends well known in the
world of fashion, of literature, and of art.   Work alter-
nates with many social pleasures and amusements.
Both being worshippers of music and the drama, concerts and theatres are an endless source of enjoyment
to them.   Perhaps one secret of their popularity may
lie in the fact that they always have a good word to
say of everyone, and it is well known to their many
friends that they may rely as confidently upon their
loyalty as upon their sympathy.

Over the well-filled bookstand in the dining-room

hangs the picture of Lady Duffus Hardy, taken in her
early married life. Except that the figure is slender
and the hair dark, the likeness is still excellent. On
one side of this painting there is a large-sized engraving of a portrait of Admiral Sir Thomas Hardy, of the
Blue Squadron, painted in 1714, and on the other is a
portrait of the late Lord Romilly, whose memory is
treasured by your hostess as that of a kind and valued
friend. The cuckoo clock opposite used to hang in
Philip Bourke Marston's study, and was bequeathed to
Miss Hardy, together with some other souvenirs, in
memory of their life-long friendship.

A photograph of Mr. Henry Irving occupies a prominent place, and leads Lady Hardy to speak of the
theatre. "I am very fond of the drama," she remarks,
"and though I can thoroughly enjoy a good melo-
drama once in a way, yet I prefer plays of a more
serious kind. I am a great admirer of Mr. Irving.
Few actors, in my opinion, excel as he does both in
tragedy and comedy. I think that the most intellectual treat I ever had was in witnessing the performances of *Othello* when Henry Irving and Edwin
Booth alternated the characters of Iago and Othello.
Irving's Iago struck me as a subtle and masterly
study. Salvini, too, realised most thoroughly my conception of Othello. He is indeed the ideal Moor of
Venice. In New York we used to enjoy immensely
the classic plays which are too seldom seen in London,
such as *Coriolanus, Julius Cæsar,* and *Virginius.*"

A visit to the theatre is in contemplation this
evening; so, having been beguiled into making an
unusually long but most enjoyable visit, you take

leave of Lady and Miss Duffus Hardy, with sympathetic admiration for the happy home life in which
daily work is sweetened by harmony and affection.
As Miss Hardy quoted the noble utterance, " Justice is
the bed rock of all the virtues," you cannot help feeling
that here are two women who at least endeavour to act
up to their ideal.

MAY CROMMELIN.

THE story of May Crommelin's life may be said to be divided into three parts. First, the period of her childish and girlish days in Ireland; next, that, when after the beginning of Irish land troubles, her family were enforced absentees, and suffering from anxieties and prolonged illness; and thirdly, during the last four years, when her London life began. The following is a brief account of her first home:—

On the east coast of Ireland there lies a long narrow neck of land, which, jutting out at the entrance to Belfast Lough, curves down by the coast of Down, and is called The Ards. Midway in it, where for an Irish mile "and a bit" the ground slopes upward from the shore, a tower rising just above the woods is a landmark for ships at sea. This is Carrowdore Castle, the home of the late Mr. de la Cherois-Crommelin, where May Crommelin (his second daughter and one of a large family) was reared.

The house, now belonging to her only brother, looks away at a dark blue belt of Irish Sea, across which on clear days after thunderstorms the Scotch coast and even houses are visible. Ailsa Craig has the appearance of a haycock on the northern horizon, and

MAY CROMMELIN

lying more southward the Isle of Man seems but a
blurred mass. Behind is the salt backwater of Strang-
ford Lough, and this arm of sea keeps the temperature
so moist that snow rarely lies long, and the humid
nature of the soil causes the garden of Carrowdore
facing south to luxuriate in giant tree-myrtles, sweet
verbenas, and even hot-house flowers growing out of
doors. It is somewhat lonely in winter when the
wind blows over the bare low hills that have caused
The Ards to be compared to " a basket of eggs," but
pleasant in summer and picturesque when its envir-
oning woods are green, when the corncrakes call from
the meadows on June evenings, and the Orange drums
beat along the lanes.

Such was May de la Cherois-Crommelin's early
home. Her present abode is a pretty flat near
Victoria Street. It seems quite appropriate that a
well-filled bookcase should be the first thing that
greets the eye as the hall door opens and admits you
into a long carpeted passage, lined with a high dado
of blue-and-white Indian matting, above which, on
art paper of the same colours, hang several framed
photographs, reminiscences of the Rhine, Nuremberg,
and the Engadine. A little way down on the left is
Miss Crommelin's writing-room, which is laid down
with Indian matting, and contains an unusually large,
workmanlike-looking writing-table, replete with little
drawers, big drawers, and raised desk. The principal
feature of this room is a carved oak fireplace, reaching
nearly to the ceiling, and which is quite original in
design and execution. There is a handsome old
oak dower chest standing near the window, here an

antique "ball-and-claw" footed table, and there a few good Chippendale chairs.

But whilst you are taking a brief scrutiny around, Miss Crommelin enters. It is very easy to describe her. She is certainly above the middle height, but looks taller than she really is by reason of her absolutely faultless figure. It is exquisitely moulded, and every movement is graceful. The good-shaped head and slender neck are well set on her shoulders, fair chestnut-coloured hair curls over a low, wide brow. The eyes, large and of the real Irish grey, are fringed with long lashes, she has a straight nose, and the expression of mouth and chin is that of dignity and repose. Her manner is peculiarly gentle and sweet, and her voice is pleasant to the ear. The long, dark blue velvet tea-gown that she wears, with its paler blue satin front folded in at the shapely waist, becomes her well, and harmonises with the artistic decorations of her pretty little drawing-room into which she has taken you. The curtains are made of some art blue fabric, the walls are pale yellow with a lighter frieze above, and are encrusted with memories of the last three or four years, when the author first set up housekeeping in London. All the woodwork is of dark walnut, as are the overmantel and *étagère*, the doors are panelled with Japanese raised paper, a long carved bracket has an excellent background of choice photographs, and there is a delightful little "cosy corner," draped with dark terra-cotta and blue tapestry, over which is a carved rail and shelf filled with odds and ends of china, pet bits of blue Dutch delft, and quaint little old brasses and bronzes from Munich and

Florence. There is an Innocenza framed in box-wood, and on the small tables yonder are some little carved wooden *stovi* such as are used in Holland, an old-fashioned brass Lucernina, and many more little souvenirs, all of which she has gathered together on foreign excursions. Amongst the pictures there is one which Miss Crommelin particularly values—it is a large and beautiful etching of Joan of Arc, by Rajon, who presented it to her shortly before his death, with an inscription in his own handwriting.

Some photographs of Carrowdore on the table close by lead you to ask her for some particulars of her people. "Mr. Smiles remarked to me," she says, "'Yours is a historical name' (he has written about us in his 'Huguenots'). I will try to think about some little family incidents, though I am afraid that to talk about my family will rather bore you, but I can briefly tell you the first that we know of them is in the archives of Ghent. In 1133 the Count of Flanders concluded an 'Accord' between the Abbot of St. Pierre de Gand and Walter Crommelin concerning the domain of Testress. In 1303, one Heinderic Crommelin was three times burgomaster of Der Kuere, near Ghent. I have been told it is strange that simple burghers had a surname in the twelfth and thirteenth centuries."

Later on came those terrible times of the persecutions in the Netherlands, when women were buried alive, and men were burned at the stake for their faith. The Crommelins fled to France, and a pious ancestor of that day wrote the history of their adventures, which record is preserved in the British Museum. It begins, "*Au nom de Dieu. Armand Crommelin et sa femme vivoient dans le Seizième Siécle, dans un tems de troubles, de guerres, de persécutions cruelles, etc."* This was their first flight. In France they prospered exceedingly by special favour of Henri IV., until came the Edict of Nantes. But acting on the old Huguenot motto, " Mieux vaut quitter patrie que foi," they chose exile rather than renounce their religion. This time, one brother escaped with difficulty to Holland, where his descendants still reside, but another, Louis Crommelin, offered his sword to William of Orange, crossed with him to England, and finally settled in the north of Ireland, where he brought Huguenot weavers and taught the linen trade, which is one of the greatest sources of Ulster's commercial prosperity. To this day his name is honoured as a benefactor, and he received a Royal grant from William III., which founded anew the fortunes of his family.

The de la Cherois, who were of a noble family in Champagne, also fled with difficulty from France. They and the Crommelins were closely connected by marriage, and also married into other families of the little Huguenot colony in Ulster. " Perhaps this keeping to themselves preserved their foreign characteristics longer and their faith stronger," says your hostess. " Then one ancestress—we have her picture at home, taken in a flowing white gown, and piled-up curls—married the last Earl of Mount Alexander. At her death she left the present County Down estate to my great-grandfather. He first, I think, took unto himself a wife of the daughters of Heth. She was a beautiful Miss Dobbs, of the family now living at Castle Dobbs in County Antrim. I must show you a photograph of her portrait. Would it not make a lovely fancy dress?—the grey gown with puffed sleeves and neck-ruffle, and wide riding-hat and feathers. Then my grandfather married the Honourable Elizabeth de Moleyns, Lord Ventry's daughter. You see her picture is scanty skirted, with the waist under the arms. My grandfather must have been rather too splendid in his ideas. Some of these were for improving the country generally, as well as his own estate, but he lost many thousands in trying to carry them into practice. I must tell you that an ancestress, Judith de la Cherois, escaped from France with her sister by riding at night across the country, their jewels sewn in their dresses. She lived to be 113, and was quite strong to the last, and though she lived fifty years in Ireland she could never speak English, which she said, with vexation, was because people laughed rudely at her first attempts.

If it be true that the girl is mother to the woman (to change the proverb), then May Crommelin still retains some characteristics of her childhood. A shy child, sensitive to an intense degree, and shrinking from the observation of strangers, her great delight when small was to be allowed to run almost wild about the woods and fields with her little brothers and sisters, and to visit all the tenant-farmers' houses, where the children from the Castle were always warmly welcomed, and regaled with tea, and oatmeal or potato cakes, in the parlour. In these later years she still retains the intense love of nature that she had then, and her descriptions of scenery have ever been praised as word-painting of rare fidelity. Taking in her impressions early she produced them later in a book called "Orange Lily," which proved how well she knew the peasant life of Ulster, a work which was declared by good judges to be absolutely faithful, while she herself was proud to find the farmers on her father's estates in Down and Antrim had copies of the book sent home from America, where it could be bought cheap, and where the many immigrants from the "Ould Country" welcomed it.

At five years of age she could read fluently, and thenceforth through childhood she read so ardently that, having then defective vision, though unfortunately it was unnoticed, it probably contributed to a delicacy of eyesight that still troubles her. All the children used to improvise, and from seven years old there hardly ever was a time when May and her elder sister had not a story, written on their copybook paper, stuffed into their pockets to read to each other at night. The girls did not go to school, but were educated by foreign governesses, and Miss Crommelin has not forgotten the miseries she and her sister went through under the tuition of one whom she calls "that charming fiend," and there is somewhat of indignation in her gentle voice as she recalls her experiences.

"I believe," she says, "that one's character is greatly influenced for life by the events of one's childhood. Mine was. A boy may be made or marred at his public school, a girl likewise looks back to her governess as the mistress of her mind and manners. We had one for three or four years who was so plausible that I am not surprised in later years, our mother used to say with regretful bewilderment she could not understand how it was that she never knew our sufferings. Ulster was gay in those days, and our parents were often absent on visits of a week or so, all through the winter. Our mother was highly accomplished, and we were always anxious to be praised by her for progress in the schoolroom. Our tormentor devised a punishment for us when she was offended (and she seemed to hate us because we were children) of not correcting our lessons. For weeks we blundered at the piano or brought her our French exercises—returned with a sneer—while swallowing our indignant tears, knowing well how our dulness and inattention would be complained of on our parents' return. She poisoned our innocent pleasures, and I can still remember how our hearts stood still at that catlike footstep, but," Miss Crommelin adds, with a laugh, " I put her into one of my books, 'My Love, she's but a Lassie,' under the guise of a cruel stepmother !" A curious incident happened to this smiling hypocrite. The servants execrated her, and one day in the nursery, when the poor little girls had whispered some new woe into the ears of two or three of the warm-hearted maids, one of them exclaimed, slowly and solemnly, the while pointing out of the window to the enemy standing below : " Madam Mosel, I wish you an illness that may lay you on your back for months!" Soon afterwards the malediction was fulfilled. The governess became ailing, took to the sofa for weeks, and was obliged to leave. Both servants and children were much awed, and quite convinced that it was a "judgment."

Next came a kindly German, who found the children

eager to be taught, and she was not loath to gratify them, but rather beyond their expectations. "I remember," says Miss Crommelin, "after a long morning and afternoon's spell of lessons, her idea of a winter evening's recreation was for my sister and self to read aloud 'Schiller's Thirty Years' War.' Meanwhile, the wind would be howling 'in turret and tree,' making such goblin music as I have never heard elsewhere. We were happy for two years under this good woman."

When about sixteen years of age, May and her sister began secretly to contribute to a paper which kindly offered to print beginners' tales on payment of half-a-crown. Alas! that bubble burst, as many a youthful writer has found out for herself.

Reared in the very heart of the country, and growing up with little or no society of other young people, the children were warmly attached to each other. May Crommelin describes her elder sister as clever, ardent, with flashes of genius; but never, unfortunately, finishing any tales, and exercising much of the same sort of influence over her as Emily Brontë over her sister Charlotte. By and by, when schoolroom days ended, came the usual gaieties of a young girl introduced into Irish county society, much livelier then than during later years. There were the usual three-days' visits to the country houses of Down and Antrim through the autumn, when pheasants were to be shot; or merry house-parties met by day at hunt races and steeplechases, and filled roomy carriages at night to drive courageously many miles to a ball. The canny northern farmers allowed no foxes to be reared, but still there was a good deal of sport to be had with the

little pack of Ards harriers, of which Mr. Crommelin
was master, and the long, cold springs were sometimes
broken by a season or two in Dublin.

Her first introduction to county society inspired
May Crommelin to write "Queenie." She did this
secretly, and about that time she went over to England
on a visit to a kind uncle and aunt, to whom she was
much attached. Alone with them, she confided the
secret of her literary venture, and coaxed her uncle to
take her MSS. to a publisher whose name caught her
eye. This he did, but declined to give the name of the
young author. She waited in breathless expectation,
and "thought it strange that a whole week elapsed
before their reply came." It arrived on a Sunday
morning—unluckily—because it was a good and wise
custom of the house, that no business letters should
be opened on that day. It was accordingly placed
in a locked cabinet with glass doors, where she
could at least gratify herself by looking at the
address, and never was a letter more tantalizing.
The next morning, however, her hopes were rewarded by the joyful news of the publishers' ac-
ceptance, with a substantial sum of money down
and a promise of so much more if the edition
sold out, which it did. On returning home she in
great trepidation told her father. He was somewhat
of a disciplinarian, and had rigid ideas on feminine
dependence and subordination, and though he did not
actually forbid her writing, he never encouraged it.
Thenceforth she wrote steadily in her own room,
sending her MSS. to the same publishers, who had
promised to take all the future works she would send

them, whilst another offered to reprint in the same way cheaper editions.

"Black Abbey" also followed; but shortly before Miss Crommelin wrote "A Jewel of a Girl," which was the result of a visit to Holland, the head of the Crommelin family settled there wrote and asked his distant kinsman to renew the acquaintance dropped for so many years. This laid the foundation of future friendship and other mutual visits, though such little breaks were few and far between, from the island bounded by "the melancholy ocean."

As yet May Crommelin's longings from childhood had been unfulfilled. She desired to travel, to see new scenes, to become acquainted with literary-helpers, critics, or advisers. Of these she knew not one, excepting that Lord Dufferin, on his rare visits at Clandeboye, had always a cheering word of encouragement for his young neighbour. The late Amelia B. Edwards, too, a friend of some relatives in England, sent her some letters of most gratefully received advice, and the Rev. Dr. Allon, editor of the *British Quarterly Review*, having once, by chance, met the young writer for two hours when he was on a visit to Ireland, became an occasional kind correspondent and a lasting friend. Others there were none during these years.

But dark days were coming. What seemed apparently trifling accidents, through horses, led to bad results. First of all, Mr. Crommelin had a fall when out hunting, the effects of which prevented his following for ever after his favourite sports, and his health declined. Then a carriage accident was the

beginning of his wife's later always increasing illness.
Their eldest daughter had not been strong, when she,
too, met with a mischance. Her horse ran away with
her, and she experienced a shock from which she never
wholly recovered. The Irish land troubles had begun;
no rents were to be expected for two years; servants
and horses had to be reduced. So, like other neighbours, they resolved to be absentees for a while in a
milder climate, rather than endure the loneliness of
the country, far from town or doctors, and they removed to Devonshire for two years, during which time
May's eldest sister died after a summer at Dartmoor.

Meantime the young author was not idle. She
wrote "Miss Daisy Dimity," "In the West Countree,"
and "Joy." These two last are both full of lovely
descriptions of moorland scenery and air, and heather
scent. Then Mrs. Crommelin became rapidly worse.
She could not bear the journey to Ireland, so they
moved to Clifton, where, after a long period of suffering, she passed away, followed a year later by her
husband. These years of hopeless illness were a
terrible strain on the family; nevertheless, during the
intervals of watching and nursing, Miss Crommelin
wrote "Brown Eyes," a remembrance of Holland,
which little work was an immense favourite; also a
sketch called "A Visit to a Dutch Country House,"
and this was translated into several Dutch papers.
Then came "Goblin Gold" in one volume, and "Love,
the Pilgrim," begun before her father's death, and
finished under the difficulties of temporary homeless-
ness. Left thus free to choose an abode on her
brother's returning to take possession of his Irish

home, May Crommelin at once resolved to come to London, and established herself in her present home in the cosy little flat. She describes this as " by far the happiest period of her life." Surrounded by the literary and artistic society she had always wished for, a favourite with all, enjoying also the companionship of a sister, and having opportunities for travelling when it suits her, she declares herself quite contented.

Since coming to London she has written a charming and spirited novel, " Violet Vivian, M.F.H.," of which she supplied the leading idea of the tale and two-thirds of the story, the more sporting part excepted; also " The Freaks of Lady Fortune." " Dead Men's Dollars " is the strange but true story of a wreck on the coast opposite her old home. Next came " Cross Roads," and " Midge," considered by many as her best book. Later " Mr. and Mrs. Herries," a sweet and pathetic story, and lastly " For the Sake of the Family." To the readers of May Crommelin's novels it is quite apparent that the idea of Duty is the keynote. Whilst all her works are remarkable for their refinement and purity of thought and style, she almost unconsciously makes her heroes and heroines (though they are no namby-pamby creations) struggle through life doing the duty nearest to hand, however disagreeable the consequences or doubtful the reward. She holds Thoreau's maxim that to *be* good is better than to try and *do* good; indeed, the first and greater proposition includes the latter, and from her youth up she has loved and taken for her motto the lines of Tennyson :—

> " And because right is right, to follow right
> Were wisdom in the scorn of consequence."

MRS HOUSTOUN

MRS. HOUSTOUN.

ONE particular Monday, near Christmas, will long be remembered as being perhaps the most terrible day hitherto experienced in an abnormally severe winter. The heavy pall of dense fog which has settled over London has disorganized the traffic and caused innumerable accidents. Great banks of snow are piled up high at the sides of the roads, a partial thaw has been succeeded by a renewed severe frost, making the pavements like ice, and causing locomotion to become as dangerous as it is detestable. Arriving at Victoria District Station early in the afternoon, with the intention of paying a visit to the veteran novelist, Mrs. Houston, in Gloucester Street, you find yourself in Cimmerian darkness, uncertain whether to turn to north or south, to east or west. A small boy passes by, from whom you inquire the way, and he promptly offers his escort thither in safety. He is as good as his word, and after a quarter of an hour's walk you arrive at your destination. Thankfully presenting him with a gratuity, and expressing surprise at his finding the road with such unerring footsteps, the

[1] Since the serial publication of these sketches, the death of the venerable writer has taken place.

child replies in a cheerful voice, "I live close by here. I have been blind from my birth; darkness and light are both alike to me"; and he goes off whistling merrily.

The septuagenarian author is upstairs in the drawing-room, lying on a long, low, comfortable spring couch, from which, alas! she is unable to move, some affection of the muscles having caused a complete uselessness of the lower limbs. She is bright and cheerful, notwithstanding; serene and patient. Her intellect is undimmed, her memory is perfect, her conversation is delightful, and her dress is suitable and picturesque. She wears a black velvet gown, which is relieved by a full frill of old lace gathered up round the wrists and throat, a crimson silk shawl on her shoulders, and a lace cap with a roll round it of the same coloured ribbon. Her hair, for which she was famous in her childhood, is still soft and abundant, and only changed from "the great ruddy mane of her youth," as she calls it, to the subdued brown and grey tints of her present age. Her eyes, of grey-blue, are bright, and light up with keen intelligence as she converses, and her voice is low and sweet. She is *grande dame* to the tips of her fingers, and the small, aristocratic-looking hands are white and well-shaped. With an old-world courtesy of manner she combines a juvenility of thought, and being a great reader, she is as well up in the literature of the day as she is in the records of the past. A brilliant *raconteuse*, Mrs. Houston possesses a fund of anecdote, as original as it is interesting.

On each side of her couch stands within her easy

reach a little table, containing her favourite authors and some writing materials, and her caligraphy is particularly neat, small, and legible. A broad verandah runs along the front of the house; in summer it is her particular care, as she superintends the training of the creepers over the wide arches, and also the arrangement of a small conservatory, which can be seen through the heavy Oriental *portières* which divide the two rooms. There, a fine plumbago creeper, with several Australian plants and ferns flourish, which give it quite a tropical appearance.

There is a great variety of old Dresden china on the mantelpieces; a Japanese screen stands near the further door. The book-cases in both rooms are well filled, and so is the large round table at the side yonder; they are kept in such method and order that Mrs. Houstoun has only to order "the eighth book on the top of the shelf at the right," or "the tenth book on the lower shelf at the left," to ensure her getting the needed volume. She calls attention to her pictures, which are mostly of considerable value. Over the piano hangs, in a Florentine frame, Sasso's copy of the Madonna del Grand Duca, a painting by Schlinglandt, which is remarkable for its extraordinary attention to detail, and others by Vander Menlen and Zucarilli. A vacant space on the wall has lately been occupied by one of Bonnington's best seascapes, which she has kindly lent for exhibition.

Mrs. Houstoun is the daughter of the late Edward Jessé, the distinguished naturalist. The family is of French extraction. He was the representative of a

P

younger and Protestant branch of the *Barons of Jesse Levas,* one of the oldest families in Languedoc, who emigrated after the revocation of the Edict of Nantes to England, and bought an estate in the county of Wilts, but when they became English country gentlemen they dropped, like sensible people, not only the distinctive *de,* but the accent on the final *e,* which marked their Gallic origin. Her grandfather was the Rev. William Jesse, incumbent of the then only Episcopalian church of West Bromwich, Staffordshire. " I have no very distinct personal recollection of him," she observes, "but I have reason to believe that his value, both as a good man and a learned divine, was duly recognized. Bishop Horne, author of ' Commentaries on the Psalms,' was at one time his curate." In 1802, Mr. Jesse (then twenty years of age) was chosen by Lord Dartmouth to be his private secretary, and four years later, through his influential chief, he obtained an appointment in the Royal Household. The duties which his post as " Gentleman of the Ewry " entailed were of the slightest, consisting merely of an attendance in full Court dress on great State occasions, to present on bended knee a golden ewer filled with rose-water to the Sovereign. The royal fingers were dipped into it and dried on a fine damask napkin, which the " gentleman " carried on his arm. For this occasional service the yearly pay was three hundred pounds, together with " perquisites " ; but though the absurd and useless office was long since done away with, whilst it existed its influence over Mr. Jesse's prospects in life was very considerable, as it enabled him to marry the beautiful daughter of Sir

John Morris, a wealthy Welsh baronet. Mrs. Houstoun's childish days were spent first at a house in the prettiest quarter of Richmond Park, and later on at a cottage close to Bushey Park. "Those were the days before the then Duke of Clarence became king, and the Sailor-Prince showed himself to be one of the most good-natured of men," says Mrs. Houstoun. "He often joined my father and me in our rides about the Park, and on one occasion he inquired of my father concerning the future of his only son."

"What are you going to do with him?" asked H.R.H.

"Well, sir," was the reply, "he has been ten years at Eton, a rather expensive education, so I entered him yesterday at Brazenose——"

"Going to make a parson of him, eh? Got any interest in the Church?"

"None whatever, sir, but——"

"Might as well cut his throat," said the Duke. "Why not put him into the Admiralty? I'll see he gets a clerkship."

The royal promise was faithfully kept. Young John Heneage Jesse got his appointment almost immediately, and worked his way up the different grades, always standing high in the opinion of his chiefs, until after a long period of service, he finally retired on a pension, and is well known in the literary world as the author of "The Court of England under the Stuarts and Houses of Hanover," and sundry historical memoirs.

Reverting to these long bygone days, your hostess says she can remember the famous philanthropist,

William Wilberforce, in whose unflagging efforts to
effect the freedom of the West Indian negroes, her
aunt, Mrs. Townsend, was so zealous and able a
coadjutrix ; she recollects to this day the childish
grudge she felt against them both, when after the
visit of the great emancipator all cakes and puddings
were strictly *tabooed*, as they contained West India
sugar, and therefore to eat them was a sin. Living
close to the home of her father's old friend, John
Wilson Croker, she became acquainted with many
world-famed and literary men ; amongst them she
mentions Theodore Hook, Sir William Follett, the
poet Moore, Sir Francis Chantrey, and Sir Thomas
Lawrence, subsequently Samuel Rogers, Mr. Darwin,
Wordsworth, the gifted Mrs. Norton, and James
Smith, the most popular and brilliant of the authors
of " Rejected Addresses."

At the early age of sixteen she became engaged, and
shortly after married Lionel Fraser, whose father died
when he was Minister Plenipotentiary at Dresden,
but in less than a year she became a widow. Mr.
Fraser, just before leaving Cambridge, had met with
an accident. In a trial of strength, an under-graduate
threw him over his shoulder : the lad fell on his head,
and was taken up for dead, but after a while recovered,
and was to all appearance the same as before ; but the
hidden evil had been slowly though surely working,
and the rupture of a small vessel in the brain brought
to a sudden close the young life of so much promise.
Inconsolable, the young widow returned to her
father's house, where she lived in close seclusion for
nearly four years, and then became engaged to Captain

Houstoun, of the 10th Hussars, second son of General Sir William Houstoun, Bart. His son George, who succeeded him, added the name of Boswall on marrying an heiress. *A propos* of that engagement, Mrs. Houstoun has an amusing story to tell. "Another of the friends," she says, "to whom we were indebted for many pleasant hours, was that courtly Hanoverian soldier Baron Knesbeck, equerry to the Duke of Cambridge. We were riding on Wimbledon Common, and I was mounted on the second charger of my betrothed, when the old Duke, on his stout bay, joined our party; my engagement had not at that time been announced, and I therefore parried, as best I could, the Duke's questions as to the horse and its owner. At last, however, the climax came, for with a wink of his eye, more suggestive than regal, His Royal Highness put the following leading question as we rode slowly on: 'Sweetheart, hey?' There was no resisting this point-blank query, and the soft impeachment had to be owned at last."

After her second marriage Mrs. Houstoun and her husband lived for a year in their yacht "Dolphin," during which time they visited Texas and the Gulf of Mexico. Later on they spent two winters at New Orleans before slavery was abolished. Then came a tour on the Continent, where they travelled from Paris to Naples in their own britska, taking four horses and two English postillions. When they stayed for any length of time at any place, the horses were saddled, and they would ride forty or fifty miles a day, revolvers in saddle pockets, into the wildest parts of the country. After a roving and adventurous time, escaping hairbreadth dangers, for Mrs. Houstoun says her husband was "as bold as a buccaneer," they returned home, where Captain Houstoun, after trying various places, finally took on a long lease Dhulough Lodge, about one hundred square miles of ground in the west of Ireland, and there for twenty years she found her lot cast. In sheer weariness of spirit she took to her pen. As a girl she had always been accustomed to correct her father's proofs, and had written some short stories and poems, but she then wrote her first novel, "Recommended to Mercy." It was so well reviewed in the *Times* that, encouraged by her success, Mrs. Houstoun followed it with "Sink or Swim," "Taken upon Trust," "First in the Field," "A Cruel Wrong," "Records of a Stormy Life," and "Zoe's Brand," which last book M. Boisse, editor of the *Revue Contemporaine*, asked permission to translate into French, but by some omission his application was never answered, and the project fell through. Some time later she wrote "Twenty Years in the Wild West" and several other novels, and she has lately finished a new story in two volumes, entitled "How She Loved Him," published by Mr. F. V. White, of whom she remarks with warmth, "He stands high amongst the publishers I have known for liberality and honour, and is one of my best and kindest friends."

"Amongst other books," says Mrs. Houstoun, "I look back with thankfulness to my novelette, entitled 'Only a Woman's Life,' the writing of which was successful in obtaining the release, after twelve years of convict life, of an innocent woman, who had been originally condemned to death on circumstantial evidence for the murder of her child. Of the death sentence I was so happy, at the eleventh hour, as to obtain a commutation."

But it is difficult to get the lonely old lady to talk much of her books, and though her memory is perfect in everything else, both past and present, she declares that she has forgotten even the names of some of her own works. She infinitely prefers to speak about those of her friends. She is devoted to Whittier's poems, and to Pope, and can quote passages at great length from this great favourite; whilst among modern novelists she prefers Mrs. Riddell and the late George Lawrence, though she says, laughing, she fears that this last shows a somewhat Bohemian taste.

"I am sure I was born to be a landscape gardener," remarks Mrs. Houstoun. "That was my real vocation in life. If you had but seen our home amongst the Connaught Mountains when I first saw it! The ' wild bog,' as the natives call the soil, reached to my very doors and windows. A wilderness of moist earth-bog' myrtle and stunted heather alone met the eye, very discouraging to such a lover of dainty well-kept gardens and flowers as I am. Towering above and beyond our roughly-built house was a mountain called Glenumra, over 3,000 feet in height, whilst in front was Muelhrae, or King of the Irish Mountains (as it is the loftiest), and a part of it effectually concealed from us all the glories of the setting sun. The humid nature of the soil was favourable to the growth of plants. I designed and laid out large gardens, and had only to insert a few feet or inches, as the case might be, of laurel, fuchsia, veronica, or hydrangia into the ground, and the slips took root, grew and flourished. Long before we left there were fuchsias thirty feet high; the veronicas, over six feet, blossomed in November. Then I built a stove-house and conservatory, where my exotic fernery was my great delight, and I spent much of my time there. All the money I earned by my writings I spent on my ferns and plants."

But the damp of the climate, the constant sitting up at night with their poor sick dependents, at whose beck and call she was ever ready, and the impossibility of procuring any medical attendance, laid the seeds of a severe neuralgic affection of the joints, from which she has never recovered, and a terrible fall resulted in a hopeless injury to both knees. She says that during her twenty years' residence in that distressful country she never knew the blessing of really good health.

Mrs. Houstoun is extremely hospitable and sociable in disposition. One of her chief regrets in being so completely laid by is that she is no longer able to give the pleasant little weekly dinners of eight in which she used to delight. She enjoys nothing more than visits from her friends, who are always glad to come in and sit with her and listen to her amusing and interesting conversation. She is a great politician and an extreme Liberal, "though," she adds, "not a Gladstonian." At the present moment she is deeply absorbed in the Stanley controversy, and, as she is a cousin of the late Major Barttelot, and was much attached to him, she naturally remarks that she "never knew anything but good of him."

But though this venerable lady is unable to entertain her friends in her former manner, she does not forget the poor and suffering. She gives little teas and suppers to aged men and women, whose sad cases have from time to time been recommended to her, at which charitable gatherings, with doors rigidly shut to exclude the smell of the poor old men's tobacco smoke, she allows them to indulge in the luxury of a pipe.

Though enduring constant pain and many long sleepless nights, she avows that she is never dull or miserable. No word of complaint or murmur passes her lips at her crippled condition. On the contrary, she expresses the deepest content and thankfulness for her many comforts and blessings, amongst which, she remarks, are her three maids, all sisters, who are as devoted to her as if they had been born in her service. They carry her up and down stairs, and wait on her, hand and foot, with tender care. "And only think," she concludes cheerfully and with a smile, "what a mercy it is that I retain my memory so well, and that my mind is so clear, whilst I lie here useless!" "Nay, not useless," is your reply, as you rise to leave, "they also serve who only stand and wait."

MRS. ALEXANDER FRASER.

A RAPID run of about an hour and a half in duration from Victoria, with just a change of carriages at Three Bridges, but no delay, and you are set down one bright, fresh morning at the pretty and picturesque station of Faygate, Sussex, which presents a curiously countrified and even primitive aspect, considering the many large properties and cottages that lie in its close vicinity. A well turned-out little carriage and pair of handsome, high-stepping chestnuts has been sent to convey you to Carylls, the lovely home of Mrs. Alexander Fraser of Durris.

The whole place is bathed in sunshine, and the air, though somewhat frosty, is wonderfully exhilarating, as you are carried swiftly along a good winding road, with trees on either side, the branches meeting overhead. Here and there, as the horses go more slowly up a gentle acclivity, you turn round to reconnoitre a little, and find that there is a charming view behind. On the left, Leith Hill, with a tower crowning it, rises up in purple tints against the horizon. On the right lies a lovely view of undulating country, broad green fields, trim hedges, brown brakes and hollows, with a background of luxuriant wood. After a short drive,

MRS ALEXANDER FRASER

the carriage turns into a gate flanked by two high turreted walls, and a neat little lodge with diamond-paned windows, peeping out of a mass of ivy, stands just within. Leaving it on the left, you go up a wide gravelled drive through an avenue of poplars; the lawns, which are undulating, and cover about three acres of ground, are laid out with low terraced walls, over which in summer time the roses trail in rich pro-fusion, and edged with a row of weeping ash and elm trees, they lie on both sides right up to the entrance of a big red brick house, lavishly covered with ivy, wisteria, and roses, with quaint gables and many-shaped chimneys, which is altogether most picturesque. A large conservatory unites the right and left wings, and once within this conservatory it is difficult to realize that it is still winter. Heated to a pleasant temperature, full of bright and rare bloom, the gentle breath of sweet-scented gardenias and tuberoses per-vading the atmosphere, cages of many-coloured foreign birds, a gleam of Moorish lamps against the greenery overhead, comfortable lounges, wickerwork tables, Turkish rugs strewn on the tesselated floor—all com-bine to make it a delightful place in which to while away the time, with book or work, in friendly con-verse, or perhaps in solitary day dreaming.

At the present moment it is passed in friendly converse. Mrs. Alexander Fraser has received you with much cordiality, and whilst lingering amongst the flowers and the ferns, the talk drifts away to India, America, and the Continent of Europe, where she tells you the earlier part of her life was spent, and that for many years past her home has been at

Carylls. She is fair and rather pale, her eyes are brown, and have a slight droop of the lids, which gives them a soft expression. The profile is just a trifle aquiline, is delicate in form, and the mouth and chin are well cut. Her hair—a little lighter in colour than the eyes, is worn in a loose, curly roll over her brow, and a thick coil on the nape of her neck. She is attired in a most becoming and well-fitting gown of black velvet and grey fur, and her manner is frank and informal.

Carylls is a very old place; a part of it, indeed, was built in 1640, but so well have all the additions and improvements of later years been carried out that the two form a truly artistic whole. Originally belonging to the well-known Roman Catholic family of Caryll, it is mentioned in Pope's poems, several of which he wrote under the old oak trees, and it is considered quite one of the show-places of this part of Sussex. Mrs. Fraser says that it suits her in every way. The air is splendid, the society is good, and she is not far enough away from town to feel out of the world. The conservatory glass door opens into a very large and lofty drawing-room with oak ceilings and great bay windows. It looks more like a foreign than an English room. An immense Indian carpet is spread over the floor, the sea-green walls are hung with many mirrors in black and gold frames, several lovely old cabinets, and plenty of Dresden, Sèvres, Chelsea, and Capo de Monti, are to be seen everywhere. Two superb silver *repoussé*-work Lucknow bowls are especially attractive; one, containing a many-leafed palm, stands on the grand piano, and in its fellow

is a large fern, the delicate fronds drooping over a
beautiful alabaster "Magdalen" close by.

"I admire these more than anything else in the
room," says Mrs. Fraser, pointing to some photographs
on an inlaid iron table. "These two are my sons,
both of them very good-looking, as you see," she
continues, smiling with very pardonable pride as
she places the pictures in your hand. And truly
she has a good right to feel proud of these handsome, noble-looking young men, one of whom is in
the uniform of the Gordon Highlanders. Here, too,
is a portrait of the Prince of Wales, with his autograph below, presented by his Royal Highness to
General Fraser, which is a much-valued gift, and
the others are pictures of different Indian viceroys
and their wives, all given by themselves, Lord and
Lady Dufferin, Lord and Lady Lytton, the latter in a
frame designed by himself, which is quite a work
of art, with a coronet in blue-and-white enamel.
An hour is passed very pleasantly amongst the many
curiosities which Mrs. Fraser has brought chiefly
from foreign lands. The room is, in fact, quite a
small museum. Going back through the conservatory into the other wing of the house, an open
door gives a peep of the dining-room in passing.
It is a good-sized room, with oak ceiling, crimson
walls, and a quantity of carved oak furniture.

But Mrs. Fraser's own particular favourite is just
beyond—she calls it her tea-room, not her study.
"Not very large," she says, "but always bright
and cheerful, and the view is so lovely from this
window. That wood was gorgeous in its autumnal

tints, and on a very clear morning Leith Hill looks as if it were close to us. My rose garden is just to the right here. I wish it was summer, that you might see it in all its glory." And the view is lovely now, as the sun peeps in and out amongst the great trees, which stand in clumps, with rustic seats beneath them.

After admiring it for a while, you turn round to have a survey of the room, and certainly endorse Mrs. Fraser's opinion. It has an oak ceiling, like the other reception rooms, and pale-green walls, that show off to advantage a number of oil paintings framed in dark crimson velvet and gold. Two are especially fine, "The Golden Horn," and "Morning on the Dutch Rivers," by an artist of some note, Fryar; and you fall in love with two exquisite little bits of Brittany, by Gregory. A large mirror in an elaborately carved frame surmounts the mantel-piece, which is laden with Satsuma ware and other Japanese, Chinese, and Indian curios. An old French marqueterie cabinet full of books stand in a recess *vis-à-vis* to a handsomely inlaid writing bureau with a silver basket of hothouse flowers on it.

Mrs. Fraser here calls attention to a number of silver vases, loving cups, hunting flasks, gongs, etc., all of which are prizes won by her sons' ponies and fox-terriers. These lie so perilously near the window as to suggest a remark to the effect that they might be stolen, but Mrs. Fraser declares that the people are wonderfully honest down in these parts of the country, and that no burglary has been heard of for thirty years or more.

Later on, whilst being regaled with all sorts of cakes and hothouse grapes, the conversation turns on literary matters. " I have no particular writing-room," says your hostess, " I generally write in the evening after dinner, with my people chattering all the time, but I am too much accustomed to that to be disturbed by it. My first essays in fiction were magazine stories. I suppose I have written over four-score of these, and they always seemed to find a good deal of favour with the leading provincial journals. I sold a story called ' Manœuvring ' for a very nice little sum to a French editor for translation into *L'Etoile*, and I was very much pleased when I got a requisition for a tale from the *Lady's Magazine* in Philadelphia, but of later years I have written about five-and-twenty three-volume novels. The first of these was called ' Faithless.' The next two : ' Denison's Wife,' and ' Not While She Lives.' After that ' Her Plighted Troth,' ' A Maddening Blow,' ' A Thing of Beauty,' and ' A Fatal Passion ' came out. These are names which recur to me at the moment out of all that I have written. I like the last best, and next to it ' A Leader of Society,' and ' The Match of the Season,' perhaps because I took the heroes and heroines from real life. More recently Mr. F. V. White has brought out my books, and they have all more or less been excellently noticed, especially ' Daughters of Belgravia,' ' The Last Drawing Room,' and ' The New Duchess,' all of which have gone into two or three editions. Occasionally I send a piece of poetry to the magazines, and it generally gets a little *kudos* from the Press, and some little time ago

I wrote a sacred song called 'Calvary's Cross,' which gained much popularity; a copy of it was very graciously accepted by the Queen." The latest of all is "A Modern Bridegroom."

Mrs. Fraser observes that she has often been asked what is her "method" in writing, and that on one occasion she received a letter from a clergyman in Nottingham, begging her to "describe it exactly." "I laughed when the letter came," she continues, "and I am ashamed to say I never answered it, because I have no method. I simply write straight on, and never copy my MSS., and pity the poor printers who have to decipher my hieroglyphics. I am very fond of recitations, too, and some years ago I studied elocution under Mrs. Stirling. Once, in her unavoidable absence, I recited two of her pieces before a large audience in St. George's Hall. I felt horribly nervous, but I suppose I did the "pathos" pretty well, for I noticed a good many people crying, and was much pleased to see them do so! I have recited several times in America also, but now I never exert myself beyond writing a novel or a short story just when I feel inclined for it."

After tea Mrs. Fraser proposes a stroll through the grounds. "It is very cold, but dry," she says, "so we might venture; but first come into the billiard-room, which is our usual postprandial resort." Passing through the hall and another conservatory, with vines thickly intersecting overhead, and full of splendid specimens of maidenhair ferns, with the vivid scarlet of geraniums between them, she takes you into a large and lofty room, panelled in oak. At the further end a flight of oaken steps leads up to a sort of daïs, from which the game can be well surveyed. The furniture is all of carved oak and crimson velvet, with the exception of two great easy chairs, whose backs and arms and legs are composed of buffalo horns, beautifully polished and mounted. These were sent to her from Russia, and are the admiration of the neighbourhood.

All round the walls hang pictures of the celebrated American trotting horses, whose performances in Central Park, New York, were a daily delight to Mrs. Fraser. A tall bookcase, carved quaintly, stands in a recess, but she tells you not to expect to see any of her own novels in it, as she invariably gives them all away, except one copy of each, which her mother, who lives with her, always confiscates, and values as her dearest possessions. This lady must have been one of the loveliest of women in her youth, and she is still wonderfully handsome and young-looking.

Mrs. Alexander Fraser comes of a good old stock. Her grandmother was a sister of Sir Wolstan Dixie, descended from the Sir Wolstan Dixie who settled at Bosworth, Leicestershire, in the time of Queen Elizabeth. On her mother's side she is related to the ancient house of Dunboyne, dating as far back as Sir Thomas Butler, or Le Botelier, in the reign of Edward II.; and she is a connection of William Makepeace Thackeray. Of this she declares herself to be "most proud," and adds :—"I consider his 'Becky Sharp' is one of the most able studies of character that was ever written. How much I should delight in his

Q

power of reading character, though perhaps he took somewhat too caustic a view of it occasionally!"

A stand close by contains the whole set of Mrs. Lovett Cameron's novels—"I enjoy her writing so much," says your hostess. "When I was younger I was *fanatica* on Ouida; but though I still admire her marvellous command of language, especially in description of scenery, I have grown too sober and prosaic and practical in my ideas and views of life to appreciate her works as I used to do."

Losing her father at a very early age, when only fifteen, Mrs. Fraser went to India, after spending two years at a school in Paris, and at the age of sixteen she married Captain, now General Alexander Fraser, C.B., sometime Member of Council, for many years Secretary to the Government of India, and only surviving brother of the late Bishop of Manchester. She describes her life in India in glowing colours. "I liked India immensely," she remarks. "Most women do, I fancy. They are so hospitable out there, and there is so much fun and 'go' in the society. Besides," she adds, laughing, "one has so much attention that one feels in a delightfully chronic state of self-complacency!"

A door at the further end leads through the fernery to the western side of Carylls, which is perhaps the prettiest part of the place. It is curiously decorated with Sussex tiles, and has an ivy-clad gable and long window in stained cathedral glass. Turning to the right, your hostess takes you round a tastefully-laid-out rosery, at the extremity of which is a glasshouse over a hundred feet in length, which is full of peach, apricot, nectarine, and other big trees. Emerging at the other door, you find yourself in a great double garden with an archway between, and the whole is enclosed within high walls covered with fruit-trees. Here are vineries and hot-houses, all in most exquisite order, for this is Mrs. Fraser's particular hobby. The day is so clear that the view all around is seen to perfection, extending to the Surrey Hills, and dotted here and there with a few white houses shown up against the dark green of the masses of firs which seem to abound in these parts. Expressing a wish to see the stables, Mrs. Fraser leads the way thither through the court-yard. Four good-looking horses stand in the stalls, and as she opens a small square window near, the black velvety muzzle of the sweetest little pony rubs against her shoulder, whilst he eagerly devours the carrot she has brought for him. "I drive this little fellow myself," she says. "I had a pair of them, 'Blink' and 'Wink,' but poor 'Wink' has gone over to the majority, I grieve to say."

A little further on are some picturesque kennels, and the inmates greet their mistress vociferously. These are the fox-terriers who won the prizes in the drawing-room. They are animals of long pedigree and long price, and are pretty well known at all the shows in England. "They are not only ornamental but useful," says your hostess. "Some are loose at night, and I pity the individual who approaches them."

Whilst leisurely rambling here and there, you stroll up to some broad stone steps (overshadowed by oaks, and with pillars on either side surmounted by large vases of flowering berberis) that lead past an upper lawn enclosed by a shrubbery, in which syringas and *Gloire de Dijon* roses hold prominent places. "These two tennis courts are in constant use in summer time," observes Mrs. Fraser, "but I really am a bit of a recluse, eschewing society as much as possible, though I thoroughly enjoy a quiet tea with my favourite neighbours. When I lived in town," she adds, "I had a charming house in Clarges-street, and used to like my Wednesday afternoons, when a number of diplomats generally looked in, and there used to be a Babel of languages going on, but long residence in the country makes one grow daily more of a stay-at-home, and I have so much to do that I never find the day too long."

Close by on the lawn lies a carefully-kept grassy mound. This is the grave of three favourite dogs, and a much deplored grey parrot. One of these dogs was a Schipperke, the breed kept by the bargemen of Belgium to guard their goods and chattels. "He was a real beauty," says your hostess, sadly, "and he travelled with me all over the Continent, then across the Atlantic, and back again. I think one really grows to care for a dog or a horse as much as for a human creature, and this pet was almost human in his intelligence."

Mrs. Alexander Fraser is warmly attached to her beautiful home, and takes the keenest interest in the improvements. She brought the design of the low double walls from the Park at Brussels, and herself superintended their building, as also the re-arrangement of the lawns. She rarely goes to town, and then only on a flying visit just to see her lawyers, or her publishers, "all the while longing to get home again," she says. She promises herself, however, to go up to stay with some friends in the season, in order to do the opera and theatres, confessing that she dearly loves a good drama. "Something that makes me weep copiously," she adds, laughing. "I dislike comic pieces."

After a stroll round the lawns to watch the glories of the setting sun, you return towards the house, passing by a piece of water enclosed by low walls, fringed all round with large weeping willows, and enter through a heated conservatory on the eastern side, not yet visited. Here is a wealth of tea roses in every shade of colour. Mrs. Fraser ungrudgingly cuts a handful of the choicest buds, and gives them to you, a welcome present indeed at this season. "Flowers," she says, "are a passion with me. I like to have them everywhere, and always have a big bunch on my table when I write." The eastern side door leads into a little room containing many Oriental treasures, notably a carved screen of sweet-smelling sandal-wood, a curious "neckbreaker" used by Indian dacoits, and some rare ivory and enamels. Conspicuous among them there stands a small inlaid table, and on it lies an evidently cherished volume, "The Life of Bishop Fraser," together with a photograph of him, in a costly frame. "He was my best friend," says Mrs. Alexander Fraser, in a low tone and with much pathos; "and my *beau idéal* of a man both personally and mentally. I felt his loss from my heart, and I am sure that thousands have done the same."

But the carriage is announced, and Mrs. Alexander

Fraser gives a whispered order to the butler, which results in a basket of large, purple hothouse grapes being brought, "to cheer you on your way back," she says. During the drive to the station she hospitably invites you to "come again when the strawberries are ripe and the roses are in bloom."

THE HON. MRS HENRY CHETWYND

THE HON. MRS. HENRY CHETWYND.

THERE is an old house in a quiet old-world street leading out of Hans Place, called Walton Place, where the Emperor Napoleon III. used to live after he left King Street, St. James's, and which was the scene of some of his famous political dinner-parties. This house, which is back to back with Jane Austen's home in London, once stood in its own gardens, but the ground was too valuable to spare for the picturesque, and it has long since been turned into a row of neat dwelling-places. Standing well back from the noisy thoroughfare and the incessant roar of traffic in the Brompton Road, there is a sense of peace and quiet about it externally which prepares you to find that within it is a home of talent, of refinement, of domestic harmony and affection.

Whilst ascending the stairs a fresh, sweet soprano voice is heard, giving thrilling expression to Tosti's lovely song, " Love Ties." On being shown into a fair-sized double drawing-room, your first impression leads to the belief that there are some good old bits of carved oak furniture to be studied, but there is more to learn about that presently. Mrs. Chetwynd is busily engaged in finishing a large coverlet of

art needlework, which she puts aside as she rises
to greet you with much grace and cordiality. She
is very fair in complexion, with large blue eyes and
softly shaded eyebrows. The hair, parted smoothly
on a broad forehead, is gathered up at the back, and
brought round the head in a plait, worn in coronet
shape in front. She is dressed in black with a scarf
of old black lace knotted becomingly round her
throat, and a bunch of violets nestles in the folds.
She has an air of high breeding, combined with
an irresistibly sweet and pleasant manner.

The musician is Mrs. Chetwynd's youngest daughter,
and you cannot resist the temptation to beg her to
indulge you with yet another verse of the song. She
good-naturedly complies, rendering the melody with
much skill and pathos. On your thanking and complimenting her, she tells you that she is a pupil of
Madame Bonner, and has never had any other teacher,
and truly she does credit to her instructress.

There is an artistic simplicity about these bright,
cheerful rooms which is very fascinating. The walls
are hung with gold-coloured paper, copied from a
pattern at Hampton Court, and taken from an Italian
palace. Carpets of electric-blue colour cover the floors,
and tapestry curtains of the same shade, with inner
ones of cream-coloured guipure, shade the windows;
close to your hostess's chair there is an enormous
Moorish brass tray mounted on a Moorshebar stand.
This was sent home by a dear absent naval son for
his mother's afternoon tea-service, but as it is so
heavy that it would require two servants to carry
it, Mrs. Chetwynd has turned it into a most appro-

priate work-table. Large plants of the "Sacred Lily
of Japan" are flowering beautifully yonder, a big
Japanese screen stands near the door, armchairs of
every shape and degree of comfort, together with a
broad couch, are placed apparently exactly where
they ought to be; nearly everything else in the
room has a story, and now the secret of the old oak
furniture is learned. You could have declared it
was a production of the seventeenth century. The
material is of cypress wood, and Miss Katherine
Chetwynd is now carving some oak, which was a
gift, and which is old, very old, inasmuch as it was
taken out of the Thames, at Blackwall, and formed
part of the planks and stakes driven in there to
keep out the Spanish Armada.   It is black with
age, but still sound.   It would appear to be a
curious present for three young girls, but Mrs. Chetwynd's daughters have a genius for wood-carving;
collecting old designs, they actually made the fireplace entirely by themselves, with its rich, broad
pattern on each side, the Rose and the Shamrock for
their father, and the Thistle entwined in compliment
to their Scottish mother, and with the help of their
brother they even fitted and placed it without the
aid of a carpenter.   Several tables, too, carved in a
variety of designs, are the manufacture of their
clever fingers, and their talents do not end here,
for on one of these tables you recognize a life-size
portrait, in red crayons, of the fair young musician
herself, executed with masterly and skilful touch by
her elder sister. The painted panels of the outer
and inner doors, as also of those which divide the

rooms, are the work of these young artists, in
thoroughly correct Japanese style, the rising sun, the
storks, and the tall flowers in raised gilt, being all
perfectly orthodox.   This talent is inherited from
their mother, for every picture on the walls is from
her own brush.   On the right hangs her large
painting from Siegert's "Liebesdienst," in the Hamburg Gallery, and she was very proud of obtaining
permission to copy it, as it was then only the second
copy allowed.   On one side of the fireplace there is
her portrait in oils of the beautiful Miss Bosville,
afterwards Lady Macdonald of the Isles, Mrs. Chetwynd's great-grandmother ; on the other "The Holy
Margaret," copied in the Dresden Gallery, a Madonna
after Rotari, and a cherub after Rubens, in all of which
pictures it is easy to see that she excels in flesh tints,
and has a fine eye for colour.

Mrs. Chetwynd is the daughter of the late Mr.
Davidson of Tulloch, by his first wife, the Hon.
Elizabeth Macdonald, one of the lovely daughters of
the late Lord Macdonald of the Isles.   Mr. Davidson
inherited, besides the family place, Tulloch Castle, the
deer forest of Inchbae, and many thousands of acres on
the West Coast, which he sold to Sir John Fowler, Mr.
Banks, and others.   He was first in the Grenadier
Guards, then member for the county, and, finally,
Lord-Lieutenant of Ross-shire.   He was noted for his
handsome person and his great kindness to everyone
around him ; a most popular landlord, he possessed a
great charm of manner, and was much in advance of
his day, especially in the matter of education.   Though
he was the best and kindest of fathers, he was strict in

discipline. His daughters were made to learn Latin and mathematics, and, besides a resident English and foreign governess, the village schoolmaster came to teach them history and geography every evening.

"It was impossible," says Mrs. Chetwynd, "to have had a happier childhood than ours, particularly up to the time of my mother's death. Though I think that education was perhaps a little overdone, we had a great deal of exercise on horseback and on foot to counteract it. We were made to keep very early hours, to be in the schoolroom at six o'clock every morning in summer and seven in winter. The piper's walking up and down playing in front of the old place at eight o'clock was the signal for our breakfast, of which we had great need, having previously studied for two hours. We then worked hard at our books till noon, when my mother always appeared at the schoolroom door with peaches, grapes, or something good in her hand; then we rode for two hours in all weathers, dined at two o'clock, worked till four, out again till six, then tea, preparation, and to bed."

It is probably just the regularity, order, and method of the happy, healthy country life of her girlhood, and the constant out-of-door exercise, which have preserved Mrs. Chetwynd's constitution so excellently, that until four years ago, when she met with a severe accident at Rugby Station—from which she has never quite recovered—she could walk long distances, and go out at night afterwards without feeling any fatigue. "The walks and rides," she continues, "that we were accustomed to take in the elastic Highland air,

sound wonderful to those who have not experienced
the ease with which one can walk there. We, as girls,
would tramp seven miles to a luncheon party, join
in any expedition, and return the whole way on foot
easily. We have often ridden twenty-five miles,
(sending other horses on early, and changing half-
way), gone out with the friends with whom we spent
the afternoon, and ridden home in time to dance at a
gillies' ball."

Another great excitement in their youth was the
acting of French and Italian plays, which were adapted
for their own capacities from *Molière, Goldoni,* etc.,
by the foreign governess, enjoying thoroughly the
applause, the dressing-up and the arranging of the
costumes, which were made in strict keeping. "But
what we did not enjoy," adds your hostess, smiling,
"was the trouble of our long and thick hair, which
as often as not was powdered for these juvenile performances, and I can remember to this day how un-
mercifully our cross French maid used to pull and tug
at it next morning."

The autumn holidays were often spent up at the
West Coast place or on the Continent. The former
was, however, the favourite holiday resort of these
happy, hardy young people, where they boated, fished,
and bathed to their hearts' content, often going off to
one of the many islands on the coast, taking books,
work, and provisions; then, sending away the boat,
they would spend half the bright, warm days swim-
ming about in the sea. When these vacations were
spent abroad the opportunity was seized to give them
the best masters to be found; "and, though we enjoyed

foreign life very much," says Mrs. Chetwynd, "we always felt we were being cheated out of our holidays. In later years my uncle, General Macdonald (known as Jim Macdonald) lived at the Ranger's Lodge in Hyde Park, and going there was always a great pleasure. He was so clever and entertaining, never too busy to enter into anything affecting his family, so overflowing with wit of the best kind, that he made one see the amusing side of the most commonplace things."

The excellent education she received, the beautiful scenery in which she was reared, the clever people (George Eliot among them) with whom she was brought in contact—all conspired to expand the young girl's mind, and to pave the way for her subsequent career as a novelist. She describes their charming supper-parties at St. Andrews, which were constantly joined by such learned men as Principal Tulloch, Professors Aytoun and Ferrier, and Sir David Brewster, who used to talk to her in the most fascinating manner about astronomy and other science, as "being an education in itself." Thackeray, too, gave her the greatest encouragement, and showed her much kindness. But the girlish days were coming to a close. In February, 1858, she married Lieutenant, now Post-Captain, the Hon. Henry Chetwynd, brother of Viscount Chetwynd, by whom she has a family of four sons and three daughters. Her first literary effort was a play, written at the early age of twelve, in which she acted with her brothers and sisters. It was really a wonderful production for so young a child, and a few years later she wrote several society verses, which were printed, and read with much amusement by her father, to whom,

however, she had not the courage to disclose the secret
of their authorship. For some years after her marriage
Captain Chetwynd held some appointments enabling
her to be constantly with him, but when the dreaded
moment for separation came, and he was ordered on
foreign service, first to the West Indies, and then to
Mexico, Mrs. Chetwynd felt the solitude of the long
evenings to be so oppressive after the little ones were
gone to bed, that for distraction she took to her pen
and wrote her first novel, called "Three Hundred A
Year." It had a good sale, though on looking back on
it now the author pronounces it to have been "ex-
cessively silly." Encouraged by this success, she wrote
"Mademoiselle d'Estanville," which was translated into
French, and had a good run. Then came "Janie"
and "Life in a German Village," which passed into
several editions. "Bees and Butterflies" came out
first in the *Pictorial World* before being published in
three volumes. This book the author considers to
have been the most successful, financially, though
"Sara" is her own favourite, and was the result of a
long study. The story is founded on fact, and the
incidents relating to the discovery of South End
smugglers were drawn from the life, Mrs. Chetwynd
having been a witness to the scene when the great
cask, supposed to contain wine, was opened, and found
full of white satin shoes, valuable lace, and other contra-
band articles. Scenes, too, in the Highlands are well
depicted in this book, whilst the sketch of Sara is carefully worked out, from her first introduction as the
"dethroned princess" in all her ignorance and absorption
in her supposed "Gift of Poetry," to the final page when,

after many vicissitudes of fortune, her soul is awakened by the love of a good man, and her really fine and noble character is fully developed.   Other books written by Mrs. Chetwynd are entitled "A March Violet," "The Dutch Cousin," and "Lady Honoria's Nieces," but though want of space prevents much comment on them, they can confidently be recommended as most pleasant reading, and all are characterized by the kindly nature, the refinement, and the noble spirit of this distinguished gentlewoman's mind. She modestly says of her works, "When I think of the great competition nowadays, I am surprised that they have held their own at all, and directly a new book is out, I always feel that I should like to recall it.   I have sold the copyright of most of my stories, but some are still in my own hands, and I have long since handed over all my literary business affairs to Mr. A. P. Watt, which I have found a perfectly satisfactory arrangement."   The author was considerably amused a few days ago on hearing that a former old servant takes in *Bow Bells* regularly in order to read her late mistress's novels, which have been reproduced and are now coming out weekly in that periodical.   Her two last books are called "Criss-Cross Lovers" and "A Brilliant Woman."

On asking Mrs. Chetwynd about her plots and taste in literature, she says : "I generally build up characters from my own experiences, a bit here, and a trait there, but I do not deliberately set to work to take pictures of people.   I think that most persons have some particular characteristic that comes out in everything they do, and to create is better than to copy. My favourite novels are written by the Gerards, and by Mrs. L. B. Walford—I find all hers charming. Besides these, I admire George Meredith's books more than any others, the one drawback being that when I have re-read one of his I cannot interest myself in anything else for a long time. I delight in history, too, history of all nations. Things which really happened absorb me intensely. I remember when a child I had curious punishments; for being untidy I had twenty lines of *Henriade* to learn by heart, or a French fable. As I could repeat the *Henriade* from beginning to end, I must have been untidy pretty often. The English governess for punishment used to make me read twenty pages of Alison's 'History of Europe' aloud in the play-hours, a fact which I once told the learned historian, and it amused him greatly. The historical punishment, however, has not deprived me of my love for history. My favourite poets are Wordsworth, Tennyson, Shelley, and Burns. I am a great needlewoman, too, and when I am ruffled by anything I take refuge in sewing a plain seam. This coverlet is from a Munich pattern, and I have finished it for my sister, Mrs. Carnegy of Lour, who began it; the tablecover is for my other sister, Mrs. Craigie-Halkett of Cramond."

It is through one of her daughters that you learn of Mrs. Chetwynd's great musical gifts. She was a pupil of Garcia, had a beautiful voice, and used to sing at many amateur concerts. She still keeps up her piano-forte playing, for which she won a gold medal, and will improvise on the piano by the hour together. Her husband and children are very proud of her performances. She has lately invented a fire-escape, which is approved of by experts and engineers, and of which more will soon be heard.

After tea, at which the party is joined by a beautiful thoroughbred Dachshund called Freda, you are taken down into the dining-room, and, in passing, just peep into a little room on the stairs, which your hostess calls her "girls' workshop," where all the wood-carving is carried on. There is a little point of interest in the dining-room which must be noticed as betokening the versatile gifts of this accomplished family. A friend had sent them a roll of paper from Japan, but, as it was found insufficient to cover the whole of the walls, Mrs. Chetwynd and her daughters put their heads together to consult as to how the balance required could be eked out. The result was, that they first distempered the uncovered part of the wall to the exact shade of the colour, and then painted it in such close imitation of the Japanese pattern, even to the native mark, that it is quite impossible to discover which is the original and which the imitation. Among the many books is a copy of "Freytag's Reminiscences," translated by Mrs. Chetwynd's second daughter, and considered by good judges to be one of the best translations from the German that has appeared for a long time. There is a picture of that grand old Highlander, Mr. Davidson of Tulloch, taken in the days when he, with your hostess's uncle, Cluny Macpherson, Fox Maule, afterwards Earl of Dalhousie, and the Duke of Abercorn, danced the first reel that the Queen ever saw in Scotland at Taymouth. By the way, Mrs. Chetwynd herself was a great per-

R

former in that line in her youth, and at some juvenile festivity she and another young Highland friend danced the reel before the late Prince Consort.

But you had forgotten thoroughly to inspect the picture of Tulloch Castle, so Mrs. Chetwynd sends for it. "I am sure," she says, "that my old home is the loveliest place in the world. Part of it is very old, and it has been (through the female line) in our family since 1300." It has an old keep, and what was once the dungeon is now a wine cellar. The house stands very high up, though almost at the foot of Ben Wyvis, and over the park you see the far-famed Strathpeffer, framed in the distance by the West Coast hills. On the other side, also over the well-wooded park, are the Cromarty Frith, and Dingwall nestling at its bend. The gardens are very large, and a good many acres are now not kept up. The approach to the front door is under a very old archway; and though a great part of the place was destroyed by fire some years ago, the walls, some of which are six feet thick, are intact. Facing the south, it catches all the sunshine, and as the hills rise behind it everything is sheltered from the colder winds, and flowers and shrubs grow most luxuriantly. Some scarlet rhododendrons of great height blossom in the winter out of doors. The place is now in the possession of Mrs. Chetwynd's nephew.

Your hostess recalls one little incident which she says was "an event in our lives. My father and Cluny Macpherson received the Queen on the occasion of her visit to Badenoch. She went to Ardverikie, then rented from Cluny by the Duke of Abercorn. My father took forty gillies with him, Cluny had as many more, and they met her majesty on the edge of the property, and escorted her in true Highland fashion. Ardverikie was afterwards sold by Cluny to Sir John Ramsden. The Queen went to Cluny Castle, and examined the many relics of 'Prince Charlie' kept there with an interest which pleased all the family much. Some of the sisters were there with my father."

You are rising regretfully to leave, when the door opens, and Captain Chetwynd comes in. This fine old sailor greets you in the same genial manner which characterises the rest of the family. He is the chief inspector of the Royal National Life-Boat Institution. He is a great organiser, is deeply interested in his work, and his wife delights to think that his talents are now turned to saving, not to destroying life. She had previously confided to you, that not only is he one of the cleverest and best of men, but also one of the most straightforward and appreciative. The good, benevolent face carries its own testimony to the fact. A more happy, united family it would be impossible to find; mutual love and confidence reign supreme; when cares and anxieties come, as to whom do they not? they are shared by all, and thus is the burden lightened.

JEAN MIDDLEMASS.

AMONG the many quiet, shady nooks and corners to be found in the "busy, toiling, but ever pleasure-loving Metropolis," where, if a student desire, she can be in the world, and yet out of its distracting roar, Brompton Square can claim to be one; not that it is really a "square" at all, but merely two long rows of houses, connected at the further end by a semi-circle composed of three or four larger houses. The gardens which separate the two lines of old-fashioned, solidly built dwellings, are thickly planted with shrubs and grand old trees, that in summer time quite shut out any view of the opposite neighbours, and ensure a delightful privacy, whilst the twittering of birds, and the cawing of the rooks, who have built their nests therein, undisturbed for many generations, would almost cheat a stranger into the belief that it is a bit out of a country village. Alas! for the poor little buds which had struggled feebly into life before the devastating blizzard! They were all untimely nipped. Spring has lingered so long in the "lap of winter," that the summer greenery is somewhat backward, yet, at last, the green shoots which have slept "through the long night" are beginning to burst out into strength, and

JEAN MIDDLEMASS

the gummy, swelling buds of the great lilacs within the railings are coming out, and are already casting a delicious perfume around the peaceful and old-world enclosure.

Nearly every house in Brompton Square is associated with the names of men and women who have left their mark in the history of London, chiefly of those who belonged to the theatrical and musical professions. On yonder side Mr. John Baldwin Buckstone, the well-known author-actor, entertained merry parties of wits. A few doors further on stands the house which Mr. Edward Fitzwilliam—famous in his day as a musical composer—inhabited. Spagnoletti, the leader of the Italian Opera orchestra, lived on the opposite side, and was succeeded in his tenancy by a famous and accomplished actress of those days, Mrs. Chatterly. Mr. James Vining, a much respected actor, owned the house which was afterwards occupied by the late Mr. Shirley Brooks. George Colman, the younger, lived and died there. Mr. William Farren, the elder, occupied one house, and owned another, which was the residence of Mr. Payne Collier, who, as Croker says in his interesting "Walk from London to Fulham," gave to the public several editions of Shakespeare, and who was long distinguished by his profound knowledge of dramatic literature and history, and his extensive acquaintance with the early poetry of England. In contradistinction to these more amusing personages, there lived in a house on the east side a man of solid and profound learning, Sir John Stoddard, who, within these walls, wrote at the age of eighty-five, a Polyglot grammar, which was much in use at schools of that period.

In addition to these world-known and histrionic names may be added those of the late Mr. Yates, Mr. John Reeve, Mr. Robson, Mr. Liston, the comedian, and Mr. Henry Luttrell, termed by Lord Byron "the great London wit," once well known in the circles of literature, the author of many epigrams, and of a volume of poetry. These have all beèn residents in Brompton Square, whilst, in later years, Mr. and Mrs. Keeley inhabited a house on the south side, and Mr. and Mrs. Chippendale lived a few doors further on.

What could be more appropriate than that Miss Jean Middlemass, author of "Dandy," "Patty's Partner," "A Girl in a Thousand," and many other bright and interesting stories, should take up her abode in this time-honoured locality, so full of literary and dramatic associations? She has settled herself in one of the larger houses in the bend of the semi-circle at the top, which was erstwhile the dwelling-place of Mr. Alfred Wigan. A spacious hall opens into two good-sized and lofty rooms, which are divided by massive doors, folded back, and draped with heavy Moorish curtains of subdued colouring.

It is all so old-fashioned as to be in thorough keeping with the exterior; but though old-fashioned, the comfortable rooms are by no means dull or gloomy. A flood of sunshine steals in through the long, high windows, lighting up the crimson coverings of the furniture, and casting a bright ray on the picture of a head of Rembrandt, by himself, which is set in a handsomely-carved oak frame of great antiquity over the mantelshelf, on which stand three old and valuable Spode jars. On one side hangs a painting by

Bowden of a lovely child, the son of Frederick Rey-
nolds, the dramatic writer, and near it is one of
Rivière's elaborately finished and exquisite miniatures
of the author's mother taken in her youth. There are
some choice bits of Dresden on a carved corner
bracket, and scattered about here and there are several
Japanese and Chinese curiosities, which have just
been sent to Miss Middlemass from the East, including
a magnificently carved junk, correct in every minute
detail. Surely the very smallest writing-table at
which author ever sat belongs to Jean Middlemass;
but that, too, was a present, and was originally made
tall enough for her to write at while standing, but as
that position was found to be quite too fatiguing it has
been cut down to suit her present requirements.
There is a beautiful old oak mounted carving on the
wall—so old that she " can remember nothing about it
or its subject," she says, " beyond the fact that we
always seem to have possessed it, and it has been
greatly admired." Above it some delightfully quaint
old china is arranged in a half circle; on either side
hang four antique engravings of great value, classical
subjects from Boucher, the French artist's paintings.
But the picture which she prizes more than all is a
life-size portrait in oils, the last work that was ever
finished by the artist Jackson. It represents the
author's grandfather. He held an appointment in the
Treasury, and was the one member of the family who
had any connection with literature, being intimately
acquainted in his youth with Sir Joseph Banks, Mdme.
de Stael, Lady Blessington, and other people of letters.
There is a look in Miss Middlemass which proclaims

the relationship. She is above the middle height, very upright, with a good figure, fair complexion, grey curly hair, and keen, bright-blue, short-sighted eyes. She is dressed in black, relieved by a little rose-coloured ribbon round the wrists and throat, tied in a bow on one side. She is sprightly and merry in nature, full of pleasant conversation, and genial in manner.

Jean Middlemass is Scottish by descent. She was born in one of the pleasant terraces surrounding Regent's Park. Naturally a clever, intelligent girl, she began to write at a very early age, and, to encourage her in this taste, when yet quite a small child her father started a magazine for private circulation only, to which she, her brothers, and several other Harrow boys used to contribute scraps and stories, aided by pieces from a few older persons to encourage the juveniles. She describes herself as having been quick at learning by heart, quick in everything, and fond of study. Plays were her chief delight, and at eight years old she had read and could repeat pages of Shakespeare, often astonishing her parents by apt quotations given with considerable dramatic power. Her youthful enthusiasm in this direction soon, however, received a check, for on one occasion, being rebuked by her mother for some trifling fault, and told how much better people would think of her if she behaved well, she pathetically replied—coolly substituting a word at the end of the first line which she considered more suitable :—

> Amen ; and make me die a good old age !
> That is the butt-end of a mother's blessing ;
> I marvel that her Grace did leave it out.

For this piece of childish and precocious impertinence, as it was deemed, she was punished by the prompt confiscation of her beloved Shakespeare, whereat she wept copiously.

"I was kept hard at my lessons," says Miss Middlemass; "no expense or pains were spared to educate me well, and I enjoyed them. My father was a great student, and himself instructed me in Latin and the rudiments of Greek. I used to attend M. Roche's French classes, and constant residence abroad has enabled me to speak French and German as fluently as English. Music I disliked from the first, and when a tiny child, if my mother were singing, I used to cry out, 'Speak it, speak it!' I do not care for music to this day, and rejoice in the exceeding thickness of the old walls of this house, which causes even the sound of neighbouring pianos to be quite undisturbing. History and biographies were always favourite studies, and I prefer reading French to English. For some years I wrote in a desultory sort of fashion, and it was not until after my mother's death, about fourteen years ago, that feeling lonely— for my four brothers all died young—I adopted writing as a profession."

At the age of eighteen, being emancipated from the school-room, Miss Jean Middlemass was brought out, made her *début* at an early Drawing Room, and enjoyed the gaieties of two London seasons, but after the death of her father the family moved to Brighton, where, later on, her inherent talent for acting asserted itself; she studied recitation and elocution, and constantly took part in amateur theatricals, sometimes playing in as many as four parts in one evening at the Royal Pavilion, coached by Mrs. Stirling. On one occasion she recited " Lady Macbeth " before a full audience at the Dome, and she was always in great request at private parties, where she used to arrange and take part in tableaux, charades, proverbs, and such like entertainments.

Miss Middlemass never acted in a theatre, though she may have had a strong desire to do so, and she smilingly confesses to being perhaps a little of the Bohemian at heart, inasmuch as she dislikes formalities and conventionalities, and loves freedom of action. She has played Esther in *Caste*, Pauline in *Delicate Ground*, Lady Aubrey Glenmorris in *School for Coquettes*, Lady Constance in a scene from *King John*, besides others too numerous to mention. Her most successful recitations have been selections from the works of Dante Rossetti, and Tennyson, Hamilton Aidé's "Lost and Found," and Hood's "Dream of Eugene Aram"; also scenes from plays—Beatrice in *Much Ado About Nothing*, and Pauline in the *Lady of Lyons*. Her memory being excellent, her *répertoire* was very large, and, according to those who witnessed her performances, her histrionic powers entitled her to a prominent position in the Thespian temple of fame, for in all that she undertook, whether in acting or reciting, she worked with indomitable energy, exhibiting the conceptions of a discriminating and educated mind, marked by the influence of a rich and cultivated taste.

"After a few years," says Miss Middlemass, "I began to publish some of my stories, and as the love of writing grew upon me more and more, I found I could not write and act too, so as the histrionic amusements were gradually abolished, I turned my attention more exclusively to my pen, and wrote my first novel, ' Lil.' My mother used to like my stories when they were out, though she never enjoyed them whilst in process of being written. I generally make out a vague plot of half a page, then draw it out into chapters, and arrange the characters. I prefer writing stories of middle or low class life, I don't know why; it came to me, and I often pick up ideas of the lower London life from standing about here and there to listen. I compose and write very quickly, going over it all several times; and I have never had much help, but have just struggled on through it alone. At night, when I go to bed, I work out all the thoughts and ideas which have suggested themselves during the day; often going to sleep in the middle of it, but in the morning it all comes back to me, and I write it out readily and rapidly."

" Lil," which is well calculated to keep alive the interest of the reader, and has, moreover, the merit of being animated in dialogue, was soon followed by " Wild George," in which the beautiful but dangerous French adventuress and her faithful old soldier servant play so prominent a part. Next came " Baiting the Trap," " Mr. Dorillon," " Touch and Go," succeeded by "Sealed by a Kiss" and "Innocence at Play." In all these works there is much insight into human nature, and the French scenes are particularly bright and life-like, betokening the author's intimate knowledge of foreign cities. " Four-in-Hand " was the sporting title

of a volume of short stories. "Sackcloth and Broad-
cloth" contains some capital sketches of clerical life
and its surroundings, about which Miss Middlemass
has had considerable experience. Perhaps up to that
date she scored her greatest success with "Dandy,"
written in 1881 ; of this book the critics and the
public were unanimous in their applause. Penetrating
into the haunts of the poorest section of humanity
in order to depict naturally and truthfully the scenes
so touchingly described therein, she gained an unusual
insight into their words and ways, their occasionally
high, their too often low standard of morality.

"Patty's Partner" is a delightful and interesting
tale of the porcelain manufacture works in the West of
England, where Miss Middlemass is as much at home
as she is in the scenes in "Dandy." It is full of
humour and clever writing. Among other of the
author's works may be mentioned "Poisoned Arrows,"
"By Fair Means," "The Loadstone of Love," and
"Nelly Jocelyn, Widow." A three-volume story published lately, entitled "Two False Moves," contains
some powerful pieces of writing, and the characters
of Derek Home, Ruth Churchill, and the Rev. John
Eagle are drawn to the life. Her last work in one
volume is entitled "How I Became Eminent."

In poetry Miss Middlemass does not as much incline
to modern writers as to the ancient classics in which
she was so early instructed. In politics she is a strong
Conservative. Until the last year or two she was, as
may be supposed, a frequent visitor at the theatre, but
being, unfortunately, so short-sighted, the necessity
for using strong glasses temporarily strained her

eyes, so that pleasure is partially laid aside for the present.

Miss Middlemass is, as usual, full of literary engagements. A new novel is being meditated, though it may not actually be begun; several short stories are in requisition, and one appeared in an early number of John Strange Winter's weekly paper. Among other enjoyments, Jean Middlemass delights in travelling; "Not in the sea part of it," she adds, smiling; "I am an especially bad sailor, and do not like being on the water. I always take the shortest sea-routes." She has made many journeys on the Continent, and in former days lived for a year in Paris. She knows her Paris well, and loves it so dearly that she has often felt that she would like to make her home in that gay and festive capital. She is equally familiar with Brussels, and has been a good deal in Germany, but only on the Rhine, passing some time at Wiesbaden, and paying what she describes as a "delightful visit to the old city of Nuremberg."

"I keep on my quarters in town," continues your hostess, "principally as a *pied-à-terre*. The severity of the long winter, then the sudden change of spring for a few days in February, following those dreadful fogs and frosts, and then the terrible gales and east winds, were all most trying, and I am again contemplating a trip abroad to more seasonable climates; first, a short tour in Holland, then on to Paris for a few weeks, and later, into North Italy, perhaps on to Venice, if the weather then be not too hot."

The brightness and vivacity of foreign life suit well Miss Jean Middlemass's happy disposition and sunny nature. Blessed with good spirits, full of clever anecdote and harmless repartee, with great conversational power, her prevailing characteristic is an utter absence of selfishness and affectation. She has a soft, merry laugh, and a kind, warm heart. With this good gift, it is almost needless to say that she goes through life making no enemies, and many friends. In her ready wit there is no sting. Before all things scandal and backbiting are an abomination to her; it has been truly quoted of this talented and amiable woman, as it has been said of many great and famous persons, "Though knowledge is power, yet those who possess it are indulgent to weaker intellects, and become as one of them in sociability and friendship."

AUGUSTA DE GRASSE STEVENS

AUGUSTA DE GRASSE STEVENS.

AMONG the younger American authors who have made their mark on the literature of the day, Augusta de Grasse Stevens takes a high stand. Highly educated and deeply read, as well versed in the political and civil history of her own country as in that of the land of her adoption, her mind expanded by much continental travel, and inheriting the talents of her brilliantly gifted parents, it is no wonder that she should have attained the depth of thought, the originality of idea, and the fluency of expression which characterise her writings. The young author, who is *petite* in stature, and slight in figure, with grey-blue eyes and brown hair, was born in Albany, on the Hudson River, the capital city of New York, a quaint old Dutch town that bears to this day many marked peculiarities of its rich founders, whose manor lands, granted by royal patent, stretched far and wide along the river banks. Her father was the Hon. Samuel Stevens, one of the most brilliant lawyers the American bar has ever produced; his opinions are still quoted in legal matters on both sides of the ocean. He was a man of the keenest intellect, and most wonderful memory; a power wherever he appeared, and one who had the reputation of never losing a case. The courtesy title was bestowed upon him by the State Legislature in recognition of his great services to that body. He was the life-long friend of such men as Chancellor Walworth, Henry Clay the statesman, and Daniel Webster, who declared that "in his opinion Mr. Stevens as a lawyer stood first in the United States, and that as a colleague he welcomed him in every case, but as an opponent he hoped each case would be the last." From Mr. Stevens' conduct of so many cases, involving important inventions, he has been called unanimously "The Founder of American Patent Law."

"Mr. Phelps, the late U.S. Minister, has often told me," says Miss Stevens, "that he, as a young man, used to travel miles to hear my father argue a case, such a lesson was it in eloquence and profound legal knowledge, and he retained as one of his happiest memories the remembrance of certain interviews he had had with him in which he learned more from my father than in hours of study and private research. My paternal grandmother was of French birth and lineage. She was Mdlle. Marie de Grasse, the daughter of Pierre de Grasse, who was a brother of the famous Admiral Comte de Grasse, the intimate friend of La Fayette, whose patriotism, like his own, was devoted to the American cause. Her parents left France in the seventeenth century, and established themselves in a country home not far from Albany. My grandmother was very beautiful, and retained her beauty to an advanced age, and it is from her we take the name of De Grasse. My great-grandfather was an ardent patriot, and I have often heard my aunt say, that stored away in the attic of their house were trunks full of 'national paper bonds,' not worth the paper on which they were printed, but which represented the sums that he had advanced to the American Government during the War of Independence, and which afterwards they were unable to redeem. My father married rather late in life, my mother being only a girl of eighteen at the time. She was very charming in manner and appearance and highly educated." On the maternal side, Miss de Grasse Stevens can trace her descent back without a break to that brave Simon de Warde who fought with the Conqueror and who fell at Hastings, and whose name is engraved on the Battle Abbey Roll, among those for whom "prayer perpetual is to be offered up" within the Abbey walls. The Wards emigrated to America some time in the year 1600, and settled in New England. They were staunch Puritans and patriots, and begrudged neither life, nor money, nor substance to the cause. General Artemas Ward, one of Washington's chief generals, early distinguished himself in the service, and he was but one in a long line of similar instances. It was while walking through an old churchyard in Connecticut that the late Samuel Brown, coming upon General Artemas Ward's tomb-stone, first saw the name that he afterwards adopted and made world-famous in a far different fashion.

Miss Stevens can remember well her great-grandfather Ward, though she was only a child when he died. He was a typical gentleman of the old school,

s

and wore to the day of his death his hair tied in a *queue*, the knee breeches, silk stockings, low shoes with gold buckles, fine cambric frill, and neckerchief of his time. Her childish recollections are full of pictures of him, and she can shut her eyes and recall without effort the long, sunny drawing-room, so still, and full of a certain awe, the trees outside bending in the summer wind, the warm crimson hangings at the wide windows, the fire on the open hearth, burning there all the year round, and the great arm-chair drawn close within its rays, in which was seated the dignified figure of her great-grandfather, Dr. Levi Ward, his beautiful clean-shaven face, slightly stern when in repose, breaking into a kindly smile at the first sound of his daughter's voice. By his side on a little table lay the great Bible, always open, which he knew literally by heart, and from which, when the blindness of old age came upon him, he could repeat chapter after chapter with unfailing accuracy. "My great-grandmother, his wife, I cannot remember," says Miss Stevens, "but she, too, was a remarkably handsome woman, and one who throughout her whole life held a distinguished position in society as well as being a leader in all philanthropic and charitable undertakings. Their beautiful home, Grove Place, Rochester, New York, was the perfection of a country seat, and about it cluster many tender memories and associations. Their daughter married my grandfather, Mr. Silas Smith, whose daughter in turn became my father's wife, and went with him to his home in Albany, where she soon won for herself a position of much responsibility, and became, puny as she was, a recognised power in all social matters. My father died when I was very young, and my earliest recollections do not date beyond his death. My mother, a young widow, returned with her little family to her father's home, Woodside, just out of Rochester, and with that dear and beautiful home all my happiest, fondest memories are knit up indissolubly. Woodside was a typical home; a large and spacious mansion set in the midst of acres of park land, gardens, and meadows. I think there never was just such a home! Everything that refinement, cultivation, and wealth could procure surrounded us, yet all was distributed and governed with so just and wise a hand that luxurious ostentation and wastefulness were never known amongst us. Here I grew from babyhood to girlhood, and to the fond remembrance and recollection of life there my thoughts turn always when I speak or think of—*home.*"

The young American author describes her mother and her system of education in touching and eloquent words. Her mother, she says, was possessed of one of those rare, unselfish natures to whom personal grief was unknown. Even in her early widowhood her first thought was for her children, and to their care and education she devoted herself unsparingly. Possessing a gifted mind and great personal attractions, a voice of unusual sweetness and power, and a heart that literally did not know the meaning of the word self, she called forth in everyone with whom she came in contact the greatest admiration and affection. "Her children loved her passionately," says Miss Stevens. "How well I can remember when I was but a tiny

mite of five, how she would gather us all around her
in the grey winter afternoons, and with me nestled
close at her knee, read to us by the hour together, but
not fairy tales or story books. She went straight to
the big heart of Shakespeare, of Longfellow, of Tennyson, of Thackeray, of Dickens, and opening the treasure-
houses of their genius, read them to us with only such
explanations and changes as necessity required to
meet the status of her youthful audience. I cannot
remember the time when Shakespeare was unknown
to me, or when the Poet Laureate, and Campbell, and
Dickens, were not dear, familiar friends. Out of this
galaxy of riches, *The Tempest, Midsummer Night's
Dream, Hiawatha,* and *Dombey and Son,* stand out
clearest in my mind. Then she would sing to us, play
to us, and so we became familiar with Mendelssohn,
Mozart, Schubert, and with all the plaintive, old
English ballads and Scotch border songs ; and in
the morning hours, while she was busy with a large
correspondence and literary work, my dear grandmother
taught us, my sister and me, to sew, cut out, and knit,
inculcating meantime many a goodly lesson in charity,
kindliness, and thoughtfulness for others. To my dear
mother, indeed, I owe all that I am. She is gone from
me now, but to her clear mind, wise criticism, and
sound judgment is due whatever literary reputation
I may have earned. I wrote for her, *she* was my
public ! "

This beloved home was ever one of open hospitality,
and to it came at all times guests of every kind. Here,
Miss Stevens tells you, her grandfather had welcomed
Talleyrand and Louis Napoleon, and here in later days

gathered many a company of literary giants whose names are now household words. After six years of widowhood her mother married the late Mr. John Fowler Butterworth, a man who was universally beloved and respected, of high position, wealth, and great personal attractions. "We all went with them to the new home in New York," adds Miss Stevens. "He was the only father I have ever known, and I loved him most tenderly."

From this time the family spent much of their time on the Continent of Europe. Miss Stevens and her sister were educated in Paris, having for their instructress a very charming and capable woman, who had been *gouvernante* to the Orleans Princesses. It was their habit to spend at least three months of every year abroad, and in this way the young girl saw much more of foreign countries than her own. Italy, Switzerland, France, Germany, the Tyrol, each were visited in turn, and such was the method of their travelling that every country and town were indelibly and individually impressed upon her memory. Rome, Florence, Geneva, Verona, Turin, Munich, Innspruck, each one and all are to her bright with particular associations. After her stepfather's death Miss Stevens and her mother settled permanently in London, where they had many friends and many family ties, her sister having married and made her home in England.

The young author's first literary efforts were begun at a very early age. "I can scarcely," she says, "remember a time when I did not scribble. My first attempt was a sermon on the text ' God is Love,' and I distinctly recollect how and where I wrote it, crouched behind a long swinging glass in my mother's bed-room, printing it off in capital letters—writing being then far beyond my attainments—and getting very hot and flushed in the effort." Her next attempt was a decided advance. Her sister and two cousins had established a small home newspaper, called the *Dorcas Gazette*, price one halfpenny, circulation strictly private and confidential, its end and aim being the helping of the "Dorcas Society," a body formed to make clothes for the poor. The circulation amounted to six copies a week, each of which had to be written out in fair round hand on two sheets of foolscap paper. To this ambitious venture she was invited to contribute, and for two years was writer in chief, furnishing serials, short stories, and anecdotes, her sister doing the political and poetical parts. "I have still," says Miss Stevens, smiling, "one or two of those old 'gazettes,' time-stained and yellow ; I look on them with the utmost respect, and feel that for harrowing plot and thrilling adventure, my 'serial' in five chapters, called 'Blonde and Brunette,' beats the record of any of my subsequent work !" Her first book, written when she was seventeen, was a small novelette called "Distance." It was published by Appleton, of New York, and was well received and reviewed. On coming to London, Miss de Grasse Stevens was asked by the proprietor of the principal American journal, the *New York Times*, to prepare for them a series of articles upon English art and artists, and for ten years she filled the position of special art critic to that paper, her letters upon London artists and their studios being the first of the kind ever written, while her account—a two-column article—of the private view and pictures at the Royal Academy, which appeared in the morning edition in New York the next day, was the first "art-cable" sent across the wires. Her first short story, written long ago, appeared in *Harper's Magazine.* She wrote it secretly, and sent it off furtively. It was called "Auf Wiedersehn," and was subsequently translated into German, and reprinted in many English papers. "After sending it off," she relates, "I waited in sickening suspense for ten long days, and when at last a letter came bearing the well-known Franklin-square stamp, I dared not open it. When I did I fell upon the floor and cried bitterly from bewildering joy! It contained a satisfactory cheque, and a request for 'more matter of the same sort.' From that moment the spell of literature held me as in a vice. I have never known a moment of purer, more unalloyed joy than that, and to it I owe my perseverance in the 'thorny path.'"

Miss De Grasse Stevens's first three-volume novel was called "Old Boston." It was originally published by Sampson Low & Co., and has since been brought out in one volume edition. Its reception was more than flattering, and the reviews upon it were such as a much older and more experienced writer might be pleased to win. The story is partly historical, and is founded on the events just preceding the siege of Boston and the declaration of American Independence. Keenly attracted beyond aught else by history, especially by the history of her own country, in which there is stored away such treasures of romance, of reality,

of poetry, and of pathetic prose—the young American
writer has, in this delightful romance of a hundred
years ago, given clear evidence of her thorough knowledge of her subject; each character is strongly indivi-
dualised; true pathos and purity of style mark every
page ; you are carried back a century, yet can feel with
unflagging interest that the persons described are living
fellow-creatures. The descriptive writing is artistically
fine, the love story is tenderly and pathetically told,
whilst the whole betokens careful study and research.
This book gained for Miss de Grasse Stevens countless
kind and flattering letters from old and, as yet, unknown friends. "Some of my dearest and most
trusty friendships," she says, "I owe to it; first and
foremost in which was that of the late Mr. Kinglake.
I had known his family in Taunton for some time,
but to 'Old Boston' I owed the friendship of the
author, which ended not with his death, for I am
certain such friendships are eternal." She contem-
plates some day writing a sequel to this book,
bringing the history part of it down to the famous
battle of Valley Forge and the bombardment and
surrender of New York.

The author's next work, "Weighed in the Balance,"
was a short story written for Mr. W. Stevens's
Magazine of Fiction, and was of the sensational
school. Over a hundred thousand copies were sold,
and for this, too, she received so much praise and so
many letters that she declares herself to have been
"greatly surprised"; among them were two which
she prized highly, one from the late Earl Granville
and the other from the late Earl Spencer, who both

wrote that the scenes being laid at Deal, the book was particularly interesting to them, especially the parts relating to the Goodwin Sands, and the historic, but decayed old town of Sandwich. This book was followed by one that caused a good deal of stir—a historical monograph called "The Lost Dauphin," in which the writer took up the mysterious fate of little Louis XVII., and advanced the theory that he did not die in the Temple but was stolen from there and carried to America, where he was deposited with the Indian tribe of the Iroquois and was eventually taken East, educated and trained as a missionary under the name of Ealeazer Williams. The book is illustrated by three portrait engravings. It called forth a storm of controversy and a great number of reviews amongst all the leading journals, the majority of which frankly accepted her hypothesis. Innumerable letters poured in from all sorts and conditions of people, mostly scholars and men interested in out-of-the-way questions. The late Mr. Kinglake was particularly keen on it, and Miss Stevens has a large packet of highly prized letters from him, devoted to the discussion of the theory that she had advanced and in which he thoroughly believed. This, from so great a scholar as the author of "Eöthen" and "The Crimea," was praise worth having. The late Robert Browning was another *litterateur* who wrote in commendation of the book, as did Mrs. Gladstone, Henry James, Mr. Russell Lowell, Miss Sewell, Mr. Phelps, and many others.

"Miss Hildreth" is the name of Miss de Grasse Stevens's next three-volume novel, which, following as it did closely after the sensation made by "The Lost Dauphin," attracted great attention both in France and England. The scenes are laid in St. Petersburg and New York, amidst the society with which she was most familiar. The plot is original, the story is conspicuous by the ability with which it is written, and proves how thoroughly and conscientiously she studies the subject that she has on hand. Very powerfully drawn is the account of the fortress prison of Petropavosk, the descriptions of scenery show how entirely the author is in touch with nature in her every aspect, while the scene of the trial betrays the logical mind and power of argument which she has inherited from her distinguished father. "Miss Hildreth" is moreover from "start to finish" deeply interesting and exciting, and displays the same experienced pen and graceful language, free from any exaggeration or straining after effect that is so conspicuous in "Old Boston." Mr. Gladstone, in his letter to her about "Miss Hildreth," after expressing his deep interest in its *motif*, writes, " I thank you very much for the work you have been so good as to send me. Both your kindness and the subjects to which it refers, make me very desirous to lose no time in beginning it." The young author has just finished a new novel in one volume, called "The Sensation of a Season," which will shortly be published, and is completing another to be called "A Romantic Inheritance." The former work is absolutely different in style, and deals chiefly with American society in London. Besides fiction, Miss Stevens writes several weekly articles for American

syndicates, and is a contributor to a South African
magazine on more abstruse subjects. She has written,
on and off, special articles, by request, for the *Saturday Review* since 1885, notably among these, papers
on " Old American Customs," and on " The position of
needlewomen in London," bearing upon the work
depôt established in Cartwright Street, Westminster,
by the Hon. Mrs. William Lowther and Miss Burke ;
also an amusing account of " Christmas in America
fifty years ago," in the Christmas number of a weekly
paper, and she has for a long time been a regular
writer on the *Argosy* staff. Mention must not be
omitted of a particular article called " The Beautiful
Madame Grand, Princesse de Talleyrand," for which
Mr. Cassell sent specially to Versailles to copy the
portrait in the Grand Gallery for the frontispiece
of the magazine. This was followed by a series
of illustrated biographical sketches in the *Lady's
Pictorial*—"American Ladies at Home in London."

When engaged on a novel Miss Stevens puts no
pen to paper. "I think it all out in my head," she
says, "before writing a word, chiefly when travelling ;
the movement of the train has a peculiar fascination
for me. I make no notes. When it is all complete in
my brain, I write straight away with no effort of
memory." But with all her increasing literary work,
Miss de Grasse Stevens finds time for a little
recreation in exercising her talents for modelling
and painting. In both of these arts she is no mean
proficient. The gift is inherited from her lamented
mother, who painted much for the Royal Family,
and who counted among her personal friends H.R.H.

Princess Louise, Marchioness of Lorne. Sir Frederick Leighton, another valued friend, used to say that her power of colouring was especially wonderful. The young author is a very early riser, and is up and out of doors every morning before seven. She writes from ten till three, and divides her time between her sister's beautiful country home in Kent and the pretty little house at West Kensington, where she stays with a dear aunt and uncle, Dr. Hand Smith, well known in the scientific world of London for his discovery of the endolithic process, about which the late Sir Edgar Boehm was so enthusiastic an admirer. This little abode may be briefly described as distinctly artistic. The rooms are olive-green in colour, and contain several cherished reminiscences of her mother. The great " Alexandre " American walnut-wood organ —both reed and wind—reaching to the ceiling, is quite unique. On a draped easel stands a large mounted plaque of gorgeous Florida poinsettias, painted by her mother in a method discovered by herself, a *replica* of the design she furnished to the Queen. Another, almost as beautiful, of different-coloured pansies, by the same beloved hand, adorns the mantelshelf. Many well-used volumes of Tennyson, Browning, Whittier, Thackeray, and of Mrs. Lynn Linton fill the bookshelves. "I delight in Mrs. Lynn Linton's books and papers," says your hostess; "I call her the Modern Crusader, and read everything that she writes with much pleasure." Among these works you notice an "In Memoriam" monograph by Miss Stevens of William Kinglake, illustrated with his portrait, and a picture of his home, Wilton House, Taunton, both of which he gave to her. There are a few good pictures on the walls: two of Morland's are especially attractive, *lunette* in shape, first proofs before letters engraved by Nutter. Yonder hang a couple of paintings of her sister's Kentish home, an old redbrick Elizabethan building, with the peculiar white facings and low white door belonging especially to the Tudor days, surrounded by park lands, lawns, and very old fruit orchards, which are at this season bright with yellow daffodils. Tradition assigns to it a veritable ghost, whose uneasy spirit walks every All Saints' Eve! A packet of letters from great men lies on a little table near. From them Miss Stevens selects some from Gladstone, Kinglake, and Irving. This last was written on the appearance of her papers in the leading Boston and New York journals on the subject of "Macbeth." She has new and pleasant work now on hand as art editor of the *Novel Review*, in which her late biographical monograph upon "John Oliver Hobbes" elicited more than ordinary comment from the general press; also a fresh and important post in connection with a smart New York society journal. "I particularly like the prospect opened out in this new field of journalism," remarks Miss de Grasse Stevens quietly, "as it gives me greater freedom of subject as well as of treatment. I am delighted, too," she adds, smiling, "with the mere thought of grappling with any little difficulties that may arise on the subject."

And to these "little difficulties" you leave the bright young American writer, feeling sure that her clever brain will guide her able pen to solve them aright.

MRS. LEITH ADAMS

(MRS. LAFFAN).

IT is a lovely day in early springtime. A gentle south-west wind is just stirring the meadows, and the young birds are chirping gaily in the hedgerows which are beginning to put forth their tiny buds. All nature seems awake and smiling; truly a fitting morn on which to visit Stratford-on-Avon, the place so fraught with memories of the immortal bard. You have been so fortunate as to make the long journey from London in the company of the well-known and popular Captain Gerard, late of the 23rd Welsh Fusiliers, and as he has been for some years a resident in these parts, he has given you the *carte du pays* and much useful and interesting information.

The town of Stratford-on-Avon is beautifully situated on the south-west border of Warwickshire on a gentle eminence rising from the bank of the Avon. As the train glides into the station, Mrs. Leith Adams is seen standing on the platform. She has come to meet you, accompanied by many dogs, who insist on jumping into the carriage as an escort home. On leaving the station the road runs past the hospital, down the wonderfully broad High-street of the town

MRS LEITH ADAMS

(MRS LAFFAN)

with its venerable houses on either side, and as the beautiful old porch of the Guild Chapel (of which Mr. Laffan is incumbent) comes into view, the pony turns down Chapel-lane and draws up at the School House.

Entering the porch into the hall you face the Head Master's study on the left, a charming room and evidently the haunt of a scholar. The next room on the same floor has two French windows opening on to the garden. In a nook by one of these windows Mrs. Leith Adams does her writing with the shades of George Eliot looking down on her, and a fine photograph of her youngest son now in Australia. Wandering about the grounds into which these windows look are six beautiful peacocks, a comical cockatoo, a seagull, so tame that it comes up when called, two white broken-haired terriers, and a wise-looking pug. On the left stands a tree with cocoanuts tied upon it, where countless blue-eyed tits congregate all day long. The wide winding staircase leads up to the drawing-room, where you find yourself among shades of olive green, and a roving glance is caught by two magnificent old china jars, standing on either side of the fire-place, once full of unguents belonging to the Knights of St. John of Jerusalem, and found in the vaults under the palace at Malta. The side window looks across the School gardens to the Memorial Theatre, a fine domed building on the banks of the river, and the three windows in the front look over New Place Gardens where lie the foundations of the house where Shakespeare died, and where in 1643 Henrietta Maria, Queen of Charles I., was hospitably received and entertained for three days by Shakespeare's daughter.

It was as the wife of the late Surgeon-General A.
Leith Adams, F.R.S., LL.D., M.D., that the author
of "Aunt Hepsy's Foundling" (by which story the
name of Mrs. Leith Adams is best known to the
public) entered on her career as a novelist. Having
been much struck during a visit to Scotland by the
character and personality of a venerable minister of
the Presbyterian Church, she resolved to attempt to
make him the centrepiece of a short story. Of this
resolve the result was "Keane Malcombe's Pupil,"
since republished under the title of "Mabel Meredith's
Love Story." Her first essay in fiction met with
instant success. Without any previous acquaintance
with, or introduction to, the present Mr. Charles
Dickens, the author offered her MS. to *All the Year
Round*. It was at once accepted and published in
the year 1876, from which time up to the present
Mrs. Leith Adams has been continuously a member
of Mr. Dickens's staff.

A more ambitious effort followed in the year 1877
when "Winstowe," her first three-volume novel, was
brought out. It bore marks of great inexperience, but
had a certain limited sale in England and a wider
one in America. In the following year "Madelon
Lemoine" was issued, a book which has made its
way steadily among a section of the community, and
is looked upon by many critics as the foremost among
the author's earlier works ; but it was not until the
publication of "Aunt Hepsy's Foundling" that her
name came prominently before the public. A remarkable notice in a leading journal resulted in a second
edition being promptly called for. This has been

followed by two other editions, each in one volume,
also one in America and one in Germany. In writing
this book Mrs. Leith Adams was inspired by the
recollections of life in New Brunswick, in which
country she had spent nearly five years with her
husband's regiment—the 1st Battalion "Cheshire."
The novelty of the scene and the freshness of its
treatment secured for the work a prompt success,
and it was spoken of by a weekly review as "an
almost perfect novel of its kind."

The author has enjoyed very exceptional advantages
as preparation for a literary career. Married at an
early age, when the impressions of a girl's life are
peculiarly vivid, she was but six months in Ireland
with the "Cheshire" when that regiment was ordered
on foreign service. Her presentation at the Irish Vice-
Regal Court, over which the scholarly Lord Carlisle
then held sway, the brilliant festivities at the Castle,
réunions at the house of Sir Henry and Lady Marsh,
where she met all the men of letters in Dublin, the
happy *camaraderie* of regimental life ; all these things,
so new to her, passed like a flash, and were exchanged
for the troopship, and ultimately for lands and societies
strangely differing the one from the other.

The sunshine, orange groves, and military pomp and
glitter of life in Malta were succeeded by the sound of
the sleigh bells over the snow, the wonders of the
sudden springtime, and the gorgeous "fall" of New
Brunswick, and, after nine years' wandering, the
beautiful coast scenery of Guernsey ; then once again
the delights of soldiering in Ireland, this time in the
South, where the lovely climate, devoted friends, and

the charm of being near home once more, have, as
your hostess expresses it, "all made the memories of
those days most dear to me."

Mrs. Leith Adams did not begin to write whilst still
a very young woman. She says of herself that
although the idea may have been in her mind, she
wished to wait until she had great stores of experience and observation upon which to draw. Some of
these experiences have been of an intense and exceptional character. During the great cholera epidemic
which visited the island of Malta in 1866—after sending home to England her only little child for safety—
she devoted herself to the care of the sick and dying
in her husband's regiment, in company with a band
of soldiers' wives, who gladly and fearlessly gave
themselves to the good work. Many of her experiences during this awful time are to be found in the
pages of "Madelon Lemoine," but in one instance
(not there alluded to) it may be said that Mrs. Leith
Adams ran extraordinary and perilous risk, such as
rendered her entire immunity from harm little short
of miraculous, whilst she also had the satisfaction of seeing the woman whom she was attending
gradually recover from the fell disease that so
seldom spares the victim that it has once attacked.

After twenty-five years' service with the old regiment, Dr. Leith Adams obtained a Staff appointment
connected with the recruiting department at the Horse
Guards, and this brought himself and his wife to
London, where they continued to reside for some
years.

It was during this period that her literary career

began. At the time of her husband's death she was
under an agreement to supply a serial story to a
leading magazine, in fact she had one, and only one,
chapter written towards that weekly instalment of
"copy" necessary during such a process, "but," she
says, "I shall ever remember with the deepest
gratitude, the prompt generosity with which the
editor, on hearing of my bereavement and of my
subsequent illness, made arrangements to give me
time." As soon as she was able to resume her pen,
Mrs. Leith Adams completed and published "Geoffrey
Stirling," first in the pages of *All The Year Round*,
and then in three-volume form. This story has had
its share of popularity, and a "picture-board" edition
of it has been issued lately.

"Amongst the many other advantages I enjoyed,"
she remarks, "I rank by no means least the society of
the many eminent and scientific men that my husband's
tastes and attainments opened to me. I can look back
upon gatherings round the hospitable board of Sir
Joseph and Lady Hooker at the Royal Society
Gardens, which included such men as the late William
Spottiswoode, P.R.S., Professor Huxley, Professor
Flower, and of foreign *savans* not a few, occasions
on which I would gladly have found myself possessed
of not two ears alone, but twenty, and when to listen
to the conversation of the charmed circle was indeed a
liberal education. At the *soirées* of the Royal Society
I used to delight in meeting all the talent of this and
many another country, and I hold the very strongest
opinions as to the unspeakable advantage that it is to
a woman to listen to highly gifted and deeply learned

men discussing questions and knowledge of the greatest and most vital importance."

In the autumn of 1883, Mrs. Leith Adams married,
en secondes noces, the Rev. R. S. de Courcy Laffan,
M.A., eldest son of the late Lieut.-General Sir Robert
Michael Laffan, K.C.M.G., R.E., Governor of the
Bermudas. Mr. Laffan is head-master of King Edward
VI. School at Stratford-on-Avon, the school at which
Shakespeare received his early education. He is a
refined scholar, a most able preacher, and on his staff
are men of high university degrees and much culture,
so that, as Mrs. Laffan, the author's lines are still cast
among intellectual surroundings.

She has thrown herself into the interests of
school-life as earnestly as she did into that of a
regiment, and of social life in London, and amidst
all the claims of her literary work contrives to find
time to give the most minute care to the health,
comfort, and happiness of the boys under her husband's roof. It is impossible to see her in their
midst, whether they be tall striplings preparing to
become defenders of their country or little fellows
in sailor suits just introduced to the surroundings
of school, with its pleasures and its trials, without
recognising, as they cluster about her in their own
sitting-rooms, or in her drawing-room, that she has
completely won their hearts and that her influence
among them is one of the factors in the rapidly
increasing success of the school. At the annual
speech day, Mrs. Laffan personally designs all the
costumes of the play, Shakespearean or otherwise,
and on the last occasion of this kind wrote the play

for the junior boys and composed the music incidental to it.

One of the later novels by Mrs. Leith Adams (who prefers to retain her former name in her literary capacity) is "Louis Draycott," in which the reader will find many traces of the influence of school life, and the study of the characteristics of boys. "No one but a woman could have filled in these tiny canvases," remarked a critic; "nor are evidences wanting of her being surrounded by the classic traditions of Stratford-on-Avon. Thoroughly imbued with Shakespeare, she has judiciously, to a certain extent, allowed him to influence her diction, but never obtrusively."

It is only natural that the author should miss in her country home the literary, musical, and artistic society of London, where she has so many friends, but she has made acquaintances too in Warwickshire, where she has the privilege of meeting men and women eminent in the world of letters. Stratford-on-Avon is of itself a shrine to which so many distinguished pilgrims, especially Americans, are drawn, that charming, unexpected meetings often take place and friendships are cemented when she takes her many visitors to see the interesting places in the town.

"Bonnie Kate, A Story from a Woman's Point of View," was the writer's next work. It had a successful career, and was followed by "A Garrison Romance," wherein military reminiscences figure largely and many characters are sketched from life. A story in the same line, entitled "Colour-Sergeant No. 1

Company," is shortly to appear, also a novel in three
volumes called " The Peyton Romance." A late small
volume, " The Cruise of the Tomahawk," was written
by Mrs. Leith Adams in collaboration with her husband and a friend; the poems with which it is
interspersed and the small illustrations are from the
pen of Mr. Laffan. At the Church Congress held at
Cardiff in 1889 she read a paper upon " Fiction viewed
in relation to Christianity," and she says that she has
some intention of giving a lecture during the present
year on the subject of " Literature as a Profession for
Women."

As regards her mode of work, she remarks : " The
plots which I find the easiest to work out are those
which have been thought over the longest : the word
' long ' here stands for a great deal. The plot and
characters of ' Bonnie Kate ' have been under consideration, and the subject of the accumulation of
constant notes for the last eight years, dating from
a visit to a Yorkshire farmstead for the express
purpose of obtaining the colouring and atmosphere
necessary to the delineation of ' Low Cross Farm.' "

Of Mrs. Leith Adams' minor works, it may be said
that "My Land of Beulah" has had a quite exceptional popularity, and "Cosmo Gordon," with its
delightful self-made man, Mr. Japp, has had its full
share of admirers. "Mathilde's Love Story," published
two years ago in the spring number of *All The Year
Round,* is a memory of Guernsey, and "Georgie's
Wooer" is a reminiscence of life in the South of
Ireland.

Mrs. Leith Adams is an ardent musician and

accomplished pianist, and as there are several good violinists among the masters and boys of Shakespeare's School, concerted music is often the order of the day, more especially at her Thursday afternoon "at homes."

There is a long gap between the publication of "Geoffrey Stirling" and that of "Louis Draycott," but various causes combined to make this so. Further very heavy bereavements, variable health, anxiety as to the health of her son (Mr. Francis Lauderdale Adams, now well known as poet and journalist in Australia), the necessity for his leaving England, the same long anxiety with the same results in the case of her younger son—a most promising boy, whose health broke down just when his prospects seemed brightest : all these causes militated for some years against continuous mental effort. The pen is now, however, once more resumed, and no doubt a group of what may be called "later novels" will be the result. In addition to the high value she places upon long consideration of a projected novel, Mrs. Leith Adams holds that to write well, you must read well. She is convinced that the style and tone of what people read thoughtfully, sensibly affects their own diction. "I am," she observes, "a devoted admirer of Mrs. Carlyle, and have read again and again those thrilling letters in which all a woman's innermost life and sorrows, and heart story are laid bare. I am of opinion that had Jane Welsh Carlyle seen fit to make literature a profession, that she would have taken rank second only to that apostle of female culture and ambitions, George Eliot. Shakespeare, Browning, Tennyson, and all biographies of great men, are the reading that

I love best. Carlyle himself only comes second to his
wife in my estimation, and at the feet of Charles
Dickens I worshipped in my girlhood. (This influence
is distinctly traceable in much of her work.) Mrs.
Gaskell, Miss Austen, Charlotte Brontë's ' Jane Eyre,'
and many of Miss Broughton's works, George Meredith,
Baring Gould, and, above all, George Eliot—these
among English fiction are my favourites, whilst in
French, Dumas' *Chevalier de la Maison Rouge*, and
many of Octave Feuillet's are my companions. If I
like a book I read it again and again ; if I like a play
I go to see it again and again. It is like learning
to know more and more of one whom you love."

Like most writers, Mrs. Leith Adams has had some
strange and funny experiences in letters from people
unknown and never to be known, and in the calm
impertinences—probably not intended—of people absolutely ignorant of literary knowledge, as for instance
when a peculiarly *banale* woman remarked to her,
" I'm sure I could write novels quite as well as you
if I were not so weak in the wrist," which was
assuredly locating the mental faculties rather low
down ; and another, a perfect stranger, who called upon
her in London and said with startling candour, " I
want to make some money, I'm going to write a novel.
How do you begin ? "

Later on, a visit to the schools is suggested, and,
escorted by your hosts, you make a tour round these
interesting premises. The schools, the chapel, and the
vicarage house form three sides of a quaint old-world
quadrangle, in which it is easy to forget for a moment
the nineteenth century, and to dream oneself back into

the middle ages. The Guild Chapel, one of the most interesting buildings in Stratford, was founded by the brethren of the Guild of the Holy Cross. The chancel dates from the thirteenth century, but the nave is of more recent construction. The next building bears an inscription, " King Edward VI. School," though its real founder was Thomas Jolyffe, one of the priests of the Guild, who built the Old Latin Schoolroom in 1482. The unpretending exterior scarcely prepares you for the quaint beauty of the interior. On entering you find yourself in a long panelled room, which is the Old Guild Hall, where the Earl of Worcester's players gave their representations in Shakespeare's day. On the same floor is a class room called the Armoury with Jacobean panelling, and a fresco of the arms of the Kings of England. A narrow staircase leads to a little room on the left, where a few years ago several 16th century MSS. were discovered. Then comes the Council Chamber with its splendid oak roof and Jacobean table, and on the wall there are two curious frescoes of roses painted in 1485 to commemorate the termination for ever of the terrible wars of the Roses. Next to it is the Mathematical Room, but it is on leaving that, and entering the Old Latin Room, that you feel impressed with the great antiquity and beauty of the building. The roof is one of the finest specimens of the open roof in the country. It was in this and the adjoining room that the poet received his education, and from it the desk which tradition assigns to him was taken. It now stands in the museum at the birthplace, which place you are duly taken to visit and also the Church of Holy Trinity, where at the

entrance to the altar, on a slab covering the ashes of
the poet, is an inscription written by himself, together
with his bust painted into a strict likeness, even to the
complexion, the colour of the hair and eyes, and you
leave all these interesting relics with a strong convic-
tion that no better cicerone could be found than Mr.
and Mrs. Laffan to do the honours of the ancient and
historic buildings of Shakespeare's School and the
" sacred places of Stratford-on-Avon "—

> " Where sleep the illustrious dead, where lies the dust
>   Of him whose fame immortal liveth still
>   And will live evermore."

JEAN INGELOW

JEAN INGELOW.

"TALENT does what it may; Genius, what it must." To no one could the definition apply more appropriately than to the well-known and gifted poetess, Jean Ingelow. She came into the world full-blown; she was a poet in mind from infancy; she was born just as she is now, without improvement, without deterioration. From her babyhood, when she could but just lisp her childish hymns, she was always distressed if the rhyme were not perfect, and as she was too young to substitute another word with the same meaning, she used simply to make a word which was an echo of the first, quite oblivious of the meaning. Every trifling incident, a ray of sunlight, a flower, a singing bird, a lovely view—all inspired her with a theme for expression, and she had a joy in so expressing herself.

Jean Ingelow was born near Boston, Lincolnshire. She was one of a large family of brothers and sisters; she was never sent to school, and was brought up entirely at home, partly by teachers of whom she regrets to say she was too much inclined to make game, but more by her mother, who, being a very clever woman of a poetical turn of mind, mainly educated her numerous family herself. Her father was a banker at Suffolk, a man of great culture and ability. "It was a happy, bright, joyous childhood," says Miss Ingelow; "there was an originality about us, some of my brothers and sisters were remarkably clever, but all were droll, full of mirth, and could caricature well. We each had a most keen sense of the ridiculous. Two of the boys used to go to a clergyman near for instruction, where there was a small printing machine. We got up a little periodical of our own and used all to write in it, my brothers' schoolfellows setting up the type. It was but the other day one of these old schoolfellows dined with us, and reminded me that he had put my first poems into type."

Many of these verses are still in existence, but the girl-poet had yet another place, and an entirely original one, where in secret she gave expression to her muse. In a large upper room where she slept, the windows were furnished with old-fashioned folding shutters, the backs of which were neatly "flatted," and formed an excellent substitute for slate or paper. "They were so convenient," she remarks, smiling. "I used to amuse myself much in this way. I opened the shutters and wrote verses and songs on them, and then folded them in. No one ever saw them until one day when my mother came in and found them, to her great surprise." Many of these songs, too, were transmitted to paper and were preserved.

Whilst on a visit to some friends in Essex, Jean Ingelow and some young companions wrote a number of short stories and sent them for fun to a periodical called *The Youth's Magazine*. She signed her contributions " Orris," and was delighted when she received an intimation that they were accepted and that the editor " would be glad to get more of them." Meantime, she went on accumulating a goodly store of poems, songs, and verses ; many were burnt and others directly they were written were carefully hidden away in old manuscript books, but the day was fast approaching when they were to see the light. In the affectionate give and take of a witty, united, and cultured family, her brothers and sisters used to laugh merrily at her efforts and often parodied good-naturedly her poems, though secretly they were proud of them. The method of bringing out this book, which was her first great success and was destined shortly to become so famous, was very curious. A brother wishing to give her pleasure offered to contribute to have her MSS. printed. This was done, and the next move was to take them to a publisher, Mr. Longman. " My mother and I went together," says Miss Ingelow ; " she consented to allow my name to appear ; we were all rather flustered and excited over it, it seemed altogether so ridiculous." Very far from " ridiculous," however, was the result. Mr. Longman at first looked doubtful, but soon recognising the merits of the work, took up the matter warmly, with the excellent effect that in the first year four editions of a thousand copies each were sold and the young poet's fame was secured. The book bore the simple and unpretending title, " Poems, by Jean Ingelow."

" It was a long time before I could make up my

mind if I liked it or not," says the author. "I could
not help writing, it is true, but it seemed to make
me unlike other people ; being one of so many and
being supposed to be sensible, and to behave on the
whole like other people, and trying to do so, and
delighting in the companionship of my own family
more than in any other, I am not at all sure that I was
pleased when I was suddenly called a poet, because
that is a circumstance more than most others which
sets one apart, but they were all so joyous and made
much fun over it."

This first volume of poems has been re-published
and yet again and again, until up to the present time
it has reached its twenty-sixth edition, in different
forms and sizes.   One of these was brought out as an
édition de luxe, and is profusely illustrated.   Jean
Ingelow's poetry is too well known and widely read to
need much comment.   In this remarkable volume,
probably the most quoted and best recollected verses
are to be found under the title of " Divided," " Song of
Seven," " Supper at the Mill," "Looking over a Gate
at a Mill," " The Wedding Song," " Honours," " The
High Tide on the Coast of Lincolnshire," " Brothers
and a Sermon," " Requiescat in Pace," " The Star's
Monument," yet when this is said, you turn to another
and yet another, and would fain name the last read
the best.   Where all are sweet, sound, and healthy ;
where all are full of feeling, bright with suggestions,
and thoroughly understandable, how hard it is to
choose !   And who has not read and heard over and
over again that exquisite song which has been set to
music no less than thirteen times, " When sparrows

build"? Also, "Sailing Beyond Seas," with the
beauteous refrain :—

> O fair dove ! O fond dove !
> And dove with the white breast,
> Let me alone, the dream is my own,
> And my heart is full of rest.

To the most superficial reader the tender and real
humanity of these entirely original poems is evident,
while to the student who goes further into the
fascinating work, deeper treasures are discovered ; you
realise more and more her own personality, her own
distinctive style, and get many a glimpse of the pure
heart and lofty aspiration of the gifted singer.

But to return to the original issue of this first
published book. In consequence of its success, Mr.
Strahan made an immediate application for any other
work by the same pen ; accordingly Jean Ingelow's
early short tales, signed "Orris," were collected and
published under the title of "Stories told to a Child."
This, too, went through many editions, one of which
was illustrated by Millais and other eminent artists.
A further request for longer stories resulted in the
production of a volume called, "Studies for Stories."

These delightful sketches, professedly written for
young girls, soon attracted children of much older
growth. While simple in construction and devoid of
plot, they are full of wit and humour, of gentle satire
and fidelity to nature. They are prose poems, written
in faultless style and are truthful word-paintings of
real everyday life.

Jean Ingelow has ever been a voluminous writer,
but only an odd volume or so of her own works is

to be found in her house. She "gives them away, indeed, scarcely knows what becomes of them," she says. Among many other of her books is one called "A Story of Doom, and other Poems," which has likewise passed into many editions. Here stand out pre-eminently "The Dreams that come true," "Songs on the Voices of Birds," "Songs of the Night Watches," "Gladys and her Island," ("An Imperfect Fable with a Doubtful Moral,") "Lawrance," and "Contrasted Songs." "A Story of Doom" may be called an epic. It deals with the closing days of the antediluvian world, while its chief figures are Noah, Japhet, Amarant the slave, the impious giants, and the arch-fiend. Her portraiture of these persons, natural and supernatural, is very powerful and impressive. "Lawrance" is unquestionably an idyll worthy to be ranked with "Enoch Arden." Told, at once, with much dramatic power and touching simplicity, there is a fresh, pure atmosphere about it which makes it intensely natural and sympathetic. One of the poems in a third volume, republished four or five years ago, is called "Echo and the Ferry," which is a great favourite and is constantly chosen for recitation. In the "Song for the Night of Christ's Resurrection," breathes the deeply devotional and sincerely religious spirit of the author who was brought up by strictly evangelical parents, yet is there no trace of narrowness or bigotry in Jean Ingelow or her writings. She is large-hearted, single-minded, and tolerant in all matters.

"It may seem strange to say so," observes your gentle hostess, whilst a smile illuminates the speak-

ing countenance ; " but I have never been inside a
theatre in my life. I always say on such occasions,
that although our parents never took us, and I never
go myself out of habit and affectionate respect for
their memory, I do not wish to give an opinion
or to say that others are wrong to go. We must
each act according to our own convictions, and must
ever use all tolerance towards those who differ from
us. We had many pleasures and advantages. There
was no dulness or gloom about our home, and everything seemed to give occasion for mirth. We had
many trips abroad too, indeed, we spent most winters
on the Continent. I made an excursion with a brother
who was an ecclesiastical architect, and in this way
I visited every cathedral in France. Heidelberg is
very picturesque, and suggested many poetical ideas,
but all travelling enlarges one's mind and is an
education."

One event which caused the keenest amusement to
these happy young people, all blessed with excellent
spirits, sparkling wit, and general enjoyment of
everything, occurred when a pretty, kindly, appreciative notice appeared in some paper of a person
called by her name. There was hardly a single
item in it that was really true, even to the
description of her birthplace, which was described
vaguely as being stationed on the sea-beach and
flanked by two lighthouses, " between which the
lonely child might have been seen to wander for
hours together nursing her poetic dreams, dragging
the long trails of seaweed after her, and listening to
the voice of the waves." This supposititious little

U

biography was productive of the greatest merriment to her brothers and sisters. The first impulse was to answer it, to disclaim the solitary wanderings and poetic dreams, and to describe the place correctly; but although urged by friends to do this, Jean Ingelow on reflection decided to let it pass, and in the end the laughter died out. "To a poetic nature," she remarks, "expression is a necessity, but once expressed, the thought and feeling that inspired it may often be forgotten. I am sure that I could not repeat one of my own poems from beginning to end just as I wrote it. I have a distinct theory too, that one is not taught, one is born to it. I was never able to make a great effort in my life, but what I can do at all, I can do at once, and having thought a good deal on any subject I know very little more than I did at first. Things come to me without striving, besides I am quite unromantic. I never wrote in a hurry. We might all be laughing and talking together, yet if I went up to my room and sat alone, I could at once write in a most sad and melancholy strain. I was not studious as a child, though I remember a great epoch in my life was reading 'The Pilgrim's Progress,' when I was seven years old, and I was perfectly well able to perceive the deep imaginative powers of it, but I always wanted to study what was not in books."

But if Jean Ingelow's books are sold by thousands in England, they are sold by tens of thousands in America. Her publishers there for many years used to send her a handsome royalty on their sales; some years ago, however, five other American publishers brought out her poetical works simultaneously, since which time she has received nothing! She is probably the first woman-poet who has met with not only world-wide popularity, but who might if it had been needful, have lived very well by the proceeds of her verse alone. A few years ago Messrs. Longman brought out, by request, a new edition of her books. Altogether, she declares herself to "have been a very fortunate woman, and almost always happy in her publishers, too."

In later years Jean Ingelow has written many prose works of fiction, notably "Off the Skelligs," "Fated to be Free," "Don John," "Sarah de Berenger," "Mopsa, the Fairy," "John Jerome," etc. "Off the Skelligs" was the first novel by the author whose name had hitherto been almost exclusively associated with verse, and it was received with more than ordinary interest. The book teems with incident ; the poetic vein may be traced in the realistic pictures of child life, in the description of the lovely scenery depicted in the yachting trip, and in the graphic and stirring account of the burning ship and rescue of its passengers. "Fated to be Free" is a sequel to the previous work. The book opens with a powerful description of àn old manor house and family over whose head hangs the mysterious blight of some unknown misfortune, which is cleverly indicated rather than described, and though tragical in the main, the sorrow is not allowed to overshadow the story too heavily, for here and there humour and wit sparkle out, while the whole betrays the writer's deep intuitive knowledge of human hearts and human lives. "Mopsa, the Fairy" has been called

"A poem in prose, for the use of children," and a better name for it could not be found. It is, as the title implies, a tale of fairyland in its brightest aspect, and is told with the purity of conception and the excellence of execution which characterise the gifted author's writings.

A few words must be said in description of the pretty house in Kensington where Miss Ingelow lives with her brother, and into which, some thirteen years ago, they removed from Upper Kensington to be further out and away from so much building. Since this removal she says, "three cities have sprung up around them!" The handsome square detached house stands back in a fine, broad road, with carriage drive and garden in front filled with shrubs, and half a dozen chestnut and almond trees, which in this bright spring weather are bursting out into leaf and flower. Broad stone steps lead up to the hall door, which is in the middle of the house. The entrance hall— where hangs a portrait of the author's maternal great-grandfather, the Primus of Scotland, i.e., Bishop of Aberdeen—opens into a spacious, old-fashioned drawing-room of Italian style on the right. Large and lofty is this bright, cheerful room. A harp, on which Miss Ingelow and her mother before her played right well, stands in one corner. There is a grand pianoforte opposite, for she was a good musician, and had a remarkably fine voice in earlier years. On the round table in the deep bay windows in front are many books, various specimens of Tangiers pottery, and some tall plants of arum lilies in flower. The great glass doors draped with curtains at the further end, open into a large conservatory where Miss Ingelow often sits in summer. It is laid down with matting and rugs, and standing here and there are flowering plants and two fine araucarias. The verandah steps on the left lead into a large and well-kept garden with bright green lawn, at the end of which through the trees may be discerned a large stretch of greenhouses, and a view beyond of the great trees in the grounds of Holland Park. On the corresponding side of the house at the back is the billiard-room, which is Mr. Ingelow's study, leading into an ante-room, and in the front is the dining-room, where the author's literary labours are carried on. "I write in a commonplace, prosaic manner," she says; "I am afraid I am rather idle, for I only work during two or three of the morning hours, with my papers spread all about the table." Over the fireplace hangs a painting on ivory of her father, and above it a portrait of her mother, taken in her early married life. This portrait, together with one of the poet herself when an infant, is in pastels, and they were originally done as door panels for her father's room; the colouring is yet unfaded.

The conversation turning upon memory—for Jean Ingelow holds pronounced theories on this subject—she leads the way back to the conservatory and points out the picture of her grandfather's house, called Ingelow House after her, with which her very earliest recollections are associated, and her memory dates back to when she was but seventeen months old! She says that "friends smile at this and think that she is romancing, but if people made attempts to recollect their very early days, certain visions which have passed

into the background for many years would rise again
with a distinctness which would make it impossible to
mistake them for inventions, and also make it certain
that the records of this life are not annihilated, but
only covered." She took some trouble to collect facts
as to "first recollections" of many people, and found
that two at least could remember events which were
proved to have happened at the age of eighteen and
twenty-two months respectively. In further support
of this theory she relates an amusing and curious
incident of dormant memory in early childhood which
actually happened in her own family. Miss Ingelow's
mother went on a visit to her own father, who
lived in London, accompanied by her infant son aged
eleven months and his nurse. One day the nurse
brought the baby into his mother's room and put him
on the floor, which was carpeted all over, where he
crept about and amused himself whilst she dressed her
mistress. When the toilet was completed, a certain
ring which Mrs. Ingelow generally wore was missing.
Search was made but it was never found and shortly
after the visit ended, and the matter was almost forgotten.
Mother and child again went on the same visit exactly
a year later, accompanied by the same nurse, who took
the boy into the same room. His mother saw him look
around him, and deliberately walk up to one corner,
turn back a bit of the carpet and produce the ring.
He never gave any account of it nor did he seem to
remember it later; he had probably found it on the
floor and hidden it for safety—it could hardly have
been for mischief—and had forgotten all about it until
he saw the place again, as he was too young when the

ring was missed to understand what the talk and search about it meant. "He was by no means a precocious child," adds Miss Ingelow, " nor did he show later any remarkable qualities in his powers of learning or remembering lessons."

She lost her mother thirteen years ago, and her father passed away before the publication of her first book of poetry—the book of which he would have been so proud. "It was a joy to me," says the poetess, "when I found that people began to read my verses, and I can never forget too my pleasure when first introduced to Mr. Ruskin and he asked my mother and me to luncheon at his house. Of course, I was far too modest to be willing to talk to him, especially in my mother's presence; but after luncheon I got away from them, leaving them in high discourse, and surreptitiously stole down to look at a bush of roses which were very much to my mind. Mr. Ruskin presently came up to me, and entered into a charming conversation. He gathered some of the flowers and gave them to me—I kept them for a long time—then we walked round a meadow close at hand which was just fit for the scythe, and afterwards he took me to see a number of the curiosities that he had collected. We soon became loving friends and his friendship has been one of the great pleasures of my life. Sir Arthur Helps, too, was for many years a dear friend."

Miss Ingelow is, as may be supposed, a great reader, though she observes, "that few people take as long a time in reading a book as she does." Her preference is for works of a religious tone, chiefly those of eminent divines. "I do not want to use the word 'fastidious,'" she adds, "but perhaps I am more *bornée* than most people in my taste in literature. Even some of Sir Walter Scott's and many of Thackeray's novels I cannot read, but I am fond of 'Vanity Fair,' and Dickens, and delight in several of Shakespeare's masterpieces, reading them over and over again."

She is "resting" for a while now. The poetic vein, she says, is not strongly upon her for the moment, but it invariably returns. Meantime it is to be hoped that the day may not be far distant when the public will rejoice to welcome yet more sweet strains from the pen of the great and gifted poet.

ANNIE S. SWAN

(MRS BURNETT SMITH)

ANNIE S. SWAN

(MRS. BURNETT SMITH).

THE well-known and popular author Annie Swan (Mrs. Burnett Smith), whose present residence is in the healthful and breezy atmosphere of Hampstead, was born at Leith, and was one of a family of seven, "the middle or 'odd' one," as she describes it, "of a particularly merry, united, and happy family." There were apparently no hereditary tendencies to literature on either side, and it was a mystery to the whole "connection" when the girl at the age of fifteen began to write short stories. At school she confesses to having been no "model" girl or having in any way distinguished herself; but she was a quick learner, and generally left her lessons to the last moment, and in play hours would gather a little knot of girls around her, and keep them amused with thrilling tales. Her home upbringing was singularly fortunate. Mr. Swan was a great agriculturist, a man of tender heart and refined mind; his sense of justice was so strong that it was proverbially said of him that he would "divide a farthing between two people rather than that either should be wronged." At first he was inclined to look on the story-writing somewhat as waste of time, but he soon recognized his daughter's natural bent, and thoroughly encouraged it. On looking back, Annie Swan acknowledges that she got her ideas—"very strong ideas"—of right and wrong from this beloved father's life and example—perhaps even more than from his precepts. To the happy, healthy out-of-door life in all weathers she owes a strong physique, for boys and girls alike indulged in all the country sports and amusements as the season might permit. "Now I come to think of it, indeed," says the writer demurely, "I believe that I was rather a harum-scarum, tom-boy sort of girl!"

Her mother combined with a refined and beautiful simplicity of character great wisdom and practical common-sense, and, while always proud of her child's writings, she held the sensible doctrine prevalent in many of the old-fashioned Scottish families, that, whatever lot in life her daughters should subsequently be called upon to fill, they would fill it none the less well for being thoroughly well trained in domestic duties. Accordingly a rule was made that in turn each girl should take a separate department in house-hold work, one week at cooking, another at the dairy, a third at the napery press, and so on, until they all became adepts in every department and well qualified to carry on the entire management of a house, great or small, the while the intellectual bent, or musical bias, or a skilful pencil was by no means ignored or thrust out of sight.

To such a character as Annie Swan's—in which, under the youthful exuberance of high spirits and love of fun, there lay a touch of her country's reticence and reserve—no training could have been more judicious. Without crushing the bright happy nature, the deeper responsibilities of life were gradually inculcated, and when the girl left home and kindred to become a wife, the knowledge that she had gained stood her in good stead; for, without drawing away the veil of sweet romance that hangs over those early days of married life, she makes no secret that in bygone years they "began on small means and saved on them." The systematic and thorough insight into domestic matters that she had gained, enabled her to order her little *ménage* with the maximum of comfort and the minimum of economy, as, hand in hand and in perfect sympathy, the young pair laughed over and surmounted little difficulties together until —the victory won—they sailed in smooth waters.

Bit by bit they collected each article of furniture with taste and judgment. Behind the glass doors of the old Chippendale bureau are many treasured pieces of Worcester, of Crown Derby, and of Wedgwood. On the walls hang water-colour sketches and views of Old Edinburgh. "These are the doctor's hobby," says his wife. The author's literary work is carried on in an upstair room that is a veritable snuggery with its warm-tinted Turkey carpet, tapestry hangings, Louis Quinze clock, and other artistic surroundings, which indicate that, although Annie Swan cultivates her intellectual faculties to the uttermost, she has not omitted the study of art combined with comfort. The large Chippendale writing-table—so neatly arranged with MSS. and proofs—shows signs of a busy but methodical writer. Here her favourite

photographs, books and reminiscences of girlhood, are
gathered together, while the great arm-chair opposite
makes a luxurious lounge for the tired physician after
a heavy day's work. In this pleasant room she works
during the morning hours, "not always wholly uninterrupted," she remarks with a smile; "but I am not
easily disturbed, and I can go on again and take up
the thread of thought without difficulty. I attribute
this to being one of a large family where it was
impossible to have a room entirely to oneself in which
to write. My usual method is to have one central
idea fixed on one central character; then the others
seem to group themselves around it. Sometimes I
have the whole plan worked out in my mind, and
the people change places, as it were. After getting
to a certain length the story seems to shape itself."

Her first book took a long time to write, and was
cut down over and over again. It was published by
a company on the "half-profits" system, but came to
an untimely end. "There were no profits," she says,
laughing, "but a considerable expenditure instead. I
was one of the victims of the company's unfortunate
speculation." Her troubles in publishing may be said
to have come to an end with this misadventure, as
the long row of neatly-bound volumes in the bookcase testify. Among them may be observed the titles
of "The Gates of Eden," "A Divided House," "Mait-
land of Laurieston," "Carlowrie," "Sheila," "A Bitter
Debt," "Aldersyde," and "A Victory Won."

Bound just inside the cover of this work is a valued
letter from Mr. Gladstone, written in the venerable
statesman's own hand, in which he remarks, "I think

it is beautiful as a work of art, and it must be
the fault of the reader if he does not profit by the
perusal. Miss Nesbit and Marget will, I hope, long
hold their places among the truly living sketches of
Scottish character." Another testimony to the merits
of this charming story is a much-prized autograph
letter from the late Lord Tennyson.

A propos of "Sheila," which is the author's own
favourite, there is a pretty incident connected with
the book. It first ran as a serial through the *Glasgow
Weekly Mail,* and while in course of publication a
travelling basket-woman wandered up on foot from
Crieff to Amulree, where the scene of the story was
laid, and called at a house to sell her wares. After
a little talk with the woman of the house she drew
a paper out of her basket, and asked to be directed to
Dalmore (the abode of the heroine, Sheila Macdonald),
as she was quite sure that lady would buy up her
whole stock-in-trade. She was very indignant when
assured that Dalmore was a purely imaginary place,
and again pointed to the copy of the *Mail,* which contained a description of the house. "When I heard the
incident," says Annie Swan, laughing, "I felt that I
had fallen in the estimation of my humble but sincere
reader, and I wished I could have explained to her the
mysteries and little necessary fictions of my craft."

Her bright, sympathetic nature leads her in general
to bring her stories to a happy conclusion. On one
occasion, however, she deviated from this rule. "St.
Vera's" has a sad ending, and while it was running
serially the young writer had so many letters im-
ploring her to avert the heroine's impending fate,

that she resolved never again to wind up in a minor key.   Among these communications the most amusing and touching was expressed with more vigour than politeness on a post card, which ran as follows : "Don't let Annie Erskine die! If you do, hanged if I read any more of your old stories!"

There is a purity and simplicity of style, withal a depth of thought and experience, that characterise all the writings of this talented and earnest worker. They are homely and wholesome in tone, the thread of the story is always interesting, and compels the reader to follow the heroine to the end.   With a keen insight into human nature, there is strength and tenderness in her stories that appeal to all hearts.   The brightness and utter absence of affectation in her own character are revealed in her works, as are also the strong religious principles that guide her life.   These have, however, led her into no narrow groove, but have rather opened out and widened her sympathies, so that, like the branches of a great tree, they spread out far and wide.

In common with most well-known authors, Mrs. Burnett Smith has a large correspondence, and receives daily budgets from young aspirants after literary fame—chiefly women—and ofttimes she is sore oppressed thinking of the vast army of women who are seeking something to do.   "Many of them, alas! are so incompetent," she remarks sadly, "and show so little qualification for, or true appreciation of, the high calling they seek to pursue, that I sometimes feel it a hopeless task trying to convince them that there is no royal road to success in literature, but that it is synonymous with incessant anxiety and effort, which an increasing reputation only makes harder instead of easier." It was owing to these innumerable letters from unknown writers upon every conceivable subject, that her magazine was instituted. They poured in largely from housekeeping women of the middle class, and, as it became too much of a tax to answer them individually, it occurred to Mrs. Burnett Smith that it would be a good plan to start a journal, which would be a kind of medium between her and her readers. The idea has been fully carried out; many readers of the *Woman at Home* regard "Over the Tea-cups" as the tit-bit of the magazine, and she has received hundreds of letters of sympathy and congratulation on its success. Much the same reasons inspired Mrs. Burnett Smith to write a late book, called "Courtship and Marriage" (Hutchinson & Co.), for so many young people wrote to her asking her for advice in these matters. This charming little book is written with mingled gravity and sweetness, and the most valuable "advice" is tendered in simple, eloquent words. Published at the small price of one shilling, this modest little volume should be distributed in, not thousands, but tens of thousands among the young; indeed, there can be but few who would not feel the better for its perusal, and be inclined to follow the wise counsel so delicately suggested. "It contains my views of life," says the author, "and," she adds, reverently, in a soft tone, "I try to live up to them."

SARAH GRAND.

WHILE on a recent visit at a country house during the pleasant informal five o'clock tea hour that precedes the sound of the dressing-gong for dinner, a lively conversation occurred which I mentally noted down with a view to future journalistic use. Its subject was Sarah Grand, and the theme was prompted by the arrival of a box of books from Messrs. Smith & Son, that had been eagerly unpacked and handed round. Among the collection were "The Beth Book," and a volume entitled "The Tenor and the Boy,' which had originally formed part of the famous "Heavenly Twins," but was just published as a separate work by itself. An animated discussion soon followed concerning the gifted author's personality, her habits and her tastes. There was a goodly company assembled—some half-dozen hunting men in pink, with mud-bespattered boots and breeches, a sprinkling of girls mostly attired in neat Busvine riding-habits, three winsome young matrons, together with a sweet old white-haired lady of the *grande dame* type. Now nothing is more varying than the different impressions produced upon people with regard to the individuality of the authors in whom

SARAH GRAND

they are interested, but who are as yet unknown to them by sight, and I listened with much amusement to the various conjectures and ideas put forth.

"I," said the genial, soldierly-looking host, meditatively, as he leaned against the mantelshelf, and caressed a favourite collie dog, "always picture her to myself as a large, dark, massive woman—commanding in presence, with black eyes, a deep contralto voice, and wearing long, stately robes of green velvet."

"But my idea," remarked the *grande dame*, in soft melodious tones, "is altogether opposite. I imagine her to be a very small, fair woman, with a very determined manner, large, pale blue eyes, and probably dressed in rather a masculine fashion."

Other opinions and suggestions were pronounced, but were all so totally unlike the reality—the actuality of the talented and womanly author, that, taking advantage of a momentary pause in the conversation, I seized the opportunity, and interpolated the remark:

"But as I have the privilege of personal knowledge of, and friendship with, Sarah Grand, I am in a position to tell you about her; and first, I will give a verbal portrait of her, which none of her friends would fail to recognize. She is something over the medium height, slight, and girlish in figure; the face of pure oval shape is crowned with soft, brown, curly hair, worn in a large, loose coil, low on the nape of her neck. She has a broad, low brow, indicating spirituality and intellect; a complexion of delicate colouring; large, grey eyes, that seem to deepen in

x

hue while she talks; a serious and somewhat sad
expression when in repose, but which relaxes into
a smile of winning sweetness, irradiating the whole
countenance when in sympathy with her company
—and," I added, "this is a true and faithful portrait
of Sarah Grand."

"Highly interesting," said our host, "but now, I,
for one, want to know more—a great deal more—
of her opinions and her proclivities, if you will so
indulge us; we seldom have the chance of meeting
with any members of the literary world in these
remote parts."

Several of the guests seconded the request, so,
overcoming my bashfulness, I proceeded to give a
brief narrative, thus:—

"Descended alike on each side from a race of
artistic and talented families, of whom it might
confidently have been predicted that, sooner or later,
they would give to the world a poet, a painter, or
an author of great note, Sarah Grand has fully
verified these expectations, and proved that *bon sang
ne peut pas mentir*, by making for herself, early in
life, a distinguished and unique name in literature.
Highly educated, and accustomed from childhood to
associate with cultured people, she was reared, so to
speak, in an artistic as well as in a good social
atmosphere, which has imbued her whole being, and
led her to cultivate to the utmost the intellectual
gifts for which she is so much renowned.   And as to
her 'opinions,' I cannot resist saying that, with every
womanly grace and charm, such as a peculiarly gentle,
quiet manner, and a low, musical voice, Sarah Grand is in

herself a proof that it is generally the most highly educated of her sex who are most refined. She holds the highest opinions on this point, and maintains, earnestly, and on all occasions, that there is no reason why women who have attained much knowledge should lose any of the charm of their feminine attributes, and that culture should not only stimulate them to increased efforts to stand by each other at all times and seasons, but also to preserve each in herself, in all its strength and glory, the respect and reverence due to womanhood."

There then was a pause which no one interrupted, so I ventured to remark, "Sarah Grand has said to me that she thinks women who cultivate the best there is within themselves will do more with a word than the too combative, with their insistence and arguments, and they should never let it be supposed that, because they advocate the 'higher education,' it unfits them for domestic duties, or renders them unable to handle a baby or darn a stocking, for, as it happens, she is quite capable of doing both; nay, even of 'making a pudding' if the necessity arose!"

At this there was a universal laugh, and when it had subsided, the young chatelaine of the house exclaimed, "Yes; but apart from darning and handling babies and the proverbial pudding-making, what about her writings? I have some of her books and shall now order all her others. Begin from the beginning!"

"Well," I replied, "I happen to know that Sarah Grand's real start in literature was made with a book called 'Ideala,' a study from life, though she had previously written several short stories and essays.

There was considerable difficulty with this work, for at that time only three-volume novels were in vogue. After many rejections, she, nothing daunted, decided to publish it at her own expense, and, having the courage of her opinions, was rewarded by seeing the book pass into four editions. That she succeeded in making herself heard and appreciated by the public is proved by the fact that although a decade of years has passed since 'Ideala' was written, a new edition of ten thousand copies has since been brought out by Mr. Heinemann. Her next important venture was a sort of sequel, 'The Heavenly Twins,' which was, as you all know, a work more widely discussed and sold than any book of the day. Two years of much preparation and thought, of patient and earnest study —for such a book could not have been written on the impulse of a moment—were expended upon that celebrated novel. Into it Sarah Grand put all that was best in herself. She sat down, not to write what is ordinarily meant by 'a novel with a purpose,' but to depict a neighbourhood with its group of characters, types evolved by close observation, with the idea of developing them on natural lines, treating them without prejudice, or making them answer to foregone conclusions. One pleasurable result of this book to Sarah Grand was the receipt of many letters from medical men, known and unknown, complimenting her upon her accurate knowledge of physiology and of pathology, while many others came from absolute strangers, women in distant lands, telling her 'that she had done more in the cause of woman and children than she would ever know.'"

"Yes, that is quite true," said the *grande dame*; "but I am glad to find that Sarah Grand's writings are by no means confined to abstruse physiological subjects. I dipped into one of her books this afternoon that I found open upon the library table — it was called 'Our Manifold Nature' — and I noticed many little touches that betray a deep poetic feeling, not to speak of a keen sense of humour that peeps out, notably in one of that collection of short stories, 'Ah Man, a Chinese Servant'; and I was touched by the pathos in another, 'Janey, a Humble Administrator.'"

"Oh," said our hostess, laughing, "I can account for that book being left open in our tidy library. I had been reading the story of 'Janey' to my little Maisie, and the luncheon-gong sounded just as I had finished. She was so much interested, and asked me many questions about Sarah Grand's childish days which I could not answer. You will win her heart for ever if you let her catechise you; but it must be after dinner, for there is the dressing-gong," and the party dispersed.

Later, the pleasant, sociable meal over, the feminine element repaired to the great drawing-room, tenanted only by a dainty little maiden of eight summers, who had been permitted the birthday treat—so beloved of childhood—of "sitting-up" some extra hours. At her mother's bidding, she rose from a low ottoman, put a tiny hand in mine, and shyly whispered, "Did Sarah Grand play with dolls when she was eight, and did she always write stories?" Both questions were easy to answer, and while the dear little one nestled confidingly against me I told her that dolls were not, perhaps, as much her companions as live pets, dogs, and animals of various sorts, and when she was quite a child an aquarium was her special delight, with gold and silver fishes and curious little green things and tadpoles, for which she used to grub about in ditches to her heart's content, and hunt for herself for specimens. Then she would ask for the books to be read to her which contained an account of these treasures, and thus got a storehouse of knowledge. She used to make up and relate little stories long before she was able to write them out, and when she was only eleven, she composed a song and set it to music. Besides all this, she could sew well, and do many pretty little bits of work. And I can tell you one thing that will please you, my little Maisie," I added, as the child scrambled upon my lap. "Even Sarah Grand often got into scrapes at school owing to over-high spirits!"

"And I can tell you one thing, my little Maisie," quoted her mother, with a merry smile, "that will *not* please you! Nurse has tapped twice at the door, and you must be off to bed." So, after a loving hug, the child obediently retired.

Next the elders took up the thread and asked, "Where does she live? Are her surroundings beautiful? and how does she dress?" Then they paused and laughingly bade me "talk on, and they would not interrupt me with any more questions." The last query was irresistible. Dress is a subject that interests—or ought to interest—all women, and Sarah Grand is by no means too much "cultivated" to neglect such an important matter. Everyone was pleased to learn that not only has she a very pretty taste of her own in dress, but not infrequently is requisitioned to supply a judicious hint or original idea when consulted by her friends as to the becomingness of this or that gown, hat, fold, or trimming.

As to her surroundings, they are naturally beautiful and artistic. Flowers are a passion, and any visitor fortunate enough to be admitted will always find them in abundance according to the season of year. Now they will be tall arum lilies grouped in bowls of blue and white Delft; anon, replaced by violets and early spring blossoms; later, by every variety of roses, and again, in their turn, by large, feathery chrysanthemums, from white to pale yellow or deep coppery brown tints.

"It is quite evident, too, that she has been a traveller," remarked a tall, handsome woman, herself a notable voyager in foreign seas. "I remember hearing of Sarah Grand in China and in Japan, where it was said that she spent some time in the house of the Mayor of a little village, to learn something of native life from the inside, and she had an English maid and a Chinese cook with her."

"Yes, that is so," I replied. "She enlarged her experience greatly by foreign travel. A prolonged tour in the East—I believe it lasted quite five years—gave her a fine opportunity of making herself thoroughly acquainted with the various types of Oriental character, and their manner of life. Egypt, Ceylon, the Straits Settlements, Shanghai, and through the beautiful Inland Sea to Japan. Always a worshipper of the sea, and of nature in its ever-changing moods, the picturesque loveliness of the Land of the Rising Sun, with its tranquillising but inspiring scenery, appealed strongly to the author's artistic temperament, as perhaps nothing else could have then done. Strolling here and there, as fancy dictated, she extended her instructive and interesting wanderings farther and farther before turning her footsteps homewards. For a while she lived in a flat at Kensington, but the calls and claims of society became very serious hindrances to her work, so, disliking crowds, and retaining her early love of out-door life, she has now made her home in the country, where among picturesque surroundings, in pure air, and under leafy trees, she can commune with nature, and pursue her art in comparative solitude."

At this juncture, the gentlemen entered and the sounds of music were heard. "We are going to have a dance in the hall," said our hostess.

"Thank you a thousand times for all the most interesting information you have given us, and," she added naïvely, "I must say, I do envy you in being personally acquainted with Sarah Grand!"

MARIE CORELLI.

IT is an open secret that Miss Marie Corelli has the strongest objection to being "interviewed," and has never even availed herself of the oft-repeated invitation to "sit for her photograph." In the circumstances, therefore, the reminiscences of sundry hours spent in her company, together with a subsequent conversation during a journey with a group of people who as yet knew her not, save through her writings, may convey some idea, not only of the personality, but also of the character of the gifted young author.

Reminiscences first. A chance meeting and a graceful act of courtesy on her part began what has since developed into a firm friendship. Some few years ago, there happened to be a particularly brilliant meeting of the popular Salon of Science, Literature, and Art. The rooms were filling fast, and the whole assembly thronged in to listen to a recitation by a clever American humorist. Gently urged on by the stream, I found myself standing near a large divan, already well filled by guests. Among them sat a little fair girl, robed in white silk, with a ribbon of the same colour round her abundant golden-brown hair. She looked so youthful as almost to suggest the idea that she could hardly yet be "out." Catching her eye, she smiled, and with a baby hand made a gesture to indicate that space could be made for me. No word was spoken until the recitation was concluded, and then, on thanking her cordially, a brief conversation on music ensued, which at once convinced me that here was no ordinary individual. Gliding on from one subject to another, the talk presently turned on the people around, and, having previously heard that Miss Corelli was expected to be present, I asked my companion if she knew her by sight. "Yes," said the young lady, demurely, "I may say that I know her fairly well, and——" But before the sentence was finished, a friend had claimed her attention and pronounced her name. Then, giving me a little mischievous bow and an arch smile, she was borne away to the refreshment room.

And as time went on, many more meetings came about, and, bit by bit, the young author's personality, surroundings, and writings became more and more familiar, and enabled me, without betraying any confidence, to enlighten the group of people afore-mentioned upon many points.

But a few days ago a journey had to be made to Hants on business. Arriving somewhat late at Water-loo, the carriages were nearly all full, and while I was hurriedly seeking for a place, a head was popped out at the window of a compartment, and I was bidden by a friendly voice to take a vacant seat therein. The voice proceeded from a bride, who, with her husband, was returning from a three months' honeymoon tour. Glancing round, it was pleasant

to note that the two remaining passengers were also
not strangers. One was an eminent divine, distinguished no less for his eloquence in the pulpit than
for his genial nature. The other was Sister ——,
a lady of renowned goodness and of ancient lineage.
Amid cordial greetings and desired introductions
the train sped on its way, and conversation soon
became general.

"I see you have our favourite book in your hand,"
said the bride; "we bought it in Paris, and all Marie
Corelli's other works in the Tauchnitz edition, and
I am ashamed to say we smuggled them over, and
are having them bound in morocco. Have you ever
seen her? and is it true that she is very tall and stout,
with prominent eyes, and an incipient moustache?"
But ere I could reply for inward mirth, the clergyman
remarked, in all good faith: "I can tell you. She was
pointed out to me in Rome, on the Prado, two years
ago. She is a majestic and massive woman, with black
hair, bound tightly round her head, dark eyes, a deep
contralto voice, and commanding presence. I was
discussing her once with our mutual friend"—turning
to me—"the late Edmund Yates, and I remember that
he said he always pictured her to himself in classic
draperies, with Greek symbols about her, and sandals."

But at this juncture the situation became too much
for my gravity, and a laugh was irresistible. "For you
are all so wrong," I exclaimed, "so funnily and entirely
wrong. *I* know her personally—have known her
for years. She is *petite*, and extremely fair, and her
eyes are grey, and deeply set, and her hair is soft
and fluffy, and curls round her head. Her voice, too, is

sweet and silvery; she is so bright and joyous in
manner, and, besides, she was not in Rome at all that
year!" After various exclamations of surprise from
my fellow-travellers, the Sister observed, with a smile:
"Well, as there is still nearly an hour before we arrive,
and we are all admirers of her books, pray tell us
all you can about her." Musing awhile to collect
my thoughts, I began with the mention of the meeting
at the Salon, and continued thus: "The *motif* of the
work 'Barabbas,' now in its sixteenth edition, was
actually conceived when Marie Corelli was at her
studies in a convent. By nature mystical and profoundly religious, she was even then vividly impressed
by the beauty and the reality of the services at the
chapel, and used to long to write down these impressions. The idea grew and strengthened until it
finally resulted in this impassioned and intellectual
work, which none can carefully read without being
struck by the powerful style of the young author, the
conscientious and earnest feeling, the reverence
for the subject, and the deeply poetic vein displayed
throughout."

"Quite true," said the clergyman; "I entirely agree
with you. Opinions may differ, always will differ,
on every subject under the sun, but, as the late Clement
Scott observed, the public taste is healthy—not morbid,
and that public taste has given a verdict for Marie
Corelli of which she has every reason to be proud; but,
pardon me, I interrupt you."

"Her works," I resumed, "have been more widely
translated than those of any living author, into Dutch,
Swedish, Russian, German, French, Modern Greek, and

Spanish. 'Barabbas,' indeed, can be found in Gujurathi, and both that and 'A Romance of Two Worlds' in Hindustani. This of itself is sufficient to indicate the popularity of her books, abroad as well as at home, where they have all passed into many editions, and are as extensively circulated now as when they were originally brought out. Her letter-boxes and autograph-albums are treasures that would tempt a collector to make raids on them, so numerous are the letters from all parts of the world—from crowned heads, from distinguished statesmen, and so forth, down to the working miners in Australia and California, who, reading her books, seem mysteriously constrained to write to her with the plain address of 'London, England,' simply to express their gratitude and admiration."

"From her writings," remarked the bridegroom, himself a "double-first" Oxford man, "it is manifest that Miss Corelli must be well versed in all the classical authors, living and dead, and is likewise a good linguist."

"That is so," I replied, "and her library is remarkable. The books are so well-worn, too. She delights in Plato, nearly knows her Shakespeare by heart, and studies Dante and Goethe in the original."

"'Thelma,' 'A Romance of Two Worlds,' and 'Ardath,'" observed the bride, "were first favourites for a long time. My husband used to prefer 'Vendetta' and 'Wormwood.' But now we think that her later books. 'The Sorrows of Satan,' 'Temporal Power,' 'God's Good Man,' 'Free Opinions freely expressed,' bid fair to run 'Barabbas,' close in public favour. They are so vivid and realistic, and so powerfully descriptive."

The Sister put in a word for "The Soul of Lilith," but confessed that she "could hardly make a choice," and added, after a pause, as she touched the crucifix at her side, "But she is of our faith, and evidently a great student of the Bible, for she is so correct in all her details."

"Yes; that is absolutely true," I answered, "which makes it the more remarkable that, quite lately, she was accused of making a 'Gospel according to Corelli,' and of inventing the two angels at the sepulchre on the Resurrection morn!"

A silence followed, and then a question—essentially feminine—was hesitatingly asked by the bride. "And her dress? the Greek fillet, the sandals, the classical draperies?"

"All purely imaginary," I said, "as poor Mr. Yates found out for himself during his last visit to Cannes, where Miss Corelli and her party were staying at the same hotel. They all became devoted friends, and enjoyed many a laugh over his preconceived notions of her. She dresses after the manner of ordinary mortals —with a difference. Possessed of highly cultivated artistic tastes, alike observable in her surroundings and costumes, she wears suitable as well as pretty clothes. The last time I went to see her, she was clad in a tea-gown composed of old gold-coloured silk, beautifully embroidered, and a darker shade of golden-hued velvet made the train which became well the childish figure and fair young face. She showed me, on her wrist, a unique bangle, a much-prized birthday gift from two friends, on which was mounted in classical design, according to an old drawing of the ancient Egyptian era, a specially rare green scarabæus, six thousand years old, purposely procured from the museum of royal scarabæi in Cairo. At my request she played to me on a peculiarly sweet-toned mandolin with much skill and expression. There were flowers grouped here and there, and on the grand pianoforte stood a large autograph picture of the King, a gift at Homburg when Prince of Wales."

Time was speeding, and but five minutes remained ere the train was to arrive at the station. Turning to the Sister, who had been listening with rapt attention, I remarked: "There is a touching incident to relate, which is not only interesting in itself but is highly indicative of the deep feeling of reverence with which Marie Corelli approached the task of writing 'Barabbas: a Dream of the World's Tragedy.' Her desk was placed opposite a picture after Guido's 'Ecce Homo,' under which a red lamp burned continuously. A friend presented her with a gold penholder, set with a single pearl at the top. With this pen alone, consecrated to the work, Marie Corelli wrote, from the first word to the last, the book which became so famous."

"It is deeply interesting," said the ecclesiastic, with a hearty handshake, as the train glided in and the party prepared to disperse. "I, for one, can assure you I never had a pleasanter journey in my life, and I shall look forward to the honour of being introduced some day to the scholarly and gifted writer."

RITA

(Mrs. Desmond Humphreys).

THE picturesque home of Rita is situated in one of
the prettiest parts of leafy Dorset. From the French
windows of the drawing-room that open on to the
garden, can be seen "the greenery," upon which
"Rita" loves to look out when writing. Among many
curios in the room where palms, ferns, plants and
flowers abound, you will not fail to notice a beautiful
Florentine lamp of great antiquity, together with a
tall Japanese cabinet, with its sliding inlaid panels,
placed near a quaint little shelf which contains saucers
to match the cups that depend from hooks below.
These are varied specimens from dragon-blue to old
"candle" china, and were parting presents from
different farmhouses near their former residence in
Devon. The mantelshelf is noticeable from the handsome bronze ornaments that adorn it, the pagoda
clock with four faces and dragon hands, the ivory
elephant, and a large animal of an extinct species
with a warlike figure seated upon it. Two lovely
little rosewood tables are devoted respectively, the
one to tiny paintings of the Christ and the Madonna
in Florentine frames, the other to a collection of finely

MRS DESMOND HUMPHREYS

("RITA")

carved specimens of Irish bog oak, such as the harp,
the spinning-wheel, and other national emblems;
while the carving of the old rosewood frames, cabinets,
brackets, and of the well-filled bookcases is especially
beautiful. For the cunningly-devised and original, if
somewhat erratic, bookshelves and nook-and-corner
adornments, "Rita's" husband, Mr. Desmond
Humphreys, is responsible. This handsome, genial
son of Erin, who is the life and soul of the house,
has indeed a genius for adapting and inventing which
is not only turned towards beautifying the house;
his ready wit and close observance of human nature,
together with an unusual wide experience of people
and of things, make him a delightful raconteur.

Born at Inverness, "Rita," at the age of four, accompanied her parents and two brothers on a long
sea-voyage to Australia, where the family made their
home for ten years. Living in a wild part of the
country, and chiefly out of doors, the lovely scenery
largely influenced her early recollections, and tended
to deepen the poetic and romantic element in her
nature, which was happily balanced by the exceptional
advantage, in that out-of-the-way spot, of being
educated until the age of fourteen with her brothers
and by their tutor, a man of great ability and of keen
judgment. He recognised the peculiarity of his pupil's
temperament, and, while judiciously preserving the
young girl's reticence and romance, he fortified her
mind with a solid foundation of reading, and cultivated particularly the art of composition. He also
took care to encourage healthful and athletic exercises,
and at an early age she became a good rider and

cricketer. Her studies and amusements were, however, alike prematurely suspended for a season, as a tendency to lung mischief caused her to be sent home, where her native Scottish air soon restored her to health.

Undoubtedly one of the peculiarities of "Rita's" books is that they seem to move in sections, so to speak. She is the very reverse of the "groovy" author, who having once made a success repeats it *ad nauseam*, until each successive book becomes a weaker and poorer repetition of the fatal No. 1, which owned the doubtful benefit of popularity. The first section of "Rita's" brain seems to have moved on romantic and imaginative lines, as, for instance, her first six books, beginning with "Vivienne," "Dian's Kiss," "Darby and Joan," "A Sinless Secret," etc., and ending with the ever-popular "Dame Durden." Then a period of foreign travel resulted in another section— "Gretchen," "Faustine," "Corinna," and "Countess Daphne," besides numerous short stories for different magazines, since published under the titles of "Vignettes," and "Brought Together." Then followed a mystical series—the result of theosophical study and the investigation of spiritism. Of these "The Seventh Dream" is the most extraordinary, being really the result of a dream which so haunted the author that she felt compelled to write it. It was begun and ended within seven days, and has a world-wide reputation, as proved by the many letters received by its writer from all places and all sorts and conditions of people. These stories were, however, but an echo of what is now fashionable.

Having temporarily exhausted the mines of speculation, "Rita" explains that she took a long rest, and
for a period was comparatively inactive before she
turned her attention to the most interesting and
attractive, as well as the most difficult, branch of
her art—namely, the character novel. "Sheba," and
"Countess Pharamond," its sequel, are characters
drawn from life, and the scenes in vivid word-
painting in both books are the scenes of the author's
childhood and early youth. In these works, too, she
has related a faithful account of her own literary troubles.
"The Ending of My Day," and "A Woman In It,"
were also life-studies, and seemed to pave the way
for the success of "Rita's" cleverest piece of work,
"Peg the Rake," which in less than two years passed
through ten editions and secured its writer well-won
fame.

Always intensely impressed by her surroundings,
the lovely scenery of Venice and Austria, so graphically described in "Gretchen," inspired "Rita" with a
ready theme. On first going to Devonshire another
marked change took place in her work, and "Asenath
of the Ford," a romance of Bideford, was received with
great enthusiasm by the press, who pronounced it to
be a country classic worthy of being ranked with
"Lorna Doone," or "Westward Ho!" Soon after this,
the versatile author—one of whose great charms is
her ever-improving variety—rapidly produced a series
of Scottish and Irish novels, the most promising being
"The Laird o' Cockpen," "Peg the Rake," and "Kitty
the Rag." A later work, "Master Wilberforce," the
study of a boy, is a masterpiece of child character

drawn from life. A long sojourn with her husband's parents in the county of Cork afforded "Rita" a fine opportunity for studying Irish scenery, life, and character.

When beginning a book, she starts with a title or perhaps one character, and the other characters and places develop mentally and group themselves around. "Peg the Rake" was written in curious circumstances, beginning at Bideford, continued at Newquay and Saltash, and finished at Teignmouth. The heroine, a woman of forty when the story opens, was only known to the author by hearsay, but when starting for the Lakes of Killarney, long after the book was finished, she came across the very person whose name had suggested it. Among other of "Rita's" novels are "Joan and Mrs Carr," a satire on the pettiness and pretensions of country society. But if you ask "Rita" whether this book, too, is drawn from life, she will smile mysteriously, shake her head, and decline to make any reply, though she confesses to having once portrayed an ancient relative too faithfully and suffered considerably thereby, for the irascible old gentleman recognised the portrait and promptly cut her name out of his will. The temptation, however, was too strong to be resisted.

"The Sinner" is the story of a sensational criminal trial which created a great stir in Cork some years ago. "Rita" acknowledges to having taken great liberties with the treatment and characters, because "fact treated fictionally is generally more attractive than fact represented as truth." But when she heard of this case, it struck her as being a good subject for a novel, and she adopted it as the basis of a plot worked out on totally different lines from the real tragedy. The author also speaks of serial engagements for the next two years, though, as a rule, she objects to tie herself down for a long period in advance.

When engaged on a new work "Rita" shuts herself up and works five or six hours a day until it is finished, sparing herself no trouble in investigating every detail so as to be absolutely sure of facts. It is often re-marked of authors who have made a great success by their early books and achieved a large popularity, that their later works have "fallen off," or that they have "written themselves out." "Rita" is happily in the reverse position, and although the books by which she made her name in early youth are still to be seen on every bookstall in the kingdom, and have never lost their hold on public favour, side by side are to be found many of her later and more popular novels. Since "The Sinner" came out, she has written a story of theatrical life which was serialised by Messrs. Tillotsen under the title of "A Daughter of the People," and is known in its volume form as "Petticoat Loose." A later novel, "An Old Rogue's Tragedy," bade fair to rival the successful "Peg the Rake." It ran into several editions, and a copy was graciously accepted and acknowledged by H.R.H. the Princess of Wales. In this book "Rita" has again chosen a heroine of an age when most writers consider the interests of life finished. "Rita," however, holds a different opinion. She maintains that the crude fancies and romantic passions of youth appeal less forcibly to the heart than the tragic sorrows and still more tragic errors of maturity. On this ground she has written a story that for pathos, force, and realism it would be hard to rival.

Her more recent works are:—"Prince Charming," "Souls," "Queer Lady Judas," and "The Masqueraders."

"Rita" loves the country and its pursuits more than the town, and is not fond of gaieties. She is of a very quiet, retiring disposition, always preferring to keep in the background, and is ever more ready to listen than to speak. If asked how she has fared at the hands of the critics, she will reply, with a merry twinkle of the dark brown eyes, that she has nothing of which to complain, though she may have had a hard hit now and then. As may be supposed, she is an ardent reader and student, and keeps up with all that is going on in fiction, in poetry, in history, and in society. The sea is her delight, "whether on it or in it." True and trustworthy in her friendships, she has the keenest perception of character, a strong sense of humour and love of fun, and falls easily from the sublime to the ridiculous; but perhaps her strongest characteristic of all is her sincere and thorough detestation of all cant and humbug.